PAUL DE MAN

Deconstr... ...n

...tic

Ideology

CHRISTOPHER NORRIS

ROUTLEDGE • NEW YORK & LONDON

Published in 1988 by

Routledge
An imprint of Routledge, Chapman and Hall, Inc.
29 West 35 Street
New York New, NY 10001

Published in Great Britain by

Routledge
11 New Fetter Lane
London EC4P 4EE

Copyright © 1988 by Routledge, Chapman and Hall, Inc.

Printed in the United States of America

Library of Congress Cataloging-in-Publication Data

Norris, Christopher.
  Paul de Man, deconstruction and the critique of aesthetic ideology.

  Bibliography: p.
  Includes index.
  1. Deconstruction. 2. De Man, Paul—Contributions
in criticism. 3. Criticism—History—20th century.
I. Title.
PN98.D43N63 1988   801'.95'0904   87–31375
ISBN 0–415–90079–4
ISBN 0–415–90080–8 (pbk.)

British Library Cataloguing in Publication Data

Norris, Christopher
  Paul de Man : deconstruction and the
  critique of aesthetic ideology.
  1. De Man, Paul
  I. Title
  801'.95'0924   PN75.D45
  ISBN 0–415–90079–4
  ISBN 0–415–90080–8 Pbk

Contents

Acknowledgments

I was greatly helped in writing this book by the willingness of friends and distant colleagues to provide copies of unpublished or otherwise inaccessible texts by de Man. In particular my thanks go to Cynthia Chase, Jonathan Culler, Neil Hertz, Tom Keenan, Dan Latimer, J. Hillis Miller, Steven Rendall, Lindsay Waters, and Andrzej Warminski, for their generous response to my requests and their dedicated work in bringing this material to light. I am also very grateful to Ortwin de Graef, who directed my attention to those articles and reviews that de Man published in Belgian periodicals during the early 1940s. Geert Lernout organized a splendid conference in Antwerp which provided an occasion for arguing out some of the ideas developed in Chapter 1. My graduate students in Rhetoric 240G at Berkeley (Summer, 1986) will no doubt recognize their own contribution at various points where the argument responds to some shrewdly aimed questions and criticisms. Chapter 5 owes much to the unique opportunity for inter-disciplinary exchange offered by those Friday afternoon seminars. Nearer home, there has been the stimulus of regular discussion with Kate Belsey, Terence Hawkes, Kathy Kerr, Nigel Mapp, Karen McDonaugh, Scott Newton, Peter Sedgewick, David Skilton, Rob Stradling, and Ian Whitehouse. I should also like to thank Roger Poole for his many helpful comments and criticisms over the past five years and more. Bill Germano it was who first put me in mind of writing a book about de Man, so I hope he now finds no cause to regret that suggestion.

Parts of this book have appeared previously in the *London Review of Books* and the journals AUMLA, *Prose Studies*, *Textual Practice*, *The Southern Review* (Adelaide), and *Southern Humanities Review* (Auburn, Alabama). My thanks to the editors and publishers concerned for permission to reprint this material in modified form.

A Note on Texts

I have not included a separate bibliography of de Man's writings since the reader will be able to find all the relevant details by going directly to the Notes and References section. For further information, there is the checklist compiled by Tom Keenan and published as an appendix to de Man's *The Resistance to Theory* (Minneapolis: University of Minnesota Press, 1986, pp. 122–27). This covers very nearly everything that appeared after 1955, when de Man started to contribute essays and reviews to French- and, later, to English-language journals. There are still sizable gaps in the record, as I explain in Chapter 6; on the one hand material from his earliest years, on the other those so-far unpublished late texts — often in the form of drafts or lecture transcripts — some of which are now being edited for press. But the Notes to this book, along with Keenan's bibliography, will give sufficient guidance to anyone intending to make a detailed study of de Man's work.

"The prudence that restrains us from venturing too far ahead in a sentence, is usually only an agent of social control, and so of stupefaction."

"This *quid pro quo* of progress and reaction makes orientation in contemporary art almost as difficult as in politics, and furthermore paralyzes production itself, where anyone who clings to extreme intentions is made to feel like a backwoodsman, while the conformist no longer lingers bashfully in arbours, literary or horticultural, but hurtles forward, rocket-powered, into the pluperfect."

"He who wishes to know the truth about life in its immediacy must scrutinize its estranged form, the objective powers that determine individual existence even in its most hidden recesses."

"The ideology of cultural conservatism which sees enlightenment and art as simple antitheses is false, among other reasons, in overlooking the moment of enlightenment in the genesis of beauty . . . The bliss of contemplation consists in disenchanted charm. Radiance is the appeasement of myth."

"The equation of the genuine and the true is untenable . . . Like gold, genuineness, abstracted as the proportion of fine metal, becomes a fetish. Both are treated as if they were the foundation, which in reality is a social relation, while gold and genuineness precisely express only the fungibility, the comparability of things . . . "

"The severance of thought is not remedied by the synthesis of mutually estranged psychic departments, nor by therapeutically imbuing reason with irrational ferments, but by self-conscious reflection on the element of wish that antithetically constitutes thinking as thinking."

Theodor Adorno, *Minima Moralia: Reflections from a Damaged Life*

For
Stephen and Christine

Introduction

In 1985 there appeared a special number of the journal *Yale French Studies* entitled "The Lesson of Paul de Man."[1] It brought together a diverse collection of essays commemorating de Man's work as a teacher, theorist, close reader of texts, and undoubtedly the single most controversial figure in present-day American literary criticism. So much one can say with confidence, given the sheer volume of commentary, admiring or hostile, that his work continues to generate. But at this point the doubts and qualifications begin to crowd in. Does his writing really belong to "literary criticism" in any sense of the term that most readers — inside or outside university departments — would recognize? Is it right to view him as an individual thinker who arrived at certain striking and (as many would argue) utterly perverse ideas about the character of textual meaning and the future of advanced literary studies? De Man would certainly have treated such claims on his own behalf with a skeptical disdain tempered by wry good humor. In her brief memoir E.S. Burt defines as a "moral trait" in de Man "what we sensed to be as complete a detachment from the claims of subjectivity or individual personality as was possible" (*YFS*, p. 11). For there was, as he argued, simply *no other way* for the study of literature to go; no question of his having single-handedly devised a new and distinctive approach to the reading of literary texts. Rather, those texts had always solicited just the kind of reading that de Man now supplied, and it was only the "blindness" of earlier critics — a blindness whose causes went deep and far back — which had so far prevented its widespread acceptance. Criticism's task for the next few decades was to carry on the business of patiently revealing those errors and delusions that had passed for truth merely through the power of entrenched belief. And this task would necessarily be conducted in a spirit of impersonal, selfless dedication which allowed the critic no room to demonstrate his or her brilliance as a virtuoso reader of texts. "Technically correct rhetorical readings may be boring, monotonous, predictable, and unpleasant, but they are irrefutable."[2] Thus de Man in his late essay "The Resistance to Theory" places the maximum possible distance between his own operations and the idea of criticism as a pretext or opportunity for pleasurable self-display.

This latter went along with the age-old practice of literary *interpretation*, a practice aimed toward discovering ever more subtle, profound, or undreamt-of levels of meaning in the text. It promoted an image of the interpreter as one specially skilled or uniquely gifted in the bringing to light of deep-laid truths. For de Man, on the contrary, these truths will most often turn out to be wishful illusions foisted onto the text by a criticism always seeking assurance of its own profundity and sympathetic grasp. In their will to reveal such occult dimensions, critics are drawn into a process of self-confirming circular exchange where nothing is allowed to resist their desire for interpretative mastery and power. Thus criticism becomes an endless celebration of its own capacity to realize meanings that were always (in some sense) *there* in the text, just waiting to be discovered, but which have hitherto gone unnoticed for want of the requisite hermeneutic skill. Such is the belief among those (like the American New Critics) who devise sophisticated techniques of reading in order to exhibit more fully the wealth of multiple meaning — of "ambiguity," "irony," or "paradox" — present in literary texts. These interpreters make a point of insisting that poetry is a special kind of language, marked off from the discourse of plain-prose reason by virtue of its sheer rhetorical complexity. So criticism errs if it resorts to paraphrase or to any form of rational explication which ignores the uniquely privileged status of poetic language. But it takes a high degree of specialized knowledge — for one thing, an elaborated system of rhetorical tropes and devices — for critics to arrive at this advanced position. Only the interpreter equipped with such knowledge will avoid the various "fallacies" of misconceived method which erase the all-important line of demarcation between poetry and other forms of discourse. Hence the New Critics' obvious conviction that theirs was the best, the most revealing, and sensitive way of interpreting texts. That is to say, it raised the art of close reading to a high point of subtlety and refinement *without* in the process losing sight of the distinction — the ontological difference — between poetry and prose. Such a program could claim its own kind of privilege *vis-à-vis* other interpretative methods while also denying any suggestion that its language might encroach upon poetry's sacred domain.

I shall have more to say about de Man's ambivalent relationship to the New Criticism. Certainly his work was much influenced, at an early stage, by the modes of close reading and rhetorical exegesis which the New Critics brought to the study of literary texts. He was also convinced like them (though for very different reasons) that the sheer complexity of literary language placed it absolutely beyond reach of paraphrase or straightforward conceptual explanation. But here the resemblances end. For de Man, the whole purpose of rhetorical study is to bring out the stark *impossibility* of knowing (as the New Critics claimed to know) just where to draw a firm juridical line between literature and other sorts of language. If he continued to make such distinctions it was only by way of insisting 1) that *all* language is to some degree "literary," in so far as it inevitably includes a certain tropological or figural dimension, and 2) that this fact is regularly ignored or suppressed by those forms of discourse (e.g. philosophy) that prefer not to acknowledge their own kinship with rhetoric or literary style. Barbara Johnson has an essay in the Yale volume ("Rigorous Unreliability") that states the main issues with characteristic elegance and force. "The relation between literature and philosophy involves the repetitive set-up and collapse of their difference . . . philosophy is defined by its refusal to recognize itself as literature; literature is defined as the rhetorical self-transgression of philosophy" (*YFS*, p. 76). Thus de Man rejects the ontological presumptions of the "old" New Criticism, the idea that poetry is somehow *sui generis*, a language possessed of its own kind of truth whose mysteries are vouchsafed only to those who resist the various tempting "heresies" of paraphrase, biography, historical source-hunting, and so forth. It is precisely this mystified notion of poetic form that de Man will deconstruct in his various writings on the aesthetic ideology of post-Romantic criticism. His point is to show that such claims always rest on a willed blindness to the omnipresence of figural language, even in writings that expressly or routinely mark themselves off from "literature" as such.

So the texts of New Criticism — as de Man reads them — turn out to question their own ontological priorities through a play of rhetorical tropes and displacements which cannot be confined to poetry alone. The more elaborate their strategies of reading, the less it appears possible to lay down rules for the proper, self-regulating discourse of critical method. These interpreters may argue — state categorically — that poems are "organic" entities, belonging to a separate realm of discourse where form is most aptly conceived by analogy with nature or the processes of natural growth. Such arguments of course go back to Wordsworth, Coleridge, and the aesthetics of transcendence identified chiefly with Romantic metaphor and symbol. They serve notice that criticism had best not confuse its own modes of conceptual understanding with the quite distinct truth-claims embodied in poetry or the language of creative imagination. But the organicist analogy begins to break down as critics become perforce more aware of the multiple, disruptive nature of poetic meaning. In de Man's words: "instead of revealing a continuity affiliated with the coherence of the natural world, it [New Criticism] takes us into a discontinuous world of reflective irony and ambiguity. . . . Almost in spite of itself, it pushes the interpretative process so far that the analogy between the organic world and the language of poetry finally explodes."[3]

And so what started out, in Coleridgean terms, as a hermeneutic quest for "unity in multiplicity" becomes in the end — and despite its own principles — an acknowledgment that no such unity is there to be found.

In this passage (dating from the mid-1950s) one already finds a clear, almost programmatic statement of the two main theses that de Man was to elaborate through nearly thirty years of intensive critical work. The first has to do with the delusory character of any such appeal to *organic* or *naturalizing* metaphors when dealing with questions of poetry, language, or representation. This is the source of that potent "aesthetic ideology" whose origins (principally in a certain misreading of Kant) and whose effects (not least on the politics of interpretation) de Man will set out to deconstruct with increasing emphasis and care. The other is his claim that our reading of critical texts can best proceed by way of noting those ironic disparities between meaning and intent that seem to characterize all systematic reflection on literary language. In the case of the critics whose work he examines in *Blindness and Insight,* "a paradoxical discrepancy appears between the general statements they make about the nature of literature (statements on which they base their critical methods) and the actual results of their interpretations" (*BI*, p. ix). It is for this reason that de Man seeks out those moments of symptomatic "blindness" in critical texts where there also exists the possibility of renewed "insight" through a reading alert to these rhetorical tensions. And this applies equally to the language of philosophy, a discourse that has always (or at least since Plato's quarrel with the poets and rhetoricians) considered itself exempt from the seductions of merely figural language. If such beliefs still hold sway — if indeed they constitute the very self-image of philosophy and the grounds for its existence as an autonomous discipline — then this can only be because (as de Man would argue) its texts have escaped, or its practitioners actively discouraged, such close rhetorical reading.

So "literature" is conserved as an operative term in de Man's criticism, but *not* in the sense of a body of writings possessing certain distinctive attributes that mark them out for privileged treatment. One could make the point simply — too simply — by saying that de Man's most "original" achievement is to have extended the techniques of rhetorical close reading developed by modern literary critics to the texts of other disciplines (like philosophy and criticism itself) where up to now those techniques have not been applied. But this might suggest that de Man is simply out to blur all forms of categorical distinction and recommend that we henceforth read every kind of text in the way that critics normally read poems or novels. Even a nodding acquaintance with de Man's work should suffice to dispel this mistaken impression. Perhaps it is the case (as he claims at one point in *Allegories of Reading*) that philosophy when analyzed in terms of its textual or rhetorical constitution will always turn out to be "an endless reflection on its own destruction at the hands of literature."[4] But this is not to say that "literature" — or literary criticism — comes out of this exchange with its traditional values enhanced by the apparent discomfiture of "philosophy." For those values have been staked precisely on the notion of literature as a *different* kind of writing, one that is defined by whatever sets it apart from (e.g.) philosophy. And it is here that de Man takes issue with just about every basic assumption in the discourse of aesthetics and literary theory. For we simply don't possess any workable concept of "literature" that would justify this defensive beating of ontological bounds or this desire to lay down terms and conditions for keeping the disciplines apart. If philosophy is in some sense compromised by its kinship with literature — its dependence on rhetorical figures — then critics seem just as anxious to maintain a safe distance from philosophy.

It is crucially by way of the *aesthetic* — a category too often simply assumed to reconcile the disjunct realms of sensuous and cognitive experience — that critics have managed to maintain such a state of epistemological innocence. For de Man, on the contrary, it is an open question "whether aesthetic values can be compatible with the linguistic structures that make up the entities from which these values are derived" (*RT*, p. 25). In fact his later work was devoted in large part to showing how this linkage remained problematical in Kant, but was eased out of sight — or simply taken for granted — by Schiller and other proponents of "aesthetic education" as a means of resolving such deep-laid antinomies. Hence the belief that language, especially the language of poetry, could unify the otherwise disparate orders of what Kant calls "sensuous intuition" and "concepts of the pure understanding." This belief persists largely unchallenged in modern criticism, and its effects — according to de Man — are responsible for much confusion. It is therefore a major part of his project to show how meaning cannot be reduced to any kind of phenomenal or sensory perception; how there always comes a point in the rhetorical study of texts where signifying structures no longer match up with any conceivable form of sensuous cognition. Such is indeed de Man's chief claim for the critical or demystifying power of textual analysis. "Close reading accomplishes this often in spite of itself because it cannot fail to respond to structures of language which it is the more or less secret aim of literary teaching to keep hidden" (*RT*, p. 24).

So de Man's work cannot easily be classified in terms laid down by the standard academic division of labor. He is perhaps best described as a conceptual rhetorician, one who perceives the linguistic (or tropological) blocks in the way of conceptual understanding, but who insists that these paradoxes cannot be resolved by appealing to a privileged aesthetic realm beyond all such hateful antinomies. It is this refusal to come down squarely on the side of either "literature" or "philosophy" which gives de Man's texts their peculiar way of resisting any kind of summary description. He is a thinker who has engaged distinctly philosophic problems — mainly in the post-Kantian tradition of epistemological critique — with a rigor scarcely equaled among other, more orthodox commentators. This comes of his insistence that the texts of philosophy can claim no special dispensation from the forms of close reading or rhetorical analysis developed by modern literary critics. But de Man is equally determined to shake criticism out of its dogmatic slumbers by showing how often its practitioners have failed to think through the nature of their own enterprise with anything like an adequate "philosophical" cogency or power of analytic grasp. Philosophers have tended to evade such problems by assuming that language — *their* kind of language — had access to a realm of clear and distinct ideas where the tropes could either be ignored (as belonging to mere "rhetoric") or safely held in check by a self-denying ordinance of style. Such was the assumption that enabled thinkers like Locke and Kant to devote short passages of their work to the problem of figural language, always with the assurance that thinking could be put straight back onto the path of rational inquiry by simply keeping watch for these telltale signs of tropological disruption. In fact, de Man argues, the figural dimension is omnipresent in philosophy, and never more powerful and seductive than at precisely those moments when philosophers think to have settled accounts with it once and for all. But this is not to say that literary critics — trained in the ways of rhetorical analysis — are necessarily much better placed than philosophers to observe those same disruptive effects. For criticism is prone to different forms of self-induced aesthetic mystification, forms which de Man sets out to analyze through the deconstructive reading of symptomatic moments in the discourse of post-Romantic critical thought.

So it is hardly surprising that his work has aroused such antagonism among philosophers and literary critics alike. Their response bears witness to de Man's notorious "techniques for making trouble," his way of unsettling all the values and assumptions that operate in both these disciplines. But of course — as de Man was the first to admit — those writings carry no kind of authority apart from what is achieved in the detailed close reading of texts. That is to say, they solicit an active, critical engagement which accepts nothing on faith and which puts up resistance at every stage on the difficult path to understanding. Few critics — and even fewer philosophers — have been willing to acknowledge the problematic status of their own most crucial arguments and truth-claims. Nor is de Man himself quite immune to the suggestion that *his* kind of rigorous, undeceiving rhetoric must give him a decided advantage over other, presumably less strong-minded critics. It comes out especially in his manner of responding to those various defenders of "mainstream" philosophical or literary readings whose only concern (as de Man often implies) is to shield their disciplines against such intrusion by "outside" pressures and interests. But this rhetoric of authority belongs to the polemical side of de Man's writing and is soon placed in doubt when he turns to the business of detailed textual explication. Here there is always an implicit understanding that *any* discourse — his own included — will occasionally be subject to those moments of constitutive error or "blindness" inseparable from true insight.

The essays assembled in *The Lesson of Paul de Man* pay his work the tribute of engaging stubbornly with its more refractory claims and not succumbing to a mood of misplaced solemn reverence. Thus Jonathan Culler asks very pointedly how we can reconcile de Man's insistence on the error-prone nature of reading with the need to make tolerable sense of his arguments despite all the obstacles they place in our way. On the one hand those arguments "focus on what resists or disrupts the hermeneutic process and repeatedly oppose an understanding which overcomes textual difficulties so as to hear in the text what it is thought to say." But on the other, as Culler remarks, "one can only make sense of his writings if one already has a sense of what they must be saying and can allow for the slippage of concepts, working to get over or around the puzzling valuations, the startling assertions, the apparently incompatible claims" (*YFS*, p. 106). Culler is not the only commentator to perceive this tension between the relentlessly demystifying drive of de Man's criticism and the fact that comprehension cannot begin without suspending that rigor at least to a certain degree. At this point one moves — like Hans-Jost Frey — to a diagnostic reading that applies de Man's lesson to his own texts and raises the question: what can possibly *motivate* such a stance of extreme epistemological scepticism? "If there is no discourse that can sustain undecidability without disavowing it, one can at least ask what the implications of this undecidability are" (*YFS*, p. 130).

Here the commentaries divide very roughly into those that seek out some humanizing pathos, some subjective *need* in de Man that drove him to adopt this self-denying ordinance, and those that follow his own injunction not to indulge in such consoling hermeneutic strategies. Minae Mizumura has an interesting piece which can be seen to oscillate between these positions. Her topic is de Man's persistent concern with ideas of sacrifice, disavowal, and renunciation, a concern that assumes ever more complex and tortuous forms in the process of his critical argumentation. For the early de Man what has to be renounced is the dream of a language that would reconcile mind and nature, subject and object in the moment of a perfect, self-present access to truth achieved through the power of poetic imagination to transcend such merely prosaic antinomies. Authentic reading would then consist in the courage to reject this temptation by facing up to the contingency of language and the fact that privileged tropes like symbol and metaphor must always depend, in the last resort, on pedestrian or un-self-deluded figures like metonymy and allegory. But the will to renounce this belief — to do without what de Man calls "the nostalgia and the will to coincide" — still goes along with a certain attachment to the idea of renunciation itself as a measure of authentic understanding. Hence the very marked existentialist tonings of de Man's early essays, the suggestion that authentic (undeluded) reading is capable of rising above such forms of seductive or naive understanding. But this standpoint presupposes at least some residual notion of the reading *self*, of a subjectivity that becomes all the more authentic as it manages to renounce the false beguilements of premature meaning and method.

According to Mizumura, there are still clear signs of this belief even in an essay like "The Rhetoric of Temporality" (1969: *BI*, pp. 187–228), often regarded as a crucial turning point in de Man's progress from a kind of covert existentialism to a thoroughgoing deconstructive or "textualist" stance. De Man himself took a distinctly Heideggerian view of this essay as marking a definite "turn" in his work, although his way of making the point — in terms of "authentic" versus "inauthentic" reading — could be seen as undermining any such claim. According to Mizumura, there *does* come about a decisive transition in de Man's thinking, but one that has to wait for the yet more extreme ascetic discipline of *Allegories of Reading* and the subsequent essays. It is a turn that takes place "only when de Man's text most rigorously works out what is implied in his own declaration that 'the cognitive function resides in the language and not in the subject'" (*YFS*, p. 92). That is to say, it can only be achieved through the act of renouncing renunciation itself, or the will to leave behind that residual pathos that attaches to the notion of authentic reading as a facing-up to the limits placed upon human understanding by the ontological gulf between subject and object, word and world. From this latter viewpoint — one that emerges in *Blindness and Insight* and which still exerts a very potent appeal in "The Rhetoric of Temporality" — it is in the nature of our predicament as *human* readers that we should always be drawn to misinterpret texts by seeking out moments of transcendent, visionary insight which language is in fact, by reason of its temporal or contingent character, unable to achieve. And to recognize this inbuilt liability of human understanding is also to associate a certain pathos with the undeceived knowledge that strives to overcome it. What occurs in the later de Man, according to Mizumura, is yet another stage in the process of renunciation, one that rejects even this last, lingering attachment to a rhetoric of human authenticity. "The shift from a concern with human errors to a concern with the problem inherent in language epitomizes his ultimate choice of language over man" (*YFS*, p. 92). It is here — at the point of renouncing every tie between language and the will to make sense of language in humanly acceptable terms — that de Man leaves behind that existential pathos that persists in his early essays.

There is undoubtedly a large measure of truth in Mizumura's observations. De Man does indeed reach a point where he seems to deny that there exists any relation between language as conceived in deconstructionist terms — conceived, that is to say, as a wholly impersonal network of tropological drives, substitutions, and displacements — and language as the expression of human meanings and intentions. The Yale volume contains one such piece, the text of de Man's last lecture, given at Cornell University in March 1983 just eight months before his death. Its topic is Walter Benjamin's elusive essay "The Task of the Translator," and de Man here presses even further than Benjamin in questioning every received assumption about language, meaning, and the powers of human communicative grasp. Translation as commonly practiced takes for granted the expressive view of language wherein words give utterance to meanings, thoughts, and intentions which can then be carried across, more or less intact, from one linguistic or cultural context to another. On the contrary, says de Man: "the problem is precisely that, whereas the meaning-function is certainly intentional, it is not a priori certain at all that the mode of meaning, the way in which I mean, is intentional in any way" (*YFS*, p. 39). Since meaning depends upon "devices" and "linguistic properties" which belong not to *us* as individual speakers but to language — language in its given, autonomous, always-already constituted nature — it is not, de Man argues, "made by us as historical beings, it is perhaps not even made by humans at all" (*YFS*, p. 39). In which case we can only be deluded, albeit (as de Man would no doubt acknowledge) *inescapably and naturally* so, if we place our faith in the human character of language and its power, by and large, to mean what we intend it to mean. To call de Man's position counterintuitive is therefore a massive understatement. Only in writers like Samuel Beckett and E.M. Cioran do we find anything like a comparable sense of this alien, unhomely character in language, its lack of all human qualities and attributes.

The Benjamin essay is by no means exceptional in this regard. Mizumura cites the well-known passage from *Allegories of Reading* where de Man takes an episode from Rousseau's *Confessions* (the story of the purloined ribbon) as a case study of the way that language works to generate narrative pretexts quite beyond the call of truth, conscience, or authorial self-justification. "Far from seeing language as an instrument in the service of a psychic energy, the possibility now arises that the entire construction of drives, substitutions, repressions, and representations is the aberrant, metaphorical correlative of the absolute randomness of language, prior to any figuration or meaning" (*AR*, p. 299). To this Mizumura might have added the extraordinary closing paragraph from his essay "Shelley Disfigured," where de Man reads *The Triumph of Life* as a poem that effectively fragments and destroys all sense of thematic coherence, of authorial presence, or humanly intelligible meaning. What the poem teaches us at last, according to de Man, is "that nothing, whether deed, word, thought, or text, ever happens in relation, positive or negative, to anything that proceeds, follows or exists elsewhere, but only as a random event whose power, like the power of death, is due to the randomness of its occurrence."[5] For the mainstream interpreters of Romanticism, language (especially the language of metaphor and symbol) stands on the side of life, creativity, and everything opposed to the random, contingent character of lifeless arbitrary signs. For de Man, on the contrary, language is everywhere shadowed by the fact of its mortal predicament, its failure to escape those random occurrences (like Shelley's own death by drowning) that block or frustrate its visionary impulse. Hence his strongly marked preference for tropes like metonymy and allegory, figures that renounce the heady seductions of a rhetoric of transcendence and thereby work to demystify the claims of that potent aesthetic ideology.

Such tropes hold out against the high Romantic dream of a perfect, unimpeded communing of mind with nature or mind with mind. They insist that understanding is at best a timebound, fragmentary, and error-prone activity which can offer no kind of hermeneutic guarantee that true communication has taken place. Thus metonymy is standardly categorized as a trope that operates on the basis of contiguity and other such random, accidental features, while metaphor has been treated (from Aristotle down) as a touchstone of artistic creativity, involving the perception of occult resemblances that transcend mere particulars of place and time. De Man does more than simply reverse this deep-laid evaluative bias. He asserts that metonymy is truer to the facts, not only of language but of human existence in the face of our common mortality. Hence his startling, and to many readers quite outrageous claim in "Shelley Disfigured": that *The Triumph of Life* is subject to the random, aleatory forces of metonymic language just as Shelley's own life was cut short by the accident of his drowning. No reading of the poem can hope to escape this "negative knowledge" by taking refuge in Romantic ideas of metaphor, symbol or organic unity. According to de Man, such readings are "powerless to prevent what now functions as the decisive textual articulation: its [the poem's] reduction to the status of a fragment brought about by the actual death and subsequent disfigurement of Shelley's body, burned after his boat capsized and he drowned off the coast of Lerici" (*RR*, p. 120). And if it seems, as de Man suspects it will, "a freak of chance to have a text thus molded by an actual occurrence," he is nonetheless prepared to go yet further and declare that "this mutilated textual model exposes the wound of a fracture that lies hidden in all texts" (*RR*, p. 120).

It is hard to know what to make of such claims, offered as they are in a tone of apodictic certainty which scarcely mitigates their scandalous character. But if one thing is clear, it is the fact that de Man's language is still haunted by ideas of sacrifice, loss, and renunciation — that he has not so much broken with this habit of thinking as attempted to generalize it far beyond the limits of any straightforward thematic understanding. Mizumura makes this point in her essay when she remarks that "he continues to speak about renunciation even in his later works when the word itself has disappeared from his text" (*YFS*, p. 94). Any reading of de Man that ignores this dimension will accept too readily his own rhetoric of impersonal rigor and detachment. Thus, in Mizumura's words, "the impression of deprivation comes closer, nonetheless, to grasping the quintessence of de Man than a placid acceptance of the extreme askesis that reigns in his work" (*YFS*, p. 97). And this connects in turn with the question of whether de Man had indeed moved "beyond " thematic interpretation to a level of generalized reflection on language and the limits of interpretative thought that no longer answered to the title of "literary criticism." Rodolphe Gasché thinks this question crucial to the whole enterprise of deconstruction in so far as it has been made over (as he argues) from the strictly philosophical concerns that animate Derrida's work into a version of applied interpretative theory that basically continues the "old" New Criticism in a more sophisticated guise. In fact Gasché takes that singular phrase from de Man's essay on Shelley — "the wound of a fracture that lies hidden in all texts" — as a measure of the distance that separates Derridean philosophy of language from its literary-critical offshoot.[6] It is not my concern at this stage to adjudicate in the matter of just what constitutes an *echt*-deconstructionist approach to issues of language and representation. But clearly the phrase is open to two kinds of reading, one of which would accept its generalizing claim — that *all* texts are subject to this dislocating force within language — while the other would point to its charged rhetorical character and the hints of a certain existential pathos that still come across in de Man's late writing.

One finds this unresolved question surfacing in various forms throughout the otherwise very diverse essays collected in *The Lesson of Paul de Man*. Several contributors (among them Culler and Michael Riffaterre) focus on the trope of prosopopeia, the figure that summons up an absent, dead, or ghostly personage by means of an act of naming that both evokes their presence and reminds us of the distance that separates them now from any power of living recall. As Culler remarks, "the status of prosopopeia and its relation to anthropomorphism is a crucial problem in de Man's conception of the lyric" (*YFS*, p. 100). The main text here is de Man's late essay "Autobiography as De-Facement," where this trope becomes a virtual synonym for what de Man calls the "privative" power of language, its way of apparently giving life and voice to the dead while in fact exposing language to all manner of ghostly possession by forces beyond its living control. The essay concludes with another of those curiously ambivalent passages where de Man's self-denying rigor of style goes along with a kind of muted intensity that suggests, once again, what an effort of repression is here taking place. Death itself, de Man writes, "is a displaced name for a linguistic predicament, and the restoration of mortality by autobiography (the prosopopeia of the voice and the name) deprives and disfigures to the precise extent that it restores" (*RR*, p. 81). Hence his frequent recourse to those passages (in Wordsworth especially) where claims for the affirmative or life-giving power of language go along with a sense of its darker, mortal implications. Such is the "latent threat that inhabits prosopopeia," namely that "by making the dead speak, the symmetrical structure of the trope implies, by the same token, that the living are struck dumb, frozen in their own death" (*RR*, p. 78).

Of course these reflections take something of their uncanny force from our knowledge of de Man's imminent death, just as — on his reading — *The Triumph of Life* cannot be understood apart from the "contingent" but utterly material fact of Shelley's drowning. And indeed it is difficult — a problem that these essays register in various ways — to observe anything like the rigorous separation that de Man's work seems to require between (in T.S. Eliot's phrase) "the man who suffers" and "the mind which creates". The elegiac tone of these essays is by no means confined to the early portion of the book which contains tributes to de Man from friends, colleagues, and students. It is there also in the pieces that engage with theoretical aspects of his work, especially where these touch upon the themes of mourning, remembrance, and poetic valediction. Thus Anselm Haverkamp contributes an essay that moves, as if inevitably, from a close reading of de Man on Hölderlin to a series of increasingly charged meditations on the failure of language to recapture — or "interiorize" — the memory of a living presence that poetry seems to hold out. "The promise is cancelled by death; death is not overcome by promise. . . . What leads Hölderlin 'beyond subjectivity' is the deconstruction of the human as echo, of lyrical subjectivity as anthropomorphism" (*YFS*, pp. 252–53). As with de Man, so with his commentators: on the one hand an argument meticulously purged of "subjective" or "anthropomorphic" residues, on the other a language that cannot in the end renounce such all-too-human implications.

Geoffrey Hartman apostrophizes both aspects of de Man in a sentence that (echoing Wallace Stevens) again moves across from recognition of the self-denying rigor to a sense of what lay behind that extraordinary style. "He made his mind increasingly more severe, and those who remember him listening fixedly to lectures by students or visitors know he could always spot the vulnerable point which turned the monumental project into a mortal project" (*YFS*, p. 7). Other contributors — among them Jacques Derrida and Yves Bonnefoy — likewise give a sense of this pervasive duality in de Man's temperament: on the one hand his warmth, generosity, and loyalty to colleagues and friends, on the other that self-abnegating spirit that marked both his writing and his conduct of personal relationships. The lyric poet Bonnefoy sets out to correct any impression we might have of de Man as a joyless, unremittingly cerebral type whose sheer mistrust of language's tendency toward forms of delusive "naturalization" led him to renounce the consoling possibilities of sensuous or physical life. Bonnefoy's essay is in one sense a kind of poetic rejoinder to de Man himself, a prose-poem of intensely metaphorical character which sets out to humanize his memory by evoking a series of emblematic scenes and settings, from Ireland to Zürich and Provence, Connecticut and California. But however strong this attachment to the natural world — "prairies and forests, waves surging among the rocks" — de Man was none the less implacably convinced that "it was and would remain inaccessible to language and moreover, even to poetry" (*YFS*, P. 328).

It is in these terms, Bonnefoy suggests, that we should seek to understand his otherwise inexplicable, not to say perverse insistence on the errors and the failures resulting from the will to reconcile language and nature, word and world. De Man "loved poetry too much to refer to it too directly, and, by so doing, engage himself in it — he preferred, as in his writing, to evoke poets rather than poetry itself, and critics rather than poets" (*YFS*, P. 328). It is a curious form of tribute, all the more so in that Bonnefoy's language is unable to conceal its allegiance to a wholly different order of poetic and human priorities. Any treatment of de Man that underrates the sheer strangeness of his work, the resistance it puts up to all our commonplace homely assumptions about language and experience, is a reading profoundly at odds with the character of that work. The following chapters are accordingly a mixture of exposition and critique, their object not only to defend his texts against various kinds of partial and polemical misreading, but also to suggest where they *ought* to be approached with a measure of argued resistance and scepticism. My reading focuses on two questions in particular: the political significance of his work and its relation to the interests of philosophy from Kant to the modern (analytical) heritage. Discussion of both has been bedeviled so far by the overly partisan attitudes adopted by de Man's disciples and detractors alike. And it has become yet more difficult with the recent, much-publicized discovery of some articles he wrote during the early 1940s for the Belgian collaborationist newspaper *Le Soir*. I hope that this book will go at least some way toward establishing more useful and productive terms for debate.

1

Allegories of Disenchantment: Poetry and Politics in de Man's Early Essays

I

The most concerted attack on Paul de Man's work has come from critics of a Marxist or left-wing persuasion, notably Frank Lentricchia and Terry Eagleton. They see in it not only a private retreat from political engagement but a last-ditch attempt to discredit every form of historical knowledge and action. "In de Man's analysis," Lentricchia writes, "the futility, the self-delusion, and the paralysis of political activity, especially oppositional political activity, would appear to be a foregone conclusion."[1] And this not simply for the reason that de Man would treat all kinds of writing — historical narratives, political manifestos, works of *Ideologiekritik* — as so many complex rhetorical structures with no direct or unmediated reference to a world of reality "outside" the text. The same could be said, after all, of those left-wing activist critics like Edward Said who insist on the materiality of signifying practice, the ways in which cultural representations can work to reinforce or to challenge and subvert systems of instituted power.[2] Lentricchia himself makes this point very firmly in *Criticism and Social Change*, where he hails Kenneth Burke as the greatest exemplar of a practice of engaged rhetorical critique, a critique that aims to transform social consciousness by revealing the mechanisms of ideological mystification. If Burke is the hero of Lentricchia's tale, de Man figures throughout as his devilish counterpart, a "nihilist" bent upon throwing up obstacles to any hope of comprehending — and thus transforming — our historical situation.

Burke is placed squarely in the long tradition (going back at least to Aristotle) that associates rhetoric not only with the business of producing suasive arguments but also with the need to defend and debate those arguments in the forum of political exchange. His entire life's work, so Lentricchia contends, is a fine vindication of rhetoric's claim to act as an energizing force in the struggle to articulate social interests and motives. For de Man, on the contrary, rhetoric is a means of disabling this project at source, of showing how language always and inevitably "dissociates the cognition from the act," thus reducing thought to an endless reflection on its own incapacity for effecting radical change. Deconstruction is the heir to that Nietzschean strain of irrationalist fatalism that reduces all thinking to the blind operation of tropes and self-engendered rhetorical forces beyond our power to control or comprehend. It thus becomes unthinkable — the merest dream of an outworn enlightenment tradition — that historical agents should seek to change their material conditions of existence by translating thought into action through a sustained effort of ideological critique. As Lentricchia reads it, de Man's is currently the most "advanced" form of this desire to neutralize political activity by showing it to rest on hopelessly naive ideas about mind, language, and reality.

Terry Eagleton concurs pretty much with Lentricchia's diagnosis, viewing the entirety of de Man's work as a covert polemic against Marxism.[3] He points to those passages in the early de Man where Heidegger's influence is still strongly marked, and where the claims of historical (especially of historical-materialist) thought are counterposed to the deeper, more "authentic" demands of an existential brooding on *Dasein*, time, and mortality. For Eagleton, the essays in *Blindness and Insight* — at least those dating from the first period of de Man's literary production — typically work to establish the following conclusions. Historical understanding is a form of false consciousness, the refuge of minds unable to contemplate the stark contingencies of human existence and authentic being-unto-death. Thus Marxism restricts its understanding to the realm of merely secular history and politics in order to avoid the tragic self-knowledge, the sense of our dispossessed or alien predicament that comes of such authentic experience. Poetry and politics are worlds apart, since poetry (on de Man's Heideggerian account of it) reveals the ontological difference between beings and Being, the gap that opens up between our everyday empirical knowledge of the world and that primordial truth whose only intimations are the signs of its existing beyond all reach of our belated, secular condition. If Marxism to some extent shares this view — if it speaks of human history in terms of a fall into reification, class division, and other such evils — still it lacks the courage or the will to press this analysis home. For de Man, in short, "the problem of separation inheres in Being, which means that social forms of separation derive from ontological and meta-social attitudes."[4] What

Marxism attempts to do is translate this unhappy consciousness, this sense of inward exile and estrangement, into a merely *historical* accident whose effects can always be reversed by the appropriate, historically punctual forms of concerted thought and action. "Marxism is, ultimately, a poetic thought that lacks the patience to pursue its conclusions to their end."[5] That is to say, it is "poetic" to the extent of acknowledging our present self-divided, unhappy condition, but falls short of poetry (authentic poetry) in seeking a secular, political issue out of all our afflictions.

Eagleton is undoubtedly right when he argues that this early Heideggerian strain in de Man goes along with a deep aversion to Marxism and the claims of historical understanding. There is also de Man's sharp denial of the idea that thought might at length overcome the "division inherent in Being" through forms of jointly intellectual and material praxis which offer at least a glimpse of alternative possibilities. In rejecting such notions the early de Man sounds a decidedly Hegelian note. "The ambiguity poetry speaks of is the fundamental one that prevails between the world of the spirit and the world of sentient substance. . . . The spirit cannot coincide with its object and this separation is infinitely sorrowful."[6] So there is no transcending this ontological gulf, this distance fixed between thought and the material objects-of-thought. Least of all can such transcendence be achieved by a Marxist criticism which — as de Man would have it — merely lacks the necessary "patience" or courage to know what the poets have always implicitly known. It is on these grounds that de Man argues (and will indeed continue to argue, through *Allegories of Reading* to his very last essays) that linguistic meaning can never be reduced to any form of phenomenal cognition; that there is simply no warrant, no evidence at all for the widespread assumption that meaning coincides with something in the nature of physical or sensuous perception. De Man's attitude to Marxism — and, more generally, to the claims of politics on literary theory — would change a great deal in the three decades that separate his earliest from his final essays. But he remained quite unswerving in this conviction that any move to short-circuit the gap between phenomenal and semantic orders of sense was merely a deluded attempt to escape the problems faced by all authentic reflection on language, thought, and reality.[7]

To the Marxist such insistence will appear just a form of stubbornly mystified thinking, one that serves to bolster an attitude of political quietism (or something worse). Thus Eagleton pointedly turns back the thrust of de Man's polemic, arguing that the "unhappy consciousness" in question is *not* the product of some timeless metaphysical malaise, some deep self-division inherent in Being itself, but more specifically the upshot of a bourgeois-liberal academic tradition run aground on the knowledge of its own historical obsolescence. "What for de Man is the irony of the human condition as such is in fact the product of a particular historical blockage, of which deconstruction is the inheritor."[8] For Lentricchia likewise, the motivating impulse of de Man's whole project is the will to block or frustrate any kind of radical critique that would move beyond theory to the realm of politically effective choices and actions. He finds the main evidence for this in de Man's 1969 essay "Literary History and Literary Modernity," where the modern is conceived in Nietzschean terms as an absolute break with all forms of historical awareness, a moment of oblivion which frees thought for action only by severing its links with a remembered past.[9] Such forgetting is vital (Nietzsche contends) because history and memory are inherently opposed to the will for radical change. They stand on the side of permanence, continuity, tradition, and everything that tends to paralyze thought by its clinging to obsolete values and ideas. "Modernity" and "history" are therefore antithetical terms, opposed not so much in a merely chronological sense as by reason of their always confronting the thinker with a drastic choice of alternatives. For Nietzsche (in his essay "The Use and Abuse of History") this amounts to the choice between a wholly inert, monument-alizing concept of tradition, one that precludes any thought of change, and on the other hand a kind of innocence regained, a posthistorical euphoria that acknowledges nothing anterior to itself. "Life," "health," "vitality," "energy," and "action" are some other names by which Nietzsche distinguishes the promise of renewal contained in this power of an absolute, radical forgetting.[10]

Lentricchia reads de Man as surpassing even Nietzsche in the will to discredit historical thought by setting it up in false opposition to a mystified concept of modernity. For de Man, this opposition is in any case deluded, since there is always a deeper complicity at work within and between the two terms, a reciprocal dependence whereby "history" is defined as the passive counterpart of modernity, and modernity as that which actively contests but also presupposes the truth-claims of history. To de Man it thus appears that "Nietzsche's most interesting moments move against — that is, 'deconstruct' — the opposition of history and life by showing them to be involved with each other in an interdependent relationship of nonopposition."[11] And this has the effect (so Lentricchia argues) of utterly immobilizing thought by denying it even that last, desperate escape route to a Nietzschean moment of pure forgetting. De Man is after all not deceived into thinking that any such move is really possible; that thought can simply break with its entire prehistory and achieve this kind of radical innocence. His intention is rather to destroy the very grounds of historical understanding by a three-stage process of reductive argument whose premises are 1) that "history" is a profoundly conservative force which works against the spirit of renewal; 2) that "modernity" is the only way out from under the dead hand of history; but 3) that since modernity itself depends on an "absolute forgetting" which is strictly inconceivable, *therefore* we should place no faith in projects that envisage any kind of radical change. If we accept these arguments, Lentricchia warns, then we can easily be led to accept also "his [de Man's] implied conclusions about radicalism and revolution," namely that these are delusive ideas without the least basis of historical or existential warrant. "The condition for action is not just forgetting — which is Nietzsche's modest point, but (de Man's inflation of the Nietzschean point) an 'absolute' forgetting, a pleonastic underscoring that hints at de Man's fundamental hostility toward the political, a stacking of the cards against action's political efficacy."[12]

There is no doubt that de Man's early essays are indeed heavily "stacked" against Marxism and against any form of critical thinking that would privilege history as the ultimate ground of interpretative method. What he always sets up in opposition to history is a certain idea of the poetic, of poetry as a deeper, more authentic knowledge undeluded by the claims of merely secular understanding. Perhaps the most striking example is his essay "Wordsworth and Hölderlin" (1966), where de Man raises questions of historical belatedness, of poetry's relation to politics, and specifically that kind of revolutionary politics that preoccupies Wordsworth in *The Prelude*.[13] One passage he singles out is the sequence of episodes in Book VI where the poet records his journeyings in France during 1790 — looking back on them, of course, from a ten-year distance and a greatly altered political perspective. Wordsworth's companions on this occasion were two young delegates to the *états généraux* whose mood of radical excitement the poet then shared although now, at the actual time of writing (1802), he views it in a spirit of chastened, postrevolutionary hindsight. As de Man remarks, such passages have often caused confusion among Wordsworth's critics, involving as they do a complex relationship of voices, time scales, and narrative levels which resist any clearcut distinction between past and present consciousness. In technical terms these problems are a matter of enunciative modality, of whether — at any given stage — we are attending to the thoughts of the young Wordsworth, recreated through sympathetic insight, or whether it is the older, disenchanted poet who supplies an ironic gloss on those thoughts. But issues of politics are never far away when interpreters take their stand on such questions. And what emerges in the course of de Man's reading is certainly of interest from this point of view.

A crucial passage in the sequence, he argues, is Wordsworth's account of the cloister of the Grande Chartreuse, representative of all those religious institutions and values threatened by the mounting revolutionary violence. De Man sees no evidence of straightforward conservative reaction in the older poet's manner of recounting this episode. "In 1802 . . . it was in no way a matter (as it often was later) of protecting the ruling religion against a social reform in which he had fully believed" (*RR*, p. 55). But there is all the same — according to de Man — a much subtler movement of recoil from the claims of political action, a movement which takes us back to those antinomies propounded in a starker, more programmatic form in the essay "Literary History and Literary Modernity." Again it is a question of two distinct attitudes to the nature of human experience, the one (political) staking its faith on the efficacy of action and the prospects for change, the other (more authentic) acknowledging the utterly contingent nature of our being-in-the-world and the overriding fact of our common mortality. Politics is seen as a means of evading these ultimate issues, a premature escape from the concerns that characterize all true reflection on the nature and limits of human understanding.

It will help to quote at length from de Man's commentary and bring out the various oppositions in play. What the radicals threaten to destroy, he writes,

> is the temporal nature of our existence. Their joy expresses itself with such self-assurance and lack of measure that it believes itself capable of reconciling the moment with eternity. They mean to possess something that endures which they fashion according to the intoxication of the act, and yet this thing that endures exists only in a nature that endures precisely because it negates the instant, just as reflection must negate the act that nonetheless constitutes its origin. (*RR*, p. 56)

De Man makes this point in a language heavy with existentialist overtones, a rhetoric more typical of his earliest essays but by no means absent from the writings of his middle period. The French revolutionaries are here identified with a will to pass directly from everyday, natural experience to a providential order that will dawn, so to speak, only under the aspect of eternity. Their "enthusiasm" knows no mortal bounds; it leaps toward a kind of premature transcendence that would raise political action to the level of revealed truth. And in so doing they ignore the constraints placed upon human knowledge by the limiting conditions of time, mortality, and chance — by the fact that there exists no ultimate, validating truth that could save such actions from their own utterly contingent historical nature.

The radicals are thus caught up in that same double-bind or disabling aporia that de Man formulates most explicitly in "Literary History and Literary Modernity." They are the creatures of an unreflecting will-to-power that can find expression only in a cycle of escalating violence, yet would surely be reduced to paralysis and terminal despair were it once to take thought and acknowledge the nature of its own historical predicament. "History is, to the extent that it is an act, a dangerous and destructive act, a kind of hubris of the will that rebels against the grasp of time" (*RR*, pp. 56–57). Where the radicals fall into bad faith is in believing that their actions will be justified *sub specie aeternitatis*, through a transfiguration of history and time brought about by revolutionary change. Such is the "intoxication of the act," a fervor that blinds them to the self-willed, arbitrary character of their own utopian imaginings. What sustains revolutionary action is the desire to create and possess "something that endures," a renewed social order that perfectly embodies the spirit of its first creation. But this belief is made possible, de Man argues, only by conceiving of history as Wordsworth conceives it, on the model of those privileged contemplative moments when mind and nature, subject and object exist in a state of perfect, unimpeded communion. It is at moments like these — visionary moments achieved by an act of sovereign creative will — that the world might seem to live up to every demand that imagination can place on it. And so this "something that endures," whether a poem or a new political order, can only be conceived in terms of the analogy with a nature which itself endures "precisely because it negates the instant, just as reflection must negate the act that nonetheless constitutes its origin" (*RR*, p. 56). In which case — as de Man clearly wishes to imply — there is a lesson to be drawn from Wordsworth's example, from his abandoning the realm of political action for that of contemplative nature poetry. This lesson has to do with the self-deluding claims of revolutionary praxis, the aporias of historical consciousness, and the power of poetry to chasten and subdue the will for radical change.

"For Wordsworth," de Man writes, "there is no historical eschatology, but rather only a never-ending reflection upon an eschatological moment that has failed through the excess of its interiority" (*RR*, p. 59). One could gloss this sentence in various ways, but they would all tend to confirm Lentricchia's diagnosis of the manner in which de Man works to problematize the claims of history and politics. Poetry is seen as the source of an undeluded wisdom that can only look back on such moments of youthful abandon from a standpoint of "interiorized" reflection which contrasts with their naive, outgoing spontaneity. Wordsworth's companions on the journey through France are victims of a zeal for translating thoughts into deeds — or utopian visions into real-life acts — which can only perpetuate the cycle of violence. Although he refuses to side overtly with the older Wordsworth against his youthful alter ego, this is undoubtedly the tenor of de Man's reading. It is reinforced by his linking the episode of the threatened cloister with the subsequent passage in

Book VI where the travelers ascend toward the Simplon Pass and the ultimate goal of their journey, only to reach it unawares through "a maze of climbing and falling paths," and so fail to register the crowning experience. At this point, as de Man notes, the poet interrupts what had up to then seemed "a simple, realistic report," and inserts a passage of twenty-four lines that "are a hymn to the imagination as the poet's highest faculty."

The remainder of this episode is taken up with an account of the poet's "dizzying" descent, one that passes through stages of extreme sensory confusion to a mood of exalted self-surrender:

> The immeasurable height
> Of woods decaying, never to be decay'd,
> The stationary blasts of waterfalls, . . .
> Were all like workings of one mind, the features
> Of the same face, blossoms upon one tree,
> Characters of the great Apocalypse,
> The types and symbols of Eternity,
> Of first and last, and midst, and without end.

These lines (Book VI, 556–72) are probably the best-known instance in Wordsworth of that moment of sublime imagining where thought overreaches all forms of adequate expression in the language of perceptual experience. They strive to articulate a sense of the mind's wrestling with those paradoxes of nature, time, and eternity that lie, in de Man's words, "at the very limit of comprehensible language." And in so doing they offer what he reads as an ironic or chastened commentary on the idea that action, as conceived by the zealots of secular change, could ever pass beyond the kind of insensate, destructive frenzy that comes of confusing political with imaginative vision. The passage can thus be seen to "summarize the relationship between history and poetry in Wordsworth." It is poetry's role to subdue the mind to a sense of its true vocation, a vocation from which it is not to be seduced by any misconceived hope of reconciling nature and history in the fulness of merely secular time. "For the interpreter of history," de Man writes, "it is never a simple and uniform movement like the ascent of a peak or the installation of a definitive social order" (*RR*, p. 58). Such simplified notions arise from a will to ignore the complexities of temporal existence — the aporias of memory, self-knowledge, and desire — that emerge through a duly attentive reading of Wordsworth's poetry. History will then appear "much more in that twilight in which . . . the crossing of the Alps was bathed, in which the coming-to-consciousness is in arrears *vis-à-vis* the actual act, and consequently is to be understood not as a conquest but rather as a rectification or even a reproach" (*RR*, p. 58).

II

It is hard to resist the conclusion that de Man is here reading Wordsworth with very definite ideological ends in view. More specifically, his account of the Chartreuse-Simplon sequence amounts to a kind of parable for critics, a lesson (so to speak) in the true sense of hermeneutic obligations and priorities. *Authentic* criticism is that which allows the precedence of poetry over politics and which sees no escape route from man's temporal predicament in calls to revolutionary action, calls that can come about only through the ignorance and blindness born of a drastically limited secular vision. The French radicals are subject to the endlessly recurrent delusion (as de Man sees it) that political change will indeed bring about the desired transformation of human existence. Theirs is "the joy in an active world in which the movement of our wishes appears to correspond to that of the age" (*RR*, p. 55). But reflective hindsight is sufficient to disclose the groundless, illusory character of all such beliefs. "Despite its doubtless healthy character," this joy must be seen to conceal a great danger, a potential for violence and destruction which the poem goes on to recognize in the threat to religious institutions and values. What allows the older Wordsworth his sense of having left such dangerous delusions behind him is essentially the wisdom that poetry provides: the knowledge that our actions can never know their ends, that consciousness is always "in arrears *vis-à-vis* the actual act," and that therefore reflection must inevitably lead to a mood of political quietism.

The French enthusiasts stake their hopes on a will to pass directly from the here-and-now of revolutionary action to the knowledge of a future that in fact lies beyond all self-assured present calculation. They lack the poet's authentic, hard-won grasp of everything that warns against this premature fusion of horizons. According to de Man, "the poet finally distinguishes himself from the hero through his care for preserving memory, even the memory of the heroic act that throws itself into the future and destroys itself in this project" (*RR*, pp. 64–65). Poetry takes rise in the moment of dwelling reflectively on those paradoxes in the nature of time, consciousness, and ethical choice which no revolutionary program can afford to admit, since its capacity for action would thereby be paralyzed. The radicals envisage a world transfigured through the power of thought, giving practical shape to their dreams by directly controlling the course of events. In this they are at one with that strain of Romantic thinking which seeks to transcend the very nature of language — its authentically temporal character — by appealing to the powers of imaginative synthesis vested in metaphor and symbol. It is this same tradition of high Romantic argument that de Man most persistently sets out to deconstruct, from its origins in the early nineteenth century to its continuation by present-day critics like M.H. Abrams.[14] Here it is primarily a matter of reversing the deep-laid aesthetic ideology that attaches a high value to metaphor and symbol at the expense of other tropes (like metonymy and allegory) that lay no claim to such transcendent visionary power. These latter possess the decisive advantage, as de Man sees it, of revealing the drive toward premature totalization that marks all forms of that chronic and recurrent delusion.

This means that the hitherto devalued terms have a certain privileged use in deconstructing the more mystified versions of Romantic belief. Thus allegory is a mode that implicitly acknowledges the *arbitrary* link between its literal, surface meaning and those other, more occult levels of sense that provide the occasion for knowing exegesis. Moreover, allegory holds out against the lure of transcendence or visionary pathos, insisting absolutely on the timebound nature of all understanding and the plain impossibility that language should achieve — as the Romantics desired — a state beyond the antinomies of subject and object, mind and nature, the temporal and the eternal. Such, for instance, were Coleridge's claims for the language of Symbol, as opposed to the generically inferior discourse of allegory. The former is conceived as bringing about "the translucence of the special in the individual, or of the general in the special, or of the universal in the general; above all, by the translucence of the eternal through and in the temporal."[15] To which de Man responds with his own opposite conviction that language is radically incapable of any such thing, and that allegory is the more "authentic" mode in so far as it accepts and perpetually rehearses the fact of this negative knowledge. In his essay "The Rhetoric of Temporality," this issue is posed in the form of a choice between rival and wholly incommensurable modes of reading:

> Whereas the symbol postulates the possibility of an identity or identification, allegory designates primarily a distance in relation to its own origin, and, renouncing the nostalgia and the desire to coincide, it establishes its language in the void of this temporal difference. In so doing, it prevents the self from an illusory identification with the non-self, which is now fully, though painfully, recognized as a non-self. It is this painful knowledge that we perceive at the moments when early romantic literature finds its true voice.[16]

Hence de Man's marked preference, not only for allegory as a trope with the power to demystify other, more grandiose and delusive figures, but also for those writers ("early romantics" like Rousseau) whose work pointedly invites or requires allegorical reading. For it is here that he locates a point of maximal resistance to the more seductive claims advanced by subsequent thinkers in the High Romantic tradition.

That this preference amounted to a strong personal investment is clear from de Man's 1971 review-essay of Derrida's *De la grammatologie*.[17] Here he takes Derrida to task for (supposedly) not having credited Rousseau with sufficient rhetorical self-awareness, or with an adequate grasp of the way in which his texts were open to deconstructive reading. For de Man, it is the mainstream *interpreters* of Rousseau whose naiveties require such treatment, and not the texts themselves (which are, as he insists, fully cognisant of everything that Derrida has to say). In fact de Man ignores the several passages in *Of Grammatology* where Derrida *does* make precisely this point — that Rousseau's writings provide all the materials for their own deconstruction — with considerable emphasis and care. But more significant in this context is de Man's anxiety to redeem Rousseau from any suggestion that his might be also a delusive language unaware of its own problematic or contradictory entailments. Derrida adverts to this question in *Mémoires* — the text of his commemorative lectures on de Man — when he asks what might account for this will to set Rousseau beyond reach of further rhetorical demystification. In fact he quotes at length from a letter in which de Man addresses the same issue. "The desire to exempt Rousseau (as you say) *at all costs* from blindness is therefore, for me, a gesture of fidelity to my own itinerary. And as *l'Essai sur l'origine des langues* [to which Derrida and de Man both make extensive reference] is one of the texts upon which I have been relying for such a long time, I must have put a certain ardor into my defense of the relative insight which I have benefited from."[18] This passage concedes a good deal to Derrida's side of the argument. But the question remains as to how far that "ardor" resulted not only from de Man's distinctive rhetorical preoccupations but also from something in the nature of an ideological *parti pris*. Such at least is the conclusion suggested by his way of allegorizing history in "Wordsworth and Hölderlin," where it is precisely the link between political action and a certain late-romantic aesthetic ideology that de Man sets out to deconstruct.

This suggestion is borne out when the essay turns to Hölderlin, the poet who figures (even more prominently than Rilke) as a constant presence in de Man's writing. Why this should be the case can best be judged from his early (1953) piece on "Heidegger's Exegeses of Hölderlin." where de Man first articulates the major themes of his work toward *Blindness and Insight*.[19] Heidegger is a gifted reader of Hölderlin, one who is peculiarly able to fathom the poetry's depth of implication through his own, closely related philosophical concerns. For it is Heidegger's intent to think back beyond the history of Western "metaphysical" thought, from Plato to the present, and give voice to that primordial experience of Being which is glimpsed obscurely in the fragments of the pre-Socratic philosopher-poets, but then progressively concealed or distorted by the claims of merely abstract, conceptual understanding. This is not the place for any detailed account of either Heidegger's thinking or Hölderlin's poetry.[20] Sufficient in this context to note that de Man finds much to admire in these late Heideggerian writings, but also that he thinks them revealingly blind to certain crucial aspects of Hölderlin's work. "For Heidegger, Hölderlin is the greatest of poets ('the poet of poets') because he states the essence (*Wesen*) of poetry. The essence of poetry consists in stating the parousia, the absolute presence of Being" (*BI*, p. 250). But de Man is able to show, through his own exegesis of several Hölderlin texts, that this is not at all what the poet actually says, that indeed he more than once denies any claim that poetry can *state* the "absolute presence of Being" in such a mode of direct, unmediated truth as Heidegger seems to require. It is unable to do so for the reason that "as soon as the word is uttered, it destroys the immediate and discovers that instead of stating Being, it can only state mediation" (*BI*, p. 259). Heidegger's readings reflect his desire to find in Hölderlin a strong precursor, a kindred spirit on the path to a wisdom that philosophy has renounced and poetry alone seems able, if fleetingly, to recover. But this desire misleads him into a falsely affirmative account of Hölderlin, a reading blind to significant details of the text.

As one example, de Man offers the line "Und was ich sah, das Heilige sei mein Wort" ("And what I saw, the Holy be my word"). The effect of a Heideggerian gloss is to ignore the pointedly subjunctive verb form ("sei"), thus converting the poet's *desire* for a union between language and the divine into a claim that such union has indeed been achieved through the power of poetic revelation. As de Man points out,

> [Hölderlin] does not say: das Heilige *ist* mein Wort. The subjunctive is here really an optative; it indicates prayer, it marks desire, and these lines state the eternal poetic intention, but immediately state also that it can be no more than intention. It is not because he has seen Being that the poet is, therefore, capable of naming it; his word prays for the parousia, it does not establish it. (*BI*, p. 258)

This passage prefigures the role that Hölderlin will play in several of de Man's later essays. On the one hand he expresses that will to transcend the antinomies of mind and nature, time and eternity that has marked the project of all "strong" poetry in the wake of Romanticism and German idealist aesthetics. On the other — and more crucially for de Man — he succeeds in resisting the powerful inducement to treat such transcendence

as a matter of achieved fact, rather than a permanent temptation in the
path of poetic understanding. If Heidegger has misread Hölderlin, his
error is by no means alien or false to the deepest concerns of Hölderlin's
thought. That "Hölderlin says exactly the opposite of what Heidegger
makes him say" is, according to de Man, "paradoxical only in
appearance," since at this advanced stage of poetic reflection "it is
difficult to distinguish between a proposition and that which constitutes its
opposite" (*BI*, p. 255). In his later work de Man will insist that
misreadings can be either "errors" or "mistakes," the latter attributable
to mere incompetence or carelessness, but the former responding to some
deep necessity in the encounter between text and commentary.[21]
Heidegger's misreadings of Hölderlin should be seen as errors, not
mistakes. That is to say, they result from a will to enlist the poet in a
quest for unmediated origins and presence which lies too close to
Heidegger's central concerns for his readings to have followed any other
path. Those readings are therefore exemplary of their kind, even though
— as de Man insists — they effectively reverse the most profound
intentions of Hölderlin's thought.

It might be thought from what I have said so far that this whole
discussion takes place at a level of rarified hermeneutic theory with no
reference to Heidegger's ill-starred political involvements. In fact de Man
does point out that the commentaries in question were produced "just
before and during World War II, and are directly linked to an anguished
meditation upon the historical destiny of Germany, a meditation that
finds an echo in the 'national' poems of Hölderlin" (*BI*, p. 254). Having
raised the question he then rather brusquely puts it out of mind as "a side
issue that would take us away from our topic." But this is sufficient to
apprise the reader — the implied reader of de Man's essay, properly alert
to its rhetorical strategies — that more is going on than might be gleaned
from this single passing reference. For there is clearly (though de Man
never spells it out) a connection between Heidegger's way with
Hölderlin's texts and the issues of political action and involvement that
preoccupy de Man in the essay "Wordsworth and Hölderlin." More
specifically, what motivates Heidegger's reading in its quest for "unmediated presence" is a certain *impetuous* quality, a desire that poetry should
here and now make good its ultimate claim, its "final promise of dwelling
in the parousia of eternity." And this desire is related to a certain lack of
hermeneutic patience on Heidegger's part, an unwillingness to rest in
uncertainties until the poetry has performed its salutary work of
chastening the desire for interpretative mastery and truth.

De Man makes the point in a passage that can scarcely be read
without some awareness of its covert political implications. "The
ineffable," he writes, "demands the direct adherence and the blind and

violent passion with which Heidegger treats his texts" (*BI*, p. 263). By contrast, it is the virtue of a deconstructive reading — although this term as yet plays no part in de Man's vocabulary[22] — to confront the desire for unmediated presence with a knowledge of its own inevitable failure to achieve this wished-for condition. Such is the implied relationship, the complex pattern of dependence, between Heidegger's exegeses of Hölderlin and de Man's commentary on Heidegger. De Man makes no attempt to conceal the extent of his indebtedness to these texts. But in place of the "blind and violent passion" that motivates Heidegger's reading, de Man will emphasize whatever resists or defers that moment of imaginary fulfillment, whatever holds out against the ultimate delusion of a poetry that *states* the plenitude of Being. "Mediation . . . implies a reflection that tends toward a critical language as systematic and rigorous as possible, but not overly eager to make claims of certitude that it can substantiate only in the long run" (*BI*, p. 263). This would all seem to place de Man in the superior cognitive position of a critic untouched by those premature seductions of hermeneutic mastery and presence that characterize Heidegger's thinking. But in fact, as a postscript to the essay makes clear, de Man is still convinced that Heidegger is too good, too faithful, and intelligent a reader of Hölderlin not to have recognized these problems and given some hint of them despite the overt drift of his essays. The postscript instead takes issue with a book by Beda Alleman (*Hölderlin und Heidegger*)[23] which he reads as having "fallen victim to an error that Heidegger's influence may indeed induce," that of measuring both the poet and the philosopher in terms of their supposed overcoming of Hegelian ("metaphysical") thought. In this power of Heidegger's readings to induce further moments of coimplicated "blindness" and "insight" de Man locates both their seminal importance and the necessity of reading them against the grain of their manifest intentions.

We can now turn back to the essay "Wordsworth and Hölderlin" with a clearer sense of its ideological bearings. What begins to emerge is an allegory of poetic consciousness in its progress beyond the perils and the pressures of active political involvement. In Wordsworth, that progress can be seen (de Man argues) in the "interiorizing" movement of thought whereby a youthful phase of activist fervor is described from the standpoint of a higher, more reflective judgment which no longer entertains such radical ideas. But this wisdom appears a kind of halfway stage, a distinctly limited achievement when set against the full demystifying rigors of Hölderlin's thought. "We abandoned Wordsworth," so the essay reveals,

> as soon as the concept of a correspondence between nature and consciousness seemed to be definitely surpassed. This overcoming —

which in Wordsworth ensues at a highly advanced point in his thinking
— belongs to Hölderlin's knowledge almost from the beginning. (*RR*, p.
59)

This suggests a distinctly Hegelian idea of poetic history. It is one in
which the mind evolves through stages of ever more complex or reflective
self-awareness, to the point of escaping its erstwhile subjection to the
crude imperatives of worldly or material circumstance. Thus Hölderlin's
achievement — the sense in which he "overcomes" Wordsworth — has to
do with his pressing reflection to the limits of this posthistorical,
postrevolutionary phase. Hölderlin is the poet in whom we can read the
allegory of a consciousness that struggles to renounce all hope in
immediate, this-worldly fulfillment. What replaces that hope is a
knowledge of the mind's self-conscious or reflective powers, its capacity
to compensate the loss of heroic self-esteem through a sense of its own
interior resources. Thus the "history" of poetic consciousness, from
Wordsworth to Hölderlin, is a passage marked by growing disenchantment with the idea that poetry — or imaginative thought of any kind —
might actively engage with issues of real-world history and politics. It is a
lesson — though de Man never quite spells this out — in the folly of
pinning one's ultimate hopes to the masthead of secular change.

There is one major theme in Hölderlin that de Man finds especially
charged and suggestive. It is the matter of his so-called "Titanism," his
dwelling on the overthrow of an old, heroic order among the gods by a
new, more complex, less obviously godlike race of divinities. From the
Titanist perspective, will translates directly into power and performative
deed, with no complicating detour through the mazy indirections of
human self-knowledge and doubt. This dream still inhabits the Romantic
idea of poetry as an active force in the world, a force on the side of
revolution and violent upheaval. It is supplanted, in Hölderlin's version
of the myth, by a consciousness that holds out against all such heroic
delusions, confronting the will with a knowledge of its own self-divided,
reflexive character. Poetry at this high pitch of development "never
allows this power to rush blindly to meet the unknown future . . . it turns
back upon itself . . . and replaces the violent temporality (*reissende Zeit*)
of action with the sheltering temporality (*schützende Zeit*) of interpretation" (*RR*, p. 63). But de Man is not content with what he calls this
"commonplace" of Hölderlin criticism — the idea that poetry, reflection,
and inwardness are straightforwardly *opposed* to their counterpart values:
Titanism, the heroic, and the life of immediate, unthinking, or precipitate
action. For it is evident from a closer reading of the texts that these
principles exist in a kind of reciprocal dependence where neither could
begin to articulate its claims except by virtue of this constant oscillating

rhythm. To suppose otherwise — to treat them as strictly antithetical values — is a mistake, de Man argues, since it leads interpretation to "glorify the power of Titanism" by raising it to the status of "an autonomous force capable of withdrawing from the control of the will" (*RR*, p. 61). And this is false to those passages in Hölderlin (of which de Man cites a number of striking examples) where there is not so much "an oppositional relationship between the activity of the Titans and that of the poet, but rather one of prematurity" (*RR*, pp. 61–62). It is this *belatedness* of consciousness *vis-à-vis* lived experience — the gap, as de Man says, that "separates the completion of an action from its understanding" — that inhibits any thought of poetry's actively impinging on the world of historical events.

So this essay comes round to much the same conclusion as de Man had arrived at in "Literary History and Literary Modernity." It reinforces what Eagleton and Lentricchia regard as the underlying message of all de Man's work: the sheer impossibility of acting for the best in any political context, since actions can never know their ends and consciousness is always fated to a knowledge of its own incapacity to foretell safely the course of events. If "history" remains an operative term in de Man's writing, it is a history entirely given over to this sense of Hamlet-like ironic detachment from the world of practical affairs. Thus "the poet and the historian converge . . . to the extent that they both speak of an action that precedes them but that exists for consciousness only because of their intervention" (*RR*, p. 65). The essay could scarcely go further in its will to problematize the nature of historical understanding and to place obstacles in the way of any other, more hopeful vision of political change. In his later work — as I have argued elsewhere[24] — de Man provides an answer to his critics on the left, an answer that effectively aligns deconstruction with the interests of Marxist *Ideologiekritik*. This involves his central claim that the discourse of modern (post-Kantian) aesthetics has rested most often on a determinate misreading of Kant and, beyond that, on a mystified ontology of meaning and value that lends itself to various, politically consequential forms of aesthetic ideology.[25] The shift is most clearly visible in his posthumous volume *The Rhetoric of Romanticism*, where essays dating from his early and middle periods (including "Wordsworth and Hölderlin") appear alongside the more overtly political productions of his last few years. But one can see why critics like Lentricchia are more forcibly struck by the conservative implications of de Man's early work.

In his Preface to that volume de Man comments wryly on the "somewhat melancholy spectacle" presented by "such massive evidence of the failure to make the various individual readings coalesce" (*RR*, p. viii). Lest the reader seek out some unconscious subplot, some covert or ulterior source of coherence, de Man goes on to make the point more emphatically. "Laid out diachronically in a roughly chronological sequence, [these essays] do not evolve in a manner that easily allows for dialectical progression or, ultimately, for historical totalization . . . If some secret principle of summation is at work here, I do not feel qualified to articulate it . . . " (*RR*, p. viii). This disclaimer is predictable, given both de Man's suspicion of all such "totalizing" concepts and his wariness of appeals to history as some kind of ultimate explanatory ground. But there is, I think, another reason why he insists so firmly on the "fragmentary aspect of the whole," and on the way that these essays "always seem to start again from scratch," so that "their conclusions fail to add up to anything." For otherwise the reader might more easily have recognized the signs of that shift in de Man's work from an attitude of political quietism — one that reads poetry expressly *against* all forms of delusive activist involvement — to a stance that finally equates right reading with the power to demystify forms of aesthetic ideology.

III

De Man's sympathetic commentators have mostly tended to ignore this shift, perhaps because they have paid too much heed to his warnings against such "totalizing" treatment. In seeking to rebut the charges of critics like Eagleton and Lentricchia, they have assumed that his work is sufficiently of a piece to warrant their addressing the question of de Man's politics as if this called for a single (albeit a nuanced and qualified) answer. In fact, as I have suggested, all the evidence points to a decisive change in the way that de Man conceived the relationship of literature, criticism, and politics. For the remainder of this chapter I want to look more closely at one possible influence on his early writings. The figure in question is Hendrik de Man, a leading left-wing activist, theoretician, and government minister in pre-war Belgian politics. Hendrik was Paul de Man's uncle, a fact alluded to in passing by Eagleton when he recalls that Antonio Gramsci, in the *Prison Notebooks*, has a series of polemical comments addressed to this Marxist-revisionist thinker. These are sufficient to give some idea of why Hendrik de Man was the focus of such widespread controversy among socialists at the time.[26] And when one turns to Peter Dodge's recent documentary study (*Hendrik de Man, Socialist Critic of Marxism*) there emerges a remarkable chapter of political history which has, I would argue, a very definite bearing on Paul de Man's early work.[27] At the very least it helps us to grasp one cause of that profound disenchantment with politics which finds oblique expression in an essay like "Wordsworth and Hölderlin."

Dodge sets out by raising the question of why this thinker, so greatly influential in his day, has now been all but consigned to oblivion:

> A figure whose intellectual contribution certainly ranks him among the leading theoreticians of the socialist movement, a pioneer sociologist of labor and industry, in his personal biography a valiant and tragic exemplar of the traumata of the West, he has simply disappeared from the history books. (Dodge, p. 4)

That this is not just a piece of dramatic overstatement on the part of his biographer becomes clear in the subsequent narration of de Man's political life and times. He was active in the Belgian socialist movement from May Day, 1902, after which de Man took part in a general strike that began in the Antwerp dockyards, argued against any compromise with existing forms of bourgeois democracy, and espoused the line of left-radical thinking advanced by German communist leaders like Karl Liebknecht and Rosa Luxemburg. At this stage he was firmly committed to a hard-line determinist version of Marxist theory, an outlook which "by its disabused political insight, scientific plausibility, and historical inevitability legitimated his own repudiation of the bourgeois world" (Dodge, p. 4). These convictions were strengthened during a period in Leipzig when de Man began writing for the radical press, forged links with prominent Marxist intellectuals, and joined in the founding of the Socialist Youth International. Under their influence he continued to oppose any form of Marxist-revisionist thinking that would question the determinate causal link between class conflict, material interests, and the looming collapse of the capitalist system.

But his views began to change over the next few years for a variety of connected reasons. A brief spell of work in England convinced him that there were indeed distinctive forms of bourgeois-democratic civil society whose effect upon the outcome of historical events must always be taken into account. And this shift of attitude was greatly reinforced by his experience during the First World War. De Man started out as a convert to the pacifist or noninterventionist arguments advanced by the Second International. That is to say, he regarded the War as basically an outcome of capitalist economic rivalries, a struggle for power in which workers and socialists should remain ideologically neutral. But this stance became increasingly hard to sustain as he witnessed the unprovoked aggression against his own country by a quasi-feudal militarist regime. After fighting in the trenches as a volunteer recruit de Man found himself compelled to acknowledge those real differences of social and political structure which existed between the contending powers.[28] "Without democracy," he now believed, "it was possible for autocratic and ruthless governments effectively to suppress and cow a strong socialist movement, as the example of the Central Powers showed; with political democracy, despite its manifold imperfections, the ultimate victory of socialism was ineluctable" (Dodge, p. 10). This conviction was further reinforced by de Man's visit to Soviet Russia in 1917, when he went as a delegate on the mission to persuade the Kerensky government to stay in the war. Its upshot for de Man, Dodge suggests, was to leave him thoroughly disenchanted with Bolshevik "revolutionary defeatism," and also by what he saw of the repressive turn in Soviet domestic policy. Soon after his return to Belgium de Man was off once more on a six-month trip to America which again had the effect of unsettling his previous beliefs. For here was a country which *had*, after all, evolved its own forms of bourgeois representative democracy, which *had* thrown its weight behind the war effort, and which yet seemed to give no hold whatsoever for the orthodox Marxist terms of analysis. More specifically, de Man was hard put to account for "the virtual absence of class consciousness in this bastion of capitalist enterprise." So his visits to Russia and America had the effect of persuading de Man that Eduard Bernstein and the revisionists were right, and that Marxism did need radically rethinking in the light of these unforeseen developments.

He undertook this task in his book *The Psychology of Socialism* (1926), the work that attracted Gramsci's attention and served as a focus for polemical debate during the interwar years.[29] Here de Man argues his case for rejecting any version of Marxism that assumes a one-sided, mechanistic, or causal relation between economic "base" and sociopolitical "superstructure." Such thinking he views as essentially rooted in nineteenth-century philosophical ideas, in particular the doctrines of determinism, rationalism, and the kind of hedonistic calculus of interests that dominated economic theory at the time. What is required, de Man argues, is a wholly different way of construing the base/superstructure metaphor, one that allows a more decisive role to the thoughts, beliefs, and conscious desires that motivate historical agents. After all, "the undoubted fact that the originators of socialist doctrines have almost invariably been bourgeois intellectuals shows that psychological motives are at work, motives that have nothing whatever to do with class interests" (Dodge, p. 144). And conversely, all the evidence of recent history — Russia, America, the lessons of the war — goes to show how little can really be explained in straightforward historical-materialist terms. For him, the mistake of "Bolshevik-defeatist" thinking lay in its refusal to take account of those significant cultural and sociopolitical differences which separate nation from nation. In much the same way, according to de Man, orthodox Marxists persistently ignore that level of conscious, reflective, or willed activity that eludes the grasp of a hard-line determinist creed. The emergence of socialist ideas — including those of Marx and Engels — cannot be accounted for on the basis of a simplified, reductive model that claims to derive from those same ideas. "They are the products, not of the cultural poverty of the proletariat, but of the cultural wealth of instructed members of the bourgeoisie . . . they spread from above downward, not from below upward" (Dodge, p. 143). What Marxism therefore needs in order to advance beyond its present, politically deadlocked condition is a better understanding of social psychology and the way that ideas, motives, and beliefs act back upon the so-called economic "base."

So Bernstein didn't in the end go far enough (as de Man sees it) in revising the claims of classical Marxist thought. He wished only to modify certain doctrines ("the theory of increasing misery, that of capitalist concentration, value and surplus value, economic crises, the intensification of the class struggle, and so on") without questioning the philosophic basis on which those doctrines rested. For de Man, that basis no longer holds good, discredited on the one hand by historical events and on the other by its failure to account convincingly for its own elaboration at the hands of bourgeois intellectuals. The only way forward, he argues, is one that abandons this outworn paradigm and accepts the idea of a "socialist creative thought" that can — indeed must — defeat any form of ironcast reductive theory. Hence de Man's argument that Marxism should now avail itself of the insights of psychology, biography, aesthetics, ethics, and all those supposedly "bourgeois" disciplines whose domain is that of conscious ideas and beliefs, rather than collective ideologies. "Socialist creative thought," he writes, "is seen to take rise in an affect, or rather in an almost infinite multiplicity of affects, derived from cultural, ethical, and aesthetic sources" (Dodge, p. 144). Such promptings cannot be explained altogether as the outcome of class interests, any more than "the beauty of a painting by Rembrandt is to be explained in terms of a chemical analysis of the pigments and the canvas — though 'in the last analysis' the picture consists of nothing more than canvas and paint" (Dodge, pp. 144–45).

This recourse to *aesthetics* as an argument against the more reductionist forms of Marxist thought is one that appears frequently in Hendrik de Man's writings. Most often it goes along with the distinction between "active" and "passive" forms of political consciousness, those that work creatively to produce new ideas and those that receive such ideas in a spirit of simple, unthinking acceptance. De Man explicitly rejects any notion that mankind can be "dichotomized" into separate classes, "those who are mental leaders and those who are mentally led." All the same he strongly suggests as much in those passages which try to define the nature of socialist creative thought. Political belief is "first and foremost a complex, an emotional state, no less in the isolated thinker who launches ideas than in the masses who accept them as symbols of their own volitions . . . In the individual thinker, it is poietic and active; in the masses, it is receptive and passive" (Dodge, p. 154). What is most striking is de Man's use of the word "poietic," here and elsewhere, to suggest both a capacity for action and a will to hold out against the pressures of conformist ideology. This will is "creative" in so far as it doesn't pass directly from stimulus to act, but dwells (so to speak) in the moment of reflecting on present and future possibilities, thus saving itself from the risks attendant on premature action. As de Man uses the term, "poietic" retains something of its Greek etymology along with those other, modern connotations that move toward the sphere of aesthetic understanding. It combines the sense of *making* — of crafting, giving shape, bringing forth new objects or actions — with the further suggestion of an inward, contemplative, self-controlled spirit that can best produce and appreciate such things. Again, de Man is careful not to imply that this spirit is the prerogative of leaders, intellectuals, or a class elite whose qualities mark them out clearly from the passive herd. "Poietic and receptive behavior denote different functions in relation to some definite happening which exerts a specific influence upon people's minds; they do not denote temperamental distinctions or varying class affiliations, per se" (Dodge, pp. 155–56). But it is none the less strongly implied that any power to resist the workings of mass psychology — or of actions performed as a kind of mere stimulus-response — must come from the reflective, interiorized resources of "socialist creative thought."

There are, I think, some interesting parallels here with Paul de Man's meditations on poetry, history, and the politics of radical disenchantment. One is reminded especially of those passages in "Wordsworth and Hölderlin" where de Man sets out the Nietzschean choice between a life of pure, unpremeditated action and one given over to a melancholy knowledge of the thinker's incapacity to act at all. Thus for Wordsworth, when he came to write the *Prelude*, "the moment of active projection into the future . . . lies for the imagination in a past from which it is separated by the experience of a failure" (*RR*, p. 58). Poetry brings the opportunity to relive that past, but only from a distance of ironically chastened self-knowledge, or a standpoint (as de Man writes) "that lies on the far side of this failure, and that has escaped destruction thanks to an effort of consciousness to make sure of itself once again" (*RR*, p. 58). This reading of Wordsworth — like so much of de Man's work — has a sense of highly charged though subdued political implications, of a consciousness indeed "making sure of itself" by an effort to *interiorize* memories and events that would otherwise threaten to overwhelm it. From the sentence I have just quoted, de Man goes on to assert categorically that "this consciousness can be had only by one who has very extensively partaken of the danger and failure." It is an oddly revealing moment, like that at the close of T.S. Eliot's "Tradition and the Individual Talent," where Eliot, having patiently argued his case for artistic "impersonality," and rejected what he takes as the Romantic misconception of poetry as a "turning loose of emotions," then abruptly sees fit to remind the reader that "only those who have personality and emotions know what it means to want to escape from these things."[30] The passage from de Man may seem to assert simply that Wordsworth's stance of mature, undeluded wisdom could come about only through his early exposure to the dangers and temptations of political life. But it also implies a degree of self-involvement, a suggestion that these pressures of ideological adjustment are not so remote from de Man's own experience.

At least this would go some way toward explaining the ambivalence that is often to be felt when de Man touches on political themes. It comes across as an intense preoccupation that is nonetheless kept at a certain remove by constantly adverting to those problems in the way of any straightforward, unambiguous form of political commitment. Hölderlin is de Man's chief exemplar in this will not to be seduced prematurely by the promise of secular deliverance. And it is always through an *intertextual* reading of Hölderlin — a reading that places him alongside some earlier, problematic figure — that de Man brings out this quality in his writing. If Wordsworth is one such figure, Rousseau is another and perhaps the most important, — since in Rousseau the relationship of writing and politics is raised to a high point of interest and complexity. For de Man, as we have seen, it is something like an article of faith that Rousseau is less deluded, less subject to the sway of aesthetic ideology, than those who avowedly followed in his path; that his texts can be read *against* their subsequent interpreters — from the major Romantics down to and including Derrida — who either take him at face value or think to expose his blind spots of rhetorical mystification. Rousseau is the strong precursor who is always demonstrably one jump ahead of any *hypocrite lecteur* who claims to have revealed the limits to Rousseau's demythologizing power.

But in his essay "The Image of Rousseau in the Poetry of Hölderlin" (1965) de Man comes very close to abandoning this position (*RR*, pp. 19–45). There is still the firm insistence that Rousseau is far advanced along the path to an ironic self-knowledge that cannot be taken in by the claims of immediate, effective historical action. Thus he figures in Hölderlin's poetry as the one who, "in reaffirming the ontological priority of consciousness over the sensuous object, put the thought and the destiny of the West back onto its authentic path . . . [who] had the wisdom and the patience to remain faithful to the limits that this knowledge . . . imposes upon the human spirit" (*RR*, p. 45). Such is

Rousseau's "image" as a guiding, tutelary presence in Hölderlin's work: the image of a thinker whose writings everywhere warn against the dangers of moving too quickly from the realm of imagination to that of practical politics. Thus in Hölderlin's poem "The Rhine" de Man finds a subtext of echoes and allusions that establish Rousseau as the voice of authentic conscience as opposed to the claims of sheer, unthinking revolutionary zeal. His counterpart is Prometheus, the Greek archetype of hubris or fateful overreaching, the figure who deludedly thought to transcend the gulf fixed between human and divine knowledge by stealing the gift of fire. Here again, de Man's reading unfolds through a series of now familiar structural oppositions, involving on the one hand the claims of heroic (or "Titanist") action, on the other a reflective consciousness that can only discountenance those claims through a knowledge of their hopelessly self-deceiving nature. "In contrast to the Promethean hero who is associated only with action, Rousseau . . . appears above all as the man of language: he listens, he speaks, he gives language . . ." (*RR*, pp. 40). The Heideggerian echoes are strong in this passage, and suggest just how complex is the network of intertextual tropes and allusions that work to establish Rousseau as a wise, undeceived precursor.

But this wisdom has a limit at precisely those points in Rousseau's more "political" texts (like the *Social Contract*) where thought oversteps the bounds of an "authentic relation to being" and seeks to legislate in terms of an "entire human community" or "general will."[31] Then he seems to fall back into the Greek or Promethean way of thinking, one that has an aspect "not merely political but revolutionary" (*RR*, p. 41). This would be Rousseau the radical reformer, the scourge of a corrupt and decadent civilization who preached a return to the natural condition of primitive innocence and grace. It is, in short, the Rousseau whose writings were to play a very active role in subsequent historical events. And de Man makes this point explicitly enough when he equates the Promethean aspect of Rousseau's thought with its power of engendering a "mad," "lawless," "intoxicating" spirit whose equivalent in political terms would be "the excessive hopes aroused by the French Revolution" (*RR*, p. 42). Such at least is the image of Rousseau that emerges *up to a point* in Hölderlin's meditation on the rival claims of history, time, and poetic self-knowledge. But then there appears — as by now we might expect — a moment of reversal in de Man's reading, a moment when Rousseau turns out after all to have prefigured the utmost that Hölderlin can achieve in the way of demystified or disenchanted hindsight. It occurs just after a passage in the poem where Rousseau is represented as a Herculean figure, "carrying the sky on his shoulders" in an image of the solitary, self-sufficient mind matching its strength against the order of divine providence. "In the joy of this triumph," de Man writes, "both the individual Rousseau and the revolutionary community that takes its origin from his solitary thinking experience the moment of greatest danger: they risk destruction by a direct confrontation with the sacred" (*RR*, p. 42). But this crisis point is no sooner reached than it gives way to another, more subdued or self-occupied strain, a poetry of redoubled thought and reflection whose emblem is the river of Hölderlin's title. Rousseau "reacts like the Rhine . . . Instead of letting himself be carried away, he makes a movement of surprised retraction, . . . and then retires in the repose of a contemplative inwardness" (*RR*, p. 42). Thus Rousseau is at last saved from the risks that attend such moments of revolutionary ardor, moments in which the poetic imagination thinks to translate will directly into deed, or to overcome the distance inevitably fixed between "authentic destiny" and the promise of secular salvation. What Hölderlin glimpses (and de Man more explicitly states) is the lesson to be read in this "exemplary" case of a thinker tempted but not overwhelmed by the claims of revolutionary action.

Nowhere do we find a more revealing instance of de Man's reading poetry as an allegory of political disenchantment, a cryptic warning against the confusion of temporal and ideal realms. It would no doubt be oversimple — a species of crudely reductive biographical fallacy — to relate this directly to the sobering memory of his uncle's experiences in the interwar years. But it is equally fallacious to suppose that de Man could have put such memories firmly behind him and carried on his critical work unaffected by this resonant case history. All the more so in that Hendrik de Man emerges as a figure whose political life was marked at every turn by an alternating cycle of activist zeal, followed by stages of intense disappointment, ironic resignation, and (ultimately) bleak despair. In the years before the Second World War he served two terms of office in the Belgian government, continued his work of Marxist-revisionist theory, and became (as Gramsci's remarks make clear) a widely discussed thinker outside his own country. When the Nazis seized power in Germany it seemed that socialism could be saved in the other European nations only by a decisive shift of policy and tactics. At this time de Man was instrumental in producing the Belgian *Plan du travail*, a document that envisaged the immediate transition to a socialist order by the left's simply taking over existing political forms and institutions.[32] As his biographer describes it, de Man's specific brief was to legitimize "in terms of the ideology of the socialist movement the possibility of undertaking effective and immediate action both to combat mass unemployment and to lay the basis for political action that went far beyond the proletariat" (Dodge, p. 290).

The *Plan* was adopted and to some extent put into practice by socialists in a series of pre-war coalitions. But with Hitler's conquest of France and the low countries de Man saw the ruin of everything he had hoped for. His last, desperate response to this calamity was to hope that Nazism might so completely undermine the institutions of a fake bourgeois democracy that perhaps, at the end of it, true socialism might yet prevail. Hence his "Manifesto" of 1940, supporting Leopold III and counseling nonresistance to the German army of occupation. Dodge sees this stance as in part the result of de Man's "refired pacifism," his extreme disillusionment with the principles that had led him, during the previous war, to invest his faith in the bourgeois democracies and their fight against oligarchical militarism. Bereft of that faith, and confronted with the prospect of utter defeat for the socialist idea, de Man "in simple desperation . . . attempted to escape by reinterpreting the Nazi movement into an instrument for the achievement of the socialist goal" (Dodge, p. 325). He died in 1953, long since convinced that all forms of socialist thinking "participated in the decadence of the capitalist world order," and that the only recourse for the thinking individual was to "cultivate his garden and hope that something of the patrimony of the ages would be thus preserved" (Dodge, pp. 16–17). It is hard to imagine a more complete story of political hopes turned to naught by the march of historical events.

The bearing of all this on Paul de Man's work must of course be a matter of conjecture. Among his hostile critics on the left it tends to loom vaguely as a hint of some near-at-hand cause for de Man's ambivalence on political issues. Thus Terry Eagleton suggests that de Man is "most interestingly viewed in the light of a bitter 'post-ideological' scepticism which belongs to the post-fascist epoch," and alludes briefly to the fact that "de Man's uncle, an ultimately disillusioned socialist, was politically involved in the Second World War period."[33] His more admiring commentators tend, understandably, to pass over the familial connection in silence or treat it as a topic of merely anecdotal interest. Juliet MacCannell is one of the few to raise the question (in a footnote to her essay "Portrait: de Man"), when she suggests that it may have been his uncle's involvement with schemes like the drastic and ill-fated *Plan du travail* that left Paul de Man with his abiding mistrust of premature totalizing theories. In support of this idea she instances the fact that de Man's essay "The Resistance to Theory" started out (at the MLA's bidding) as a "plan" or program for the future of literary studies, but was finally rejected by its sponsors when the topic proved to be theory's inbuilt "resistance to itself," and not just the pressure of institutional conservatism. From this we can see, she writes, "how little of the 'leader'

— or Mafia don — there was in Paul de Man."[34] Clearly MacCannell is writing with an eye to those opponents (like Lentricchia) who have remarked on the seeming disparity between de Man's belief that interpretative issues are finally "undecidable" and his frequent way of making that point in a downright, even authoritarian style. Her purpose is to insist that, in his writing and teaching alike, de Man was always maximally alert to the dangers of programmatic theory. So where Hendrik de Man "staked a great deal on the belief that the Marxist version of historical development would 'naturally' prevail over the evident decadence of capitalism," Paul de Man was perhaps "scrupulous to a fault to avoid repeating the mistakes of his notorious relative."[35]

But there is sufficient truth in Lentricchia's observation to suggest that the problem goes deeper and cannot be attributed to simple misreading on the part of hostile commentators. What characterizes Paul de Man's style is a rhythm that alternates between claims of an assertive, self-assured, even apodictic character, and moments of ironic reflection when those claims are called into doubt. Such is the pattern we have traced in his essays on Rousseau, Wordsworth, and Hölderlin, a pattern marked by this constant oscillating movement of critical thought. And the same might be said of Hendrik de Man, in so far as his writings manifest a sequence of intensifying conflict between the principles of action and reflection, revolutionary hope on the one hand and self-chastening irony on the other. The final paragraph of "Wordsworth and Hölderlin" comes close to an explicit statement of this conflict as it bears on Paul de Man's reading of literary history. Romanticism, he writes,

> necessarily appears to us in a Titanic light which no amount of demythologizing can entirely dissolve. Whence issues our bifurcated attitude toward a phenomenon that always unduly attracts or repels us, depending on whether we accent the aspect of renewal or of danger. (*RR*, p. 65)

Lentricchia and Eagleton are right to detect a mood of profound political disenchantment in de Man's early writings. It is a mood that repeatedly generates his sense that consciousness must choose between stark alternatives: *either* the life of unthinking, spontaneous action (with all its dangerous consequences) *or* the kind of inward, contemplative life that can never bring itself to act in any way. For Eagleton, this marks de Man as the spokesman of a bankrupt ideology pushed up against the limits of articulate self-knowledge, one that effectively "displaces the dilemmas of the liberal intellectual under late capitalism into an irony structural to discourse as such."[36] There is certainly a measure of truth in this assessment, at least as applied to the early texts. But we shall better understand why this should be the case if we also grasp something of the pressured situation — the background of complicated motive and circumstance — that left such a mark on de Man's characteristic strategies of argument.

2

De Man and the Critique of Romantic Ideology

I

In his essay "Sign and Symbol in Hegel's *Aesthetics*," de Man addresses what he takes to be the crucial and unresolved problem inhabiting all versions of high-Romantic or symbolist aesthetics.[1] This problem has to do with the relationship between art and philosophy, and the fact (as de Man argues) that Hegel's compulsion to *theorize* the nature of art leads to a series of discrepancies or blind spots in his argument which undermine his own explicit claims. I want to look closely at this essay, along with another of de Man's late productions, "Phenomenality and Materiality in Kant."[2] Together they present a detailed working out of de Man's arguments on the topic of Romantic ideology, a topic that focused all his major concerns, from the early essays collected in *Blindness and Insight* (1971) to the posthumous volume *The Resistance to Theory* (1986). In Kant and Hegel de Man reads a series of persistent contradictions, aporias, or antinomies which characterize the discourse of Romanticism and continue to vex modern thought in its attempts to make terms with that problematic heritage.

What is at issue here is the high valuation of artistic creativity vested in privileged poetic tropes, especially metaphor and symbol. This valuation goes along with the Romantic belief in art as the manifestation of genius, of creative powers that lie beyond the reach of mere craft, learning, or applied technique. Metaphor and symbol supposedly transcend the order of quotidian language and perception. They give access to a realm of intuitive or visionary insight where thought overcomes its enslavement to the laws of time, contingency, and change. The true mark of genius is the power to create such moments out of time, moments when the mind can contemplate nature and its own "inner" workings with a sense of achieved harmony, a sense that such distinctions have fallen away in the act of unified perception. And this power.has been associated, at least since Aristotle, with metaphor above all other tropes — since metaphor is the means by which language renews its creative resources and breaks with routine, stereotyped habits of thought. For a long line of critics and theorists — including the present-day mainstream interpreters of Romanticism — metaphor becomes the very touchstone of aesthetic value, that which distinguishes the language of poetry from other, straightforwardly referential or cognitive uses. This assumption cuts across the widest differences of ideological and poetic belief. It unites a high Romantic like Shelley (for whom poetry revealed the visionary heart of human existence by stripping away the "veil of familiarity" from everyday objects and events) with an anti-Romantic, classicizing thinker like T.S. Eliot, one who firmly rejected such claims as a kind of blasphemous overreaching, but who still placed his faith in the power of poetry to renew our habits of perception by "dislocating" language to creative ends of its own. The Russian Formalists (and Roman Jakobson after them) likewise identified the "poetic function" in language with the predominance of metaphor over other, more prosaic kinds of trope. From their methodological point of view, metaphor seemed to exhibit most strikingly that shift of linguistic focus — from an emphasis on content or "message" to a concern with matters of form, structure, and style — which again provided the groundwork of a generalized poetics. In one form or another — as de Man argues — this high valuation of metaphor typifies just about every variety of modern (post-Romantic) critical approach.

In Hegel's *Aesthetics* it is symbol, rather than metaphor, that occupies this privileged position.[3] For Hegel, the symbolic is the highest form of art, the most advanced stage that aesthetic consciousness can reach in its striving for a realm of unified knowledge and perception beyond the antinomies of alienated spirit. "Nowhere else does the structure, the history, and the judgment of art seem to come as close to being systematically carried out, and nowhere else does this systematic synthesis rest so exclusively on one definite category . . . called the aesthetic" (SS, p. 762). Art holds out the utopian promise of a knowledge that would reconcile the hitherto disparate orders of sensuous intuition and conceptual understanding. It does so by restoring a sense of physical or concrete immediacy to those elements of meaning, structure, or form that would otherwise belong on the side of abstract intellection. The symbol represents this unifying power at its highest stage of development, since here (as Hegel argues) we witness the capacity of art to transcend or reconcile all those antinomies that plague the discourse of conceptual reason.

It is in terms of this saving imaginative vision that other Romantic theorists — Coleridge among them — will put forward their claims for poetry as a source of secular salvation. For Coleridge, poetic genius partakes of an essentially "organic" creativity, a condition of restored natural grace where mind is at one with the external world and rejoices in the exercise of its own spontaneous powers. It is here — in the moment of supposedly transcending all commonplace limits of thought and perception — that the symbol (or a certain beguiling idea of the symbol) asserts its paramount claims. For Coleridge, such moments are characterized "by the translucence of the special in the individual, or of the general in the special, or of the universal in the general; above all by the translucence of the eternal through and in the temporal."[4] And this can only come about through the grace of genius manifest chiefly in privileged tropes like metaphor and symbol, tropes that reveal a creative power which is also a kind of second nature, a token of the "one life, within us and abroad" envisioned by poets like Wordsworth and Coleridge. Thus in Hegel's *Aesthetics*, as de Man writes, "the symbol is the mediation between the mind and the physical world of which art manifestly partakes, be it as stone, as color, as sound, or as language" (SS, p. 763).

This follows from Hegel's all-embracing dialectic, his conception of the history of Mind (or Spirit) as a world-historical progress through successive phases of increasing self-consciousness and interiorized reflective grasp. The beginning of this journey is the state of primitive sense-certainty where the mind has not yet learned to distinguish subject and object, inward and outward realms of experience, and therefore exists in a kind of rich but confused harmony with nature. (This idea finds a parallel in Freud's account of the infant as passing through a phase of "polymorphous," undifferentiated instinct and desire, and in Lacan's development of the Freudian thesis in terms of a pre-Symbolic "imaginary" stage where desires are as yet unbounded by the Oedipal law that sets limits to the self and prohibits such forms of anarchic self-gratification.[5]) As consciousness evolves, so it comes to recognize the difference between itself and the objects of its knowledge and desire, the ontological gulf that opens up as soon as reflection starts out on its arduous course of discovery. This recognition is both necessary and painful. It is the only way forward for consciousness in its overcoming of naive sense-certainty and its progress toward a reflective, philosophical grasp of its own prehistory. But this advance goes along with a deepening sense of the mind's estrangement from nature, its confinement to a realm of ideas, concepts, and representations which enjoy nothing of that primitive, spontaneous being-in-the-world.

This ambivalence in Hegel is of course reproduced in numerous texts of Romantic poetry, criticism, and philosophy. It is the basis of Schiller's widely influential distinction between "naive" and "sentimental" art, the one existing in a state of undisturbed (because largely prereflective) proximity to nature, the other able to evoke that state only from a distance of self-consciousness, nostalgia, and ironic hindsight. There is the same underlying pattern to be found in those poems of Wordsworth and Coleridge that look back regretfully to a period in childhood when the visionary sense of communion with nature was as yet untouched by the dislocating, alien effects of self-consciousness and adult knowledge. But this sentiment of loss goes along with the faith that such communion *can* be restored, if only momentarily, by acts of creative imagining that overcome the ontological and temporal void fixed between subject and object, mind and nature. In fact it has been argued — notably by M.H. Abrams — that this is precisely the organizing principle and characteristic form of the "greater romantic lyric."[6] It involves, according to Abrams, a three-stage dialectical movement of thought, from recollection of an erstwhile innocence and grace, through despair at the mind's present sense of having lost the strengths and consolations of nature, to a newly found mood of tranquility and hope based on a wise acceptance of this same predicament. As with Schiller, the mind takes comfort in a knowledge that all is not lost, that the pleasures of reflective or "sentimental" thought may compensate for whatever is relinquished in the way of spontaneous, natural instinct. And it is chiefly through the agencies of metaphor and symbol that poetry achieves this restorative vision. Thus it comes about, according to Abrams, that "nature is made thought and thought nature, both by their sustained interaction and by their seamless metaphorical continuity."[7]

Such a reading finds copious evidence to support its case in the canonical texts of English Romanticism, including the Odes of Wordsworth and Keats and the Coleridge "Conversation Poems." And it also acquires a more generalized sense of philosophical conviction from the echoes of Hegelian dialectic that accompany its major claims. For Hegel likewise, art promises to restore that happy reciprocal relation between mind and nature, subject and object which was once a matter of spontaneous "natural" grasp. But it does so at a higher dialectical stage of the progress toward reflective self-knowledge, a standpoint from which that earlier condition can appear only as naive and deluded. Hence the preeminence of the symbol in Hegel's aesthetic discourse. For "symbolic art" is that which not only reconciles mind and nature (like metaphor in the passage from Abrams above), but also incorporates a power of inward or phenomenological reflection on its own nature, history, and genesis. In de Man's words:

the commanding metaphor that organizes this entire system is that of interiorization, the understanding of aesthetic beauty as the external manifestation of an ideal content which is itself an interiorized experience, the recollected emotion of a bygone perception. (SS, p. 771)

It is for this reason, de Man conjectures, that Hegel's *Aesthetics* has found so many echoes among critics (like Abrams) in the mainstream Romantic line of descent. The allusion to Wordsworth ("emotion recollected in tranquillity") is an index of this strong elective tie. What Hegel provides is the basis (or, as de Man would have it, the *putative* basis) for a working faith that poetry can indeed make good its ultimate promise; that language can recapture those moments of inward communing with nature when mind overcomes the melancholy knowledge of its own self-estranged or belated predicament. "Hegel is indeed, from the relatively early *Phenomenology* to the late *Aesthetics,* preeminently the theoretician of internalization, of *Er-innerung*" (SS, p. 771). His entire philosophy is built upon this root conviction: that mind can aspire to true knowledge only through a thinking back into the history of cultures, life forms, ideas, and representations that mark the various stages of its progress to date. *Erinnerung* — or the power of active, living memory — is both the key to this triumphal progress and the means by which reflection may at last overcome the conflicts and antinomies of philosophic reason still present in thinkers like Kant.

Hence the importance of aesthetics for Hegel, and — more specifically — of the symbol as a means of fulfilling (or appearing to fulfill) this high promise. "*Er-innerung*, recollection as the inner gathering and preserving of experience, brings history and beauty together in the coherence of the system" (SS, p. 771). It is this Hegelian movement of "interiorization" — this inward turn toward living memory as a source of redemptive insight — that has shaped the reading of English Romanticism offered by interpreters like Abrams. This reading claims warrant as a faithful account of what these poets manifestly wrote, thought, and intended. That is to say, it can point to numerous passages in their work where imagination is indeed credited with a power of overcoming the limits of quotidian knowledge and perception; where language (most often the language of metaphor and symbol) seems to take on an "organic" or quasi-natural power of creativity; and where the poet celebrates a power of living recollection that transcends all mere contingencies of time and change. So much is a matter of plain self-evidence as long as one takes the word for the deed, assuming — like Abrams — that there *must* be a power vested in metaphor and symbol that enables this passage from the level of declarative statement to the level of achieved effect. And this assumption is indeed a staple of

Romantic criticism, as de Man shows in his essay "The Rhetoric of Temporality," where he gathers a number of representative statements from various present-day commentators. Thus Earl Wasserman takes it as read (so to speak) that Coleridge is genuinely able to reconcile "the phenomenal world of understanding with the noumenal world of reason."[8] And Abrams likewise states it as a matter of demonstrable truth that "the best Romantic meditations on a landscape, following Coleridge's example, all manifest a transaction between subject and object in which the thought incorporates and makes explicit what was already implicit in the outer scene."[9] Once again, the measure of true Romantic genius is its power to reconcile antinomies, to create (through metaphor and symbol) an autonomous realm of unified thought and perception.

For these critics, the assertion of an "organic" relationship between mind, nature, and language is not to be regarded merely as a topos, a recurrent theme or preoccupying metaphor. On the contrary, they press as far as possible toward *literalizing* the metaphor, taking it in earnest as a sign that poetry can indeed transform the very nature and condition of language. Such is the suasive force of this aesthetic ideology that critics are led to invest in its claims to the point of forgetting that it is, after all, a species of analogy or fiction, and not in any sense a truth about the workings of language. De Man finds a classic illustration of the point in W.K. Wimsatt's well-known essay "The Structure of Romantic Nature Imagery." Wimsatt argues that there *did* indeed occur a marked shift in the currency of poetic language at around the turn of the eighteenth century. He sets out to analyze the effects and the extent of this change by comparing two sonnets, one by Coleridge and one by Coleridge's early mentor, the poet William Lisle Bowles. What chiefly differentiates these two productions is, according to Wimsatt, the greater specificity of surface detail in the Coleridge poem, its "more faithful observation of the outside object," and — paradoxically — its achievement of a more authentic "inwardness", a sense that it communicates "experiences of memory and of reverie that stem from deeper regions of subjectivity than in the earlier writer" (cited in *BI*, p. 194).[10] Again, Wimsatt is not content to regard this difference as simply a matter of Coleridge's having achieved a more effective, condensed, or metaphorically striking treatment of his theme. In fact he is not overly impressed by this performance, but thinks it a useful pointer to much greater things. Thus "the meaning might be such as we have seen in Coleridge's sonnet, but it might more characteristically be more profound, concerning the spirit or soul of things — 'the one life within us and abroad.' And that meaning especially was summoned out of the very surface of nature" (*BI*, p. 194).[11]

This statement is remarkable partly for the fact that Wimsatt was a chief theorist and spokesman for the American New Criticism. That is to say, his sympathies were far removed from the kind of neo-Romantic position that Abrams and Wasserman clearly represent. For the New Critics — like Eliot before them — Romanticism figured as a source of manifold tempting errors and delusions. In particular, it tended to blur the distinction between poetry and subjective experience, the line that Eliot insisted should be drawn between "the man who suffers" and "the mind which creates." This classicist demand for impersonality in art was translated by the New Critics into a series of prescriptions for the practice of responsible reading. Hence the various "fallacies" — biographical, intentionalist, and so forth — which Wimsatt and his colleagues regarded as well-nigh heretical confusions. Indeed, one of Wimsatt's last essays was a polemical piece taking on what he saw as the threat to this position posed by critics like J. Hillis Miller, those who were engaged at the time in a form of applied phenomenology (or "criticism of consciousness") aimed at breaking down the ontological distinction between author, work, and reader response.[12] Such excursions struck Wimsatt as exhibiting a willful disregard for the standards of disciplined, objective response established by New Critical method. So it is surprising to find him, in the essay on Coleridge, equating the highest achievements of Romantic poetry with its power to efface ontological differences, to reconcile mind and nature, subject and object, experience in its "noumenal" and "phenomenal" aspects.

But in a sense this bears out de Man's contention: that the Hegelian assumptions of post-Romantic criticism cut across the widest divergences of method and principle. In his early essay "Form and Intent in the American New Criticism," de Man shows how the anti-intentionalist case rests on a misunderstanding of its own main premise; how poetic "intentionality" doesn't involve "[the] transfer of a psychic or mental content that exists in the mind of the poet to the mind of a reader," but rather "the activity of a subject regardless of its empirical concerns, except as far as they relate to the intentionality of the structure" (*BI*, p. 25). In short, the New Critics were right to reject any simplistic appeal to authorial intentions, but wrong to suppose that their methods were or could be "objective" in the sense of breaking altogether with intention-alist premises and assumptions. De Man goes on to show how New Criticism mistook the nature of its own privileged metaphors, notably (again) that of the poem as a kind of "organic" entity. "Because such patient and delicate attention was paid to the reading of forms, [these] critics pragmatically entered into the hermeneutic circle of interpretation, mistaking it for the organic circularity of natural processes" (*BI*, p. 29). New Criticism can therefore be seen — despite its more dogmatic disavowals — as belonging very much to the post-Romantic or Hegelian history of thought.

Wimsatt himself gives a hint of this when he describes the poem as a "concrete universal," an autonomous structure of inwrought meaning which compels a due respect for its objective mode of existence.[13] But the phrase of course derives from Hegel, and carries along with it a range of suggestions that complicate Wimsatt's programmatic message. These include the antinomies of mind and nature, subject and object, the inwardness of reflective self-knowledge and the various forms of phenomental or naturalized perception that mark the stages of Hegelian dialectic. As de Man writes, "these categories are susceptible to infinite refinement, and their interplay can undergo numberless combinations, transformations, negations, and expansions" (SS, p. 771). In Wimsatt's usage, the term "concrete universal" seems designed to keep these suggestions at bay, to insist on the objective character of poetic meaning, and hence its existence in a realm apart from the vagaries of idealist or speculative thought. But this attempted sublimation of the term's prehistory cannot disguise its Hegelian provenance and its involvement with all those coimplicated themes and metaphors that make up the heritage of Romantic-Symbolist aesthetics. In de Man's words (from the late essay on Hegel):

> The dialectics of internalization make up a rhetorical model powerful enough to overcome national and other empirical differences between the various European traditions. Attempts, for instance, to mediate between Hegel and English Romantics such as Wordsworth, Coleridge and Keats often turn around the distinctive topoi of internalization . . . In all these instances, Hegel can be invoked as the philosophical counterpart of what occurs with greater delicacy in the figural inventions of the poets. (SS, p. 771)

We can now perhaps appreciate the far-reaching character of de Man's proposed revision to the standard history of modern (post-Romantic) critical thought. He is suggesting that this history has been programmed or determined in every last detail by the system of "commanding metaphors" that Hegel most consistently expounds. This system comprehends not only the poetics of Romanticism but all those schools and movements in the wake of Romanticism which supposedly rejected its claims.

Thus when Eliot (and the New Critics after him) set out to rewrite the canonical Tradition of English poetry, they did so by means of an historical myth which expressly devalued the Romantics but implicitly invoked a whole series of arch-Romantic values and assumptions. If there did indeed occur, as Eliot thought, a "dissociation of sensibility," a cultural malaise that set in some time toward the mid-seventeenth century, then the only possible standard by which this decline could be measured is that of the "organic" or unified sensibility, a condition of reconciled thought and sensibility conceived very much in Hegelian terms.[14] And this is exactly the kind of language that Eliot uses when writing about Shakespeare, Donne, and other such exemplars of English poetry at its finest. Thus Eliot's avowed antipathy to Romanticism goes along with a covert adherence to its whole working system of evaluative terms and categories. As with Hegel, so with Eliot's potent mythology: the aesthetic becomes a privileged ground on which poetry (or a certain idea of poetry) lays down the terms for historical understanding. And the same applies (so de Man argues) to other, more recent varieties of critical thought. Thus Hans-Georg Gadamer speaks for the enterprise of modern hermeneutics when he affirms the superiority of symbol over allegory, since the language of symbolism opens the way to a deeper, more intimate communion of minds between text and interpreter.[15] And again this involves a very marked preference for that period of Romantic speculative thought when such organicist metaphors attained their greatest prominence. For Gadamer, in short, "the valorization of symbol at the expense of allegory" coincides with "the growth of an aesthetics that refuses to distinguish between experience and the representation of this experience." Furthermore, it is the "poetic language of genius" that transcends such prosaic distinctions and "can thus transform all individual experience into general truth" (*BI*, p. 188). There is thus a very direct line of descent from the poetics of Romanticism to the methods and principles of modern hermeneutic philosophy.

De Man argues to much the same effect in his late (1982) essay on Hans-Robert Jauss and the project of *Rezeptionsaesthetik*.[16] In Jauss he detects a certain impatience with those problems and resistances so often encountered in the close reading of literary texts. What links this project to the wider hermeneutic enterprise is its tendency to repress or evade such problems and seek out a meaning that would ultimately reconcile text, history, and present awareness in a consummate merging of interpretive horizons. Jauss's inclination, understandably enough, is to avoid paying too much attention to "linguistic factors that threaten to interfere with the synthesizing power of the historical model" (*RT*, p. 63). His method is staked on a working faith that criticism can achieve such understanding if it first takes account of the cultural differences that separate past and present, the text as a product of its own historical epoch and the critic's response as likewise conditioned by latter-day beliefs and expectations.[17] What sets this project apart from Gadamer's version of hermeneutic method is the greater specificity of Jauss's excursions into the history of variant readings. By making full allowance for these — by treating the text's interpretative afterlife as an integral aspect of its meaning for subsequent readers — Jauss can hope to make terms with the fact of cultural relativity and change.

For de Man, there is a question whether Jauss's historical procedure "can indeed claim to free itself from the coercion of a model that is perhaps more powerful, and for less controllable reasons, than its assumed opponents believe" (*RT*, p. 58). This model is Hegelian and consists, once again, in the regular substitution of *aesthetic* ideas and values for the detailed labor of textual close reading. At a certain stage in Jauss's essays there always occurs — according to de Man — a moment of assumed convergence or identification between history, meaning, and phenomenal perception. That is to say, his method inherits the terms of that deep-laid aesthetic ideology which equates the nature of language and meaning with the nature of empirical experience. Thus Jauss tends to think of reception-history in terms borrowed from the formalist and phenomenological lexicon, notably those of "concretization" and the "defamiliarizing" power of aesthetic devices. If understanding transcends the obstacles of temporal and cultural distance, it does so by *perceiving* those salient features of the work that stand out against the various implicit "horizons" of past and present response. Such analogies work by assimilating language to the order of phenomenal cognition, or assuming that questions in the province of textual interpretation can be answered in terms that ultimately derive from the realm of cognitive psychology. Responsive readings are "the outcome of a reception by means of which the individual work becomes part of a landscape against which new works will, in turn, be silhouetted" (*RT*, p. 59).

What gives this model such persuasive power is its way of translating spatial or perceptual metaphors into a semblance of epistemological rigor. Reception-history can then be envisaged as a series of questions and answers, a process of constant interrogative exchange between past and present "horizons" of knowledge. "As the answer metamorphoses into a question, it becomes like an individual, tree, or portrait set within a stylized landscape and it reveals, by the same token, a live background behind its background, in the form of a question from which it now can itself *stand out*" (*RT*, p. 59). Thus Jaussian aesthetics rejoins that tradition of phenomenalist thinking about art and language that runs from Hegel to the various present-day forms of hermeneutic philosophy. Its claims are underwritten in the last analysis by its assumption that language is a natural, organic phenomenon; that linguistic structures are there to be *perceived*, like objects in the natural world; and that the process of interpreting texts is best understood in terms deriving from the activity of sensuous cognition. For Jauss, then, "the condensation of literary history and structural analysis occurs by way of the category of the aesthetic and depends for its possibility on the stability of this category" (*RT*, p. 64). But it is precisely this stability that is called into question by de Man's insistence on the way that language fails to match up with the order of phenomenal or sensuous experience. Such correspondence could only obtain if the organicist metaphor was more than just that, if linguistic structures were somehow truly consubstantial with the world of natural processes and forms. This illusion is perhaps inescapable, or by now so deeply ingrained in the post-Romantic temper of speculative thought that it has become fundamental to much of our thinking about art, language, and aesthetics. But it nonetheless remains an illusion, and one that de Man thinks responsible for manifold errors and failures of reading.

Hence his reservations with regard to Jauss and the otherwise highly appealing project of historical *Rezeptionsaesthetik*. This program can sustain its ambitions only in so far as it assumes the ultimate compatibility of phenomenal and linguistic modes of apprehension. For de Man, on the contrary, "all the obstacles to understanding . . . belong specifically to language rather than to the phenomenal world; consequently, the expectation that they could be mastered by analogy with processes that stem from the psychology of perception is by no means certain" (*RT*, p. 62). It is only by dint of a covert appeal to that aesthetic ideology — to the notion of art as possessing a power to reconcile concepts with sensuous intuitions — that Jauss can make such impressive claims for the scope and power of his method. More specifically, it is at the point where hermeneutics seeks to incorporate a fully historical dimension that Jauss falls back into familiar Hegelian ways of thought. History can be rendered amenable to the purposes of aesthetic understanding only by a move that overcomes the obstinate, resistant signs of textual difference by assimilating language to a model of transcendent, unitary thought and perception. Hence, de Man argues, the continuing suasive efficacy of that model, the appeal it exerts upon critics and theorists of otherwise very diverse persuasion. To resist this appeal involves a labor of demystifying thought which goes clean against some of our deepest, most "natural," and perhaps — de Man admits — ineradicable ideas about language and experience. But to raise it into a full-scale applied methodology is nonetheless to risk very real distortions of critical understanding.

II

De Man typically asserts this need for a watchful, resistant practice of reading in a language that carries strongly marked ethical overtones.

"The aesthetic is, by definition, a seductive notion that appeals to the pleasure principle, a eudaimonic judgment that can displace and conceal values of truth and falsehood likely to be more resilient to desire than values of pleasure and pain" (*RT*, p. 64). So when de Man speaks of the "resistance to theory" — as in the title of a late essay and the posthumous collection of which that essay forms a part — his use of the phrase is distinctly double-edged. On the one hand it denotes the overt *hostility* to literary theory among critics who regard it as an alien, subversive discourse, or at best a mere distraction from the common pursuit of true judgment which is all that criticism can hope to achieve. This response is familiar enough, from F.R. Leavis's famous refusal to "philosophize" when challenged by René Wellek in 1937, [18] to the various attacks on deconstruction, poststructuralism, and other such recent theoretical trends. It reflects the deep attachment to commonsense-intuitive values and assumptions which has characterized the discourse of literary criticism from Matthew Arnold to Leavis and beyond. To this extent, the "resistance to theory" is a matter of largely institutional forces and pressures, a resistance that comes, so to speak, from outside and defines itself in straightforwardly adversarial terms. But there is also, according to de Man, a resistance internal to theory itself, a point at which that enterprise comes up against problems resulting from its own methodological commitments. It is here precisely that de Man locates the source of those persistent errors, confusions, and misreadings that critics are prone to when their judgment is in the grip of some powerful *a priori* theory. The effect — as with Jauss — is to generate a kind of prematurely synthesizing method, an approach that takes for granted the ultimate compatibility of linguistic, historical, and aesthetic values.

Hence the seductive power of any theory that promises to reconcile these disjunct dimensions, to provide an all-embracing hermeneutic model that would overcome every such resistance. Close reading is to this extent the active antithesis of "theory" in its more doctrinaire or reductive forms. That is to say, it forces the critic to recognize those problematic elements of meaning, structure, and style which hold out against a reading intent upon reducing them to consistency with its own fixed ideas. This is one reason why de Man often praises the American New Critics, despite what he sees as their unfortunate tendency to raise certain privileged rhetorical tropes (paradox, irony, etc.) into a species of premature aesthetic ontology. For there was always, he argues, a strong countervailing impulse in their work, a devotion to the business of close reading and detailed textual explication which put up a resistance to such preconceived aesthetic absolutes. We might recall that de Man became acquainted with New Critical practice soon after his arrival in America, at a time (the early 1950s) when it was set to bring about the most far-reaching changes in the way that literature was taught and understood. Its emphasis on close reading and its apparent unconcern with larger, "philosophical" issues would no doubt have struck him all the more forcibly for the fact that up to then he had been very much influenced by thinkers like Heidegger, Sartre, and Blanchot for whom such issues were inseparable from the interests of literary criticism.

In his late essay "The Return To Philology" de Man recollects both the impact of New Criticism and, in particular, the impression made by that salutary insistence on patient, meticulous close reading. Students were encouraged to suspend their habitual beliefs and expectations, to read with an eye to details that resisted a straightforward assimilative grasp. They started out, as de Man puts it, "from the bafflement that such singular turns of tone, phrase, and figure were bound to produce in readers attentive enough to notice them and honest enough not to hide their non-understanding behind the screen of received ideas that often passes, in literary instruction, for humanistic knowledge."[19] So the New Criticism itself promoted a certain "resistance to theory," at least in so far as it practiced the virtues of textual close reading and allowed them to deflect, subvert, or undermine its own more ambitious "ontological" claims. It is the same kind of scrupulous regard for the letter of the text that de Man brings to bear on Jauss's project of *Rezeptionsaesthetik*. That project is distinctly Hegelian in its will to overcome all signs of difference, of disruptive or heterogeneous sense, and thus restore the text to an order of self-present meaning and truth. It does so primarily by means of the resort to aesthetic perception as a bridge between the sensuous (or phenomenal) and the purely linguistic aspects of textual understanding. Thus Jauss tends to ignore certain kinds of apparently anomalous, deviant, or unmotivated detail, elements of so-called semantic "freeplay" whose effects, since they derive from the letter of the text, and appeal to what seems a merely "literal" reading, therefore very often "escape from the network of hermeneutic questions and answers." What enables him to set such details aside — to regard them (implicitly) as not worth serious attention — is that same deep-laid aesthetic ideology that always knows *in advance*, so to speak, which are the pertinent or signifying features, those that will respond to the right kinds of question.

For de Man, on the contrary, "whenever the aesthetic is invoked as an appeal to clarity and control, whenever, in other words, a symptom is made into a remedy for the disorder that it signals, a great deal of caution is in order" (*RT*, p. 64). This caution takes the form of an extreme (to some minds perverse) attentiveness to textual detail, coupled with an equally rigorous scepticism as regards the claims of interpretative theory or method. When such claims have the appearance of matching up perfectly with "the more objective properties of language revealed by linguistic analysis," then — says de Man — the suspicion must arise that "aesthetic judgment has trespassed beyond its legitimate epistemological reach" (*RT*, p. 64). Thus Jauss's indifference to certain kinds of wordplay — puns, ambiguities, proper names that take on a semantic or signifying function — goes along with his express aversion to poststructuralist theory and its doctrine of the "arbitrary" sign. What is threatening in both cases is the idea that texts may exhibit structures of meaning that answer to nothing in the nature of a properly intuitive and natural response. When Jauss "on rare occasions" does take note of such wordplay, its effects are "quickly reaestheticized before anything unpleasant might occur" (*RT*, p. 65). That is to say, he always refers them back to some governing sense of *aesthetic* fitness, relevance, or purpose which in turn presupposes the perfect match between linguistic and phenomenal orders of perception. What Jauss's method cannot entertain is the possibility that these orders might *not* in fact be linked in such a close and unproblematical fashion; that reading may at any time come up against "linguistic factors" that "threaten to interfere with the synthesizing power of the historical model." That model is powerful enough to produce all manner of interpretative blind spots and evasions through the will to preserve its truth-claims intact. De Man indeed goes so far as to assert that "the ultimate aim of a hermeneutically successful reading is to do away with reading altogether" (*RT*, p. 56). In other words, it tends toward a point of maximally self-assured method and grasp where no counterevidence — no difficulties met with in the process of reading — would suffice to deflect or to complicate that aim.

For de Man, therefore, the "resistance to theory" has both a negative and a positive aspect. On the one hand "theory" is the willingness to question received ideologies of language, literature, and historical method which otherwise succeed in imposing their values in the form of self-evident, commonsense knowledge. To this extent theory is a liberating force, an active critique of those aesthetic beliefs and preconceptions that characterize the discourse of modern (post-Romantic) thought. The "resistance" to it would then be an index of the strength, depth, and tenacity of purpose mustered on the side of that aesthetic ideology. But there is also, as we have seen, a sense in which the phrase turns back upon itself, implies that the resistance in question may be as much a matter of reading *against* theory as of theorizing the blindspots in other, naive or self-deluded readings. This is much more what preoccupies de Man in his essays on Jauss, Riffaterre, and other proponents of a literary theory that aspires to methodological completeness and rigor.[20] In these critics, "the resistance to theory . . . is a resistance to language itself or to the possibility that language contains factors or functions that cannot be reduced to intuition" (*RT*, pp. 12–13).

What prevails in their reading is always the desire that texts should make sense according to some historical, aesthetic, or hermeneutic model that overcomes any obstacles in its way. In such cases the "resistance to theory" is itself a very strong theoretical *parti pris*, but one that protects its own methodological assumptions by not exposing them to textual problems and resistances that might jeopardize its whole project.

So theory is a strictly impossible venture in so far as it aims — as most theories do — to achieve a sense of having thoroughly mastered the relevant problems and issues. To de Man, such illusions are precisely what criticism has to give up as it comes to recognize those deviant linguistic structures, or elements of rhetorical "undecidability," that work to undermine any form of self-assured hermeneutic understanding. "Nothing can overcome the resistance to theory since theory *is* itself this resistance" (*RT*, p. 19). Theory, that is to say, in the form of an applied rhetoric that would mark exactly those points of divergence between what a text says — the stubborn materiality of the words on the page — and what the various critics have made it say for theoretical and ideological reasons of their own. Rhetorical readings of this kind are, de Man suggests,

> The most elastic theoretical and dialectical model to end all models and they can rightly claim to contain within their own defective selves all the other defective models of reading-avoidance . . . They are theory and not theory at the same time, the universal theory of the impossibility of theory. To the extent however that they are theory . . . rhetorical readings, like the other kinds, still avoid and resist the reading they advocate. (*RT*, p. 19)

This extraordinary passage brings out all the tensions and paradoxes that run through de Man's late essays. It presents a number of provocative theses in a language of straightforwardly constative or truth-telling force which scarcely seems to brook any kind of dissenting response. Yet in each case this authoritative stance is directly undercut by what the passage goes on to suggest: namely, that there is no vantage point from which *any* kind of theory, de Man's included, could possibly claim to control or comprehend the workings of figural language.

The fact that this conclusion is arrived at nonetheless through a series of assertive propositions — sentences that claim to state the truth about language, or at any rate the lesson that no such truth can finally, properly be stated — is a difficulty that de Man never seeks to deny. It is addressed most directly in one of the essays on Nietzsche from *Allegories of Reading*, where he begins by contrasting two dimensions of language, the "constative" and "performative," and ends by effectively collapsing that distinction or revealing its undecidability in any given case. Nietzsche goes as far as possible toward showing up the inherently rhetorical nature of all those concepts, categories, and truth-claims that "philosophy" accepts at face value.[21] Like de Man, he suspects that we are imposed upon by language to the point of forgetting how our notions took rise from certain long-since naturalized tropes or figures of thought. And one major target of Nietzsche's sceptical critique is precisely that phenomenalist set of assumptions which maintains the primacy of physical perception (or some analogue thereof) at every level of thought and language.

For Nietzsche, this amounts to no more than a species of persistent rhetorical illusion, brought about by the trope of *metalepsis* (or reversal), the figure that substitutes cause for effect through a covert exchange of priorities. Thus in Nietzsche's words (from a passage entitled "Phenomenalism of the Inner World"):

> pain is projected in a part of the body without having its origin there; [conversely] the perceptions which one naively considers as determined by the outside world are much rather determined from the inside; . . . the fragment of outside world of which we are conscious is a correlative of the effect that has reached us from outside and that is then projected, *a posteriori*, as its "cause." (cited in *AR*, p. 109)

De Man is careful to state that he is not so much concerned with Nietzsche's specific "thesis" at this point as with "the manner in which the argument is conducted." That is to say, the relevance of this passage for de Man's purposes has nothing to do with any claims it may make as to the causes of pain, the nature of perception, or human experience in general. What he wishes to examine is the structure of an argument that approaches the limits of intelligible discourse by attributing every last concept and category to the workings of language or rhetoric. Thus de Man is not obliged to go along with some of Nietzsche's more immoderate or downright nonsensical claims, like the wholesale dismissal of causal explanations as a species of rhetorical imposture. Rather, he is concerned to isolate the source of that *particular* phenomenalist error that dominates the thinking of aesthetic philosophers from Hegel to the present. And Nietzsche provides a most effective means to this end when he shows that, in some cases at least, rhetoric assists in the effacement or forgetting of its own operations by allowing us to think of language in naively phenomenalist terms.

This brings us back to the constative/performative distinction, one that de Man takes over from speech-act theory but puts to work in ways undreamt of by J.L. Austin.[22] For it is an unavoidable consequence of Nietzsche's arguments that they must themselves be subject to the same degree of epistemological scepticism that they bring to bear on other, more confident varieties of philosophic truth-claim. That is to say, Nietzsche demonstrates that language is in some sense performative through and through; that every speech-act has a certain rhetorical dimension, even (or especially) those that would appear to state self-evident, *a priori*, or factual truths. And this would have to apply equally to every proposition that Nietzsche himself puts forward concerning the ubiquitous character of rhetoric, the illusory nature of commonsense or philosophic truths and the errors produced by taking them at face value. And yet of course Nietzsche is no more able than de Man to escape the necessity of arguing his case in propositional or assertoric terms. They are both in the position of stating it as a matter of fact that language can never — or only by a species of rhetorical self-deception — state *anything* as a matter of fact. De Man is very conscious of this double-bind predicament and finds it everywhere prefigured in Nietzsche's texts. So we shouldn't, he warns, be persuaded to read those texts as displaying "an irreversible passage from a constative conception of language to a performative one" (*AR*, p. 126). For there are too many signs in Nietzsche's writing of that need to state the fallacy of constative truth-claims in a language that inevitably falls back into the very mode of utterance it wishes to denounce. And yet, according to de Man, "Nietzsche has earned a right to this inconsistency by the considerable labor of deconstruction that makes up the bulk of his more analytical writings" (*AR*, p. 131). In other words — and the same might be said of de Man — there is a saving readiness in Nietzsche's texts to problematize their own most crucial working assumptions, and not take refuge in a premature appeal to method and system. "Considered as persuasion, rhetoric is performative but when considered as a system of tropes, it deconstructs its own performance" (*AR*, p. 131) Once again, the "resistance to theory" is one that takes rise from within the theoretical project itself, and which comes about only through that project's capacity for questioning its inbuilt values and commitments.

This has all taken us a long way around from that original question as to the bearing of deconstructionist theory on the Romantic ideology of genius. But the connection is not, after all, so remote if de Man's arguments hold good and it can indeed be shown that the whole development of modern critical thinking derives from a certain endemic confusion of language (or the signifying structures of language) with the order of phenomenal cognition. For then it would appear — as de Man implicitly argues — that "genius" is very much an idea resulting from the will to find *proof* of exactly that ideal convergence between mind and nature, language and whatever belongs to the world of sensuous experience. It is in Kant that these issues first achieve the status of primordial questions that philosophy must address before it can claim any warrant to pronounce on matters of epistemic, ethical, or aesthetic judgment. For de Man, Kant's thinking is a reference point from which to assess the various errors, misreadings, and ideological mystifications that have subsequently overtaken the history of critical and philosophic thought. I shall therefore now turn to Kantian aesthetics to draw out some further implications of de Man's late essays.

III

For Kant, genius is "a talent for producing that for which no definite *rule* can be given."[23] The productions of genius have this as their characterizing mark: that no amount of learning, acquired skill, or imitative talent can possibly suffice for their creation. Aesthetic perception is therefore distinguished from *theoretical* understanding — from the kind of knowledge that mainly preoccupies Kant in his first *Critique* — by its not conforming to the cardinal rule that every intuition be brought under an adequate or corresponding concept. It is precisely this incommensurable nature of artistic genius that sets it apart from science, theory, and the labors of enlightened (epistemological) critique. Thus "the concept of beautiful art does not permit the judgment upon the beauty of a product to be derived from any rule which has a *concept* as its determining ground, and therefore has as its basis a concept of the way in which the product is possible" (*KS*, p. 418). This is why Kant rejects any form of phenomenalist aesthetic that would treat art as possessing the power to reconcile concepts with sensuous intuitions. Such thinking fails to register what is distinctive in the nature of aesthetic experience: namely, the capacity of genius to create new forms, ideas, and images that exceed all the bounds of theoretical (or rule-governed) understanding. The author of such works "does not himself know how he has come by his Ideas," and certainly lacks the kind of knowledge that would allow him "to devise the like at pleasure or in accordance with a plan" (*KS*, p. 419). Whence the basic difference between art and all other forms of cognitive activity: that in art there is no question of intellectual *progress*, of collective advance through a shared application of the truths discovered by previous thinkers.

Kant's great example here is Newton, a figure whose intellect indeed took him voyaging into strange seas of thought, but whose findings, once established, opened up the trade routes of received, communal knowledge. Such scientific truth-claims are warranted precisely by their power of bringing intuitions under concepts, or showing that determinate rules can be given for the understanding of natural phenomena. Thus "Newton could make all his steps, from the first elements of geometry to his own great and profound discoveries, intuitively plain and definite as regards their consequence, not only to himself but to everyone else" (*KS*, p. 420). But this is not the case with those whose genius lies in the production of beautiful artworks. Theirs is a strictly *incommunicable* gift which cannot be taught, reduced to precepts, or in any way simply handed on. Such genius produces individual creations for which the mold (so to speak) is broken with each new endeavor and allows of no progressive building on previous achievements. Or more exactly, if artists can indeed learn from their great precursors, the lesson is more by way of general inspiration than anything pertaining to form, style, or technique. For genius, according to Kant, is "imparted to every artist immediately by the hand of nature; and so it dies with him, until nature endows another in the same way, so that he only needs an example in order to put in operation in a similar fashion the talent of which he is conscious" (*KS*, p. 420). So art exists at the furthest possible remove from that spirit of enlightened, cooperative enterprise that for Kant belongs to both science and philosophy in its aspect of rational critique. Art may be said to "stand still" in the sense that its productions exhibit no signs of advancing toward an enlightened consensus on the "rules" of judgment or taste.

This is why Kant rejects the idea that beauty resides in the object of aesthetic contemplation. If this were the case, then there could be no clear distinction between theoretical knowledge (that which applies concepts to the realm of sensible intuitions) and aesthetic understanding (that which allows us a privileged grasp of our own appreciative faculties at work). Kant is very firm about this need to resist any form of phenomenalist reduction. Aesthetic judgement contributes nothing to our knowledge of the objects that solicit its regard. Of course those objects must possess certain attributes, qualities that mark them out in the first place as capable of arousing such response. Otherwise art would be an empty concept and aesthetics would lack any claim to exist as a self-respecting discipline of thought. But we are equally mistaken, Kant argues, if we assimilate whatever is distinctive in the act of aesthetic judgement to those properties supposedly inherent in the object itself. For beauty is not determined by any concepts (or rules) that would find adequate exemplification in the features — or objective characteristics — of this or that artwork. It should rather be sought in the manner of our responding to such features, or the way that our various faculties are engaged in the act of aesthetic understanding. And this is where the experience of art differs essentially from other forms of cognitive experience. "In order to decide whether anything is beautiful or not, we refer the representation, not by the Understanding to the Object for cognition but, by the Imagination (perhaps in conjunction with the Understanding) to the subject, and its feeling of pleasure or pain" (*KS*, p. 375). Such is the inward or transcendental turn in Kantian aesthetics, the movement away from all forms of phenomenalist reduction. In the act of responding sympathetically to a beautiful object, the mind is thrown back (so to speak) upon its own resources, required to seek a sense of purposive relationship or harmony *not* between sensuous intuitions and concepts of the pure understanding (as in all forms of theoretical knowledge), but rather between those various faculties whose interplay thus defines the nature of aesthetic experience. "The judgment of taste is therefore not a judgment of cognition, and is consequently not logical but aesthetical, by which we understand that whose determining ground can be *no other than subjective*" (*KS*, p. 376).

But of course Kant is at pains to make clear that this "subjective" character of aesthetic judgment does not amount to a species of relativism in matters of artistic taste. To pronounce a work beautiful is always to claim a validity for one's judgment that cannot be compared with the expression of mere personal *preference* in this or that regard. Thus one may (indeed must) be content to differ with other people on the question of what makes a good wine, a satisfying meal, or a pleasant way of spending one's time. Such opinions are specific to the judging individual and can lay no claim to universal validity. It would be folly, Kant says, to "reprove as incorrect" another person's sentiments in the hope of persuading them to see reason and admit one's own superior taste. But this principle — "de gustibus, non est disputandum" — cannot apply in the realm of aesthetic judgment, any more than with issues of ethical reason. Here it is question of requiring assent to one's evaluative statements, or putting them forward as considered judgments with a claim to universal validity. So the reflective individual learns to distinguish between matters of idiosyncratic taste and matters of absolute or principled judgment. "Many things may have for him charm and pleasantness; no one troubles himself at that; but if he gives out anything as beautiful, he supposes in others the same satisfaction — he judges not merely for himself, but for everyone, and speaks of beauty as if it were a property of things" (*KS*, p. 384). So the argument here goes by way of analogy, deriving the universal character of aesthetic judgments from our need to treat them *as if* they related to qualities somehow objectively present in the work or natural phenomenon concerned.[24] But what is really at issue in such judgments is the utterer's fitness to pronounce them with authority owing to his or her possession of the requisite taste or appreciative powers. And this means that there is, after all, a realm of properly subjective judgments whose nature is nonetheless universal (or prescriptive) in so far as they effectively demand our assent and brook no denial on grounds of mere personal taste.

Kant attaches the highest importance to this legislative aspect of aesthetic judgment. Thus it cannot be a matter, as Hume had argued, of the social interests that are best served by our reaching some measure of agreement on questions of good taste and beauty. For this could be no more than an *empirical* fact about our present social arrangements, and so a source of value only as related to our short-term motives and interests. To see the limits of such thinking, Kant argues, "we have only to look to what may have a reference, although only indirectly, to the judgment of taste *a priori*" (*KS*, P. 381). For even if reflection does find traces of self-interest or social motivation, still we are compelled by the very nature of such judgments to accord them a validity beyond anything accountable on those terms alone. At this stage, according to Kant,

> taste would discover a transition of our judging faculty from sense-enjoyment to moral feeling; and so not only would we be the better guided in employing taste purposively, but there would be thus presented a link in the chain of the human faculties *a priori*, on which all legislation must depend. (*KS*, pp. 381–82)

So there exists an analogy between aesthetic judgment and practical reason (or ethics), as well as that other which Kant perceives between aesthetics and the order of phenomenal cognition. Both are in the nature of "as if" arguments — designed to give universal import to aesthetic values while *not* confusing them either with purely theoretical knowledge, on the one hand, or with ethical judgment on the other. Thus Kant insists that art take its place as a "link in the chain" of human faculties, an indispensable link, to be sure, but one whose role in the total system — the Kantian "architectonic" — needs defining with considerable care and circumspection. Otherwise aesthetics will overstep the limit of its own legitimate domain, with untoward results not only for itself but for the whole enterprise of enlightened critique.

We can best understand what de Man has to say about Kant, Hegel, and the subsequent discourse of "aesthetic ideology" if we read his work against this background of contesting truth-claims and legislative faculties. It will then become clear that he, like Kant, is concerned to set limits to the play of seductive metaphors and analogies that characterize aesthetic understanding; that he sees a real danger in the various moves to extend or annul those limits, to apply aesthetic notions *directly* to other domains of knowledge; and that this is what leads him to treat such attempts with an unrelenting suspicion. I have already tried to show how this argument takes shape in de Man's readings of Hegel and Jauss. It fastens on those moments of critical "blindness" where thought falls prey to the phenomenalist delusion, the idea that language — especially the language of metaphor and symbol — can become in some way consubstantial with the world of natural objects and processes, and so transcend the ontological gulf between words (or concepts) and sensuous intuitions. There is not a single essay of de Man, at least after the early 1960s, that doesn't raise this issue in one form or another. In *Blindness and Insight* it is posed in terms of those various interpretative methods and approaches — from the American New Criticism to the continental schools of phenomenology, existentialism, and Marxist aesthetics — which all of them at some point hold out the prospect of an ultimate reconciliation between language and nature, word and world. In *Allegories of Reading* the focus shifts to a more rhetorically sophisticated mode of critique, one that brings out the inherent strains, contradictions, or moments of aporia that develop as language strives to efface all the signs of its failure to achieve such a natural condition.

The best-known example is the section on Proust (*AR*, pp. 57–78) where de Man takes a single, exemplary episode — the young Marcel reflecting on the solitary pleasures of reading and their superiority over other, more extrovert or outdoor kinds of enjoyment — and shows how the passage in fact turns on the systematic privilege attaching to metaphor, as opposed to pedestrian or routine tropes like metonymy.[25] Metaphor is on the side of inwardness, imagination, contemplative withdrawal, and all that belongs to the realm of pure, self-delighting creative reverie. Metonymy, by contrast, is a literalistic trope that works on the basis of external or real-world relationships, those (like contiguity) which allow no room for exploring the freedoms of a rich imaginative life. Thus the passage presents a veritable "allegory of reading," one where every detail reinforces the idea that it is somehow *better* for Marcel to be sitting indoors with a book — thus allowing his mind the full scope of its self-sufficient inward resources — than leaving his room and suffering all the nuisances, perils, and distractions of the outside world. As de Man reads this passage,

> two apparently incompatible chains of connotations have thus been set up: one, engendered by the idea of "inside" space and governed by "imagination," possesses the qualities of coolness, tranquility, darkness as well as totality, whereas the other, linked to the "outside" and dependent on the "senses," is marked by the opposite qualities of warmth, activity, light, and fragmentation. (*AR*, p. 60)

Metaphor connotes "totality" along with its other positive values because, unlike metonymy, it implies that special power of creative imagination to evoke a whole world of unified thought and feeling untouched by the crass contingencies of everyday life. What is more, it suggests a yet higher stage in the totalizing process, a moment of consummate or hypostatic union when the very difference between inward and outward realms would at last fall away, and imagination reign supreme through the gift of metaphorical insight. Thus Marcel "finds access to the 'total spectacle of Summer,' including the attractions of direct physical action, and . . . possesses it much more effectively than if he had been actually present in an outside world that he then could only have known by bits and pieces" (*AR*, p. 60). What the passage from Proust therefore seeks to convey is a sense of radically transformative vision whose enabling trope is metaphor and whose claim is nothing less than to have overcome all the bad antinomies of rational (prosaic) thought.

But there are, according to de Man, rhetorical forces at work in this passage which effectively resist and subvert that claim. For the metaphors that carry the main weight of implication also turn out, on a closer reading, to depend on a certain tropological sleight of hand, a covert series of "exchanges and substitutions" whose structure is undeniably *metonymic* in the last analysis. De Man makes this point in a few remarkable pages whose sheer complexity of detailed textual exegesis defies any attempt at paraphrase. But the upshot is to show 1) that the inner realm of Marcel's imagining has to borrow its descriptive terms at every point from the "contingent," "fragmentary" world of natural experience; 2) that this amounts to a virtual undoing of metaphoric truth-claims through the effects of a generalized metonymy; and 3) that any reading which accepts those claims at face value will be blind to what is *really* going on in the Proustian text, and thus complicit with the force of "seduction" exerted by its leading metaphors and analogies. "A rhetorical reading of the passage reveals that the figural praxis and the metafigural theory do not converge and that the assertion of the mastery of metaphor over metonymy owes its persuasive power to the use of metonymic structures" (*AR*, p. 15). In which case — as de Man goes on to argue — we shall have to recognize some large obstacles in the way of any critical reading, aesthetic philosophy, or theory of language that thinks to negotiate or short-circuit the passage from linguistic signs to the order of perceptions and natural experience.

This may come down to an ultimate choice between "aesthetically responsive" and "rhetorically aware" readings, those which go along with the metaphoric drift for its yield of imaginative pleasure, and those which hold out against such easy satisfactions for the sake of a better, less deluded understanding. De Man makes some pretence of even-handedness in this. He declares that the two kinds of reading are "equally compelling," and denies that it is possible to read at all without in some measure submitting one's judgment to the suasive operations of metaphor. But the terms in which de Man presents this choice — on the one hand "seduction," naive enjoyment, a relaxed and pleasurable complicity with the text, on the other an ethos of undeceiving rigor, a determination not to be thus beguiled or seduced — can leave no doubt as to which is for him the right option. "The relationship between the literal and the figural senses of a metaphor is always," he writes, "metonymic, though motivated by a constitutive tendency to pretend the opposite" (*AR*, p. 71). This tendency is a product of the same deep-laid aesthetic ideology that de Man finds at work in the texts of critics and philosophers after Kant. It is "constitutive" in the sense that it is *not* a mere mistake or local aberration that could always be corrected in the wisdom of critical hindsight. Rather it is a kind of permanent temptation to which thought is subject whenever it approaches the complex terrain of language, ideology, and aesthetic understanding. That the error persists through such a range of texts — poems, novels, works of philosophy, critical theory, and so forth — should be evidence enough that its sources go deep into our "natural," received, or commonsense grasp of these matters.

This is why de Man insists that his chapter on Proust has nothing in common with the usual literary-critical forms of thematic or interpretative discourse. Since it does, after all, single out an episode in which *reading* — the reading of imaginative literature — figures as a central theme, one might be forgiven for assuming that this was what sparked de Man's interest in the passage, and that therefore his chapter is an ingenious example of thematic commentary in the modern reflexive or self-conscious mode. Not so, de Man urges, "for we cannot *a priori* be certain to gain access to whatever Proust may have to say about reading by way of such a reading of a scene of reading" (*AR*, p. 57). That is to say, the exemplary value of the episode lies not so much in its thematization of issues that happen to engage de Man's interest, but in the fact that it raises these issues at a level of generalized import beyond any such local concern. "The question is precisely whether a literary text is *about* that which it describes, represents, or states" (*AR*, p. 57). And for de Man that question must clearly be answered in the negative. The problems encountered in reading a fictional text like *Du Côté de chez Swann* cannot be distinguished in any rigorous or clearcut way from those presented by Hegel's *Aesthetics* or other such works of philosophy and theory. In each case there is the choice between simply accepting what the text has to say — reading along with its persuasive drift — and deconstructing the figural devices by which such effects are achieved. Thus the real dividing line is that which separates readings that are somehow imposed upon by forms of rhetorical mystification from readings that possess the rhetorical means to resist such unwitting collusion.

This question crops up again later in *Allegories*, when de Man is discussing Rousseau's very diverse literary output and the problems encountered by orthodox scholarship in fixing generic distinctions. What emerges in the course of de Man's reading is a pattern of rhetorical crossings and exchanges that defeats the best efforts of rigid classification. This applies as much to a fiction like *Julie ou La Nouvelle Héloïse* as to a piece of ethical-religious argument like the *Profession de foi*, or for that matter a political treatise like the *Social Contract*. "If we choose to call this pattern an allegory of unreadability, or simply an allegory, then it should be clear . . . that no distinction can be made between [these] texts from the point of view of a genre theory based on rhetorical models" (*AR*, p. 247). Models, that is to say, whose justification derives from the orthodox parceling out of discursive domains into those where utterances are assessed according to constative (logical or referential) criteria, and those where no such standards apply since they belong to the realm of metaphor, fiction, or suasive ("rhetorical") language. What de Man brings out with considerable force in his chapters on Rousseau is the way that these distinctions begin to break down under close textual scrutiny. Thus with the *Profession de foi* and *Julie*, "the fact that one narrates concepts whereas the other narrates something called characters is irrelevant from a rhetorical perspective" (*AR*, p. 247). For they both pose problems of interpretative grasp which cannot be resolved by assigning them to any one genre or category of discourse.

With the *Social Contract* likewise, it is an error to suppose that "the assumed inconsistencies and contradictions of the political theorist [can] be explained away by calling them 'literary'" (*AR*, p. 257). The result of such typecast classifications is simply to foreclose the more difficult question of how these texts are rhetorically structured in ways that cut across all conventional generic borderlines. And this question is crucial, de Man argues, since reading conventions — no matter how dubious their epistemological grounding — have very real consequences in the realm of ethical and political action. To claim (as he does) that the *Social Contract* exemplifies linguistic problems and aporias that are also to be found in purely "fictional" writing is by no means to deny its influence on the course of real-life events. Indeed, "the redoubtable efficacy of the text is due to the rhetorical model of which it is a version . . . [and] this is also why textual allegories on this level of rhetorical complexity generate history" (*AR*, p. 277). Such passages should not be read as expressions of a deeply conservative drive to reduce all history to the mere play of rhetorical tropes and devices. De Man is absolutely clear about the ways in which a text like the *Social Contract* can "generate history" to the point of provoking revolutions in the sociopolitical sphere. What he wants to define with more precision is the source of that "redoubtable efficacy" in the various linguistic forms of persuasion and argument which enable such effects to take place. "In the description of the structure of political society, the "definition' of a text as the contradictory interference of the grammatical with the figural field emerges in its most systematic form" (*AR*, p. 270). But this is also to say that political theory cannot do without a theory of the text or a rhetoric that seeks to understand the complex, overdetermined relationship between writing and the world of actions and events.

IV

This is why Kant remains a constant point of reference for de Man's critique of aesthetic ideology. In the Kantian system there is a rigorous attempt to articulate the various forms of knowledge — pure reason (epistemology), practical reason (ethics) and aesthetic judgment — while respecting the boundaries between them and checking the tendency for each to intrude upon issues beyond its own proper competence or scope. As we have seen, it is de Man's conviction that one of these categories — the aesthetic — has indeed very often overreached itself, to the detriment of clear thinking about issues of epistemology, ethics, and politics. This is really what is at stake in his reading of the passage from Proust, where the "totalizing" power of metaphorical language seems to give access to a self-sufficient realm of imaginary deeds and experiences untouched by the otherwise obtrusive demands of everyday, practical life. Thus the passage sets out "to attempt the reconciliation between imagination and action and to resolve the ethical conflict that exists between them" (*AR*, p. 64). If this were possible — if metaphor could *really* make good its visionary claims — then the reader could identify wholly with Marcel in his conviction that the life of solitary imagining transcends all practical needs and obligations. This desire would be satisfied at a stroke "without leaving a residue of bad conscience." But to go along with this reading is to fall into errors which cannot be justified or absolved by any appeal to the increased aesthetic pleasure which the passage then yields. A "literal and thematic" approach of this kind would "have to favor metaphor over metonymy as a means to satisfy a desire all the more tempting since it is paradoxical: the desire for a secluded reading that satisfies the ethical demands of action more effectively than actual deeds" (*AR*, p. 67).

Such a reading is manifestly in bad faith in so far as it substitutes the self-centered pleasures of a solitary life for the active engagement with real-life decisions and concerns that would break this charmed circle of inward communing. In de Man's early work — including many of the essays collected in *Blindness and Insight* — this issue is posed in more overtly Sartrian or existentialist terms. Inauthentic readings are those that project onto the text some notion of organic or unitary form that would point back to its originating source in a moment of pure, self-sufficient creative inspiration. What these readings must perforce ignore is any sign that language may become entangled with dimensions of contingent or metonymic sense that prevent it from ever achieving this wished-for condition. To read authentically is to know such delusions for what they are; to accept that language *cannot* in the end break free of its temporal and contingent character, no matter how strong the appeal of metaphor and its "constitutive tendency to pretend the opposite." By the time of *Allegories*, de Man has adopted a more chastened and self-denying style, one that admits only occasional, unguarded hints of this earlier existentialist ethos. But it is still detectable in his reading of Proust, where the suasive powers of aesthetic ideology are identified in ethically loaded terms that would scarcely make sense otherwise. "Precisely when the highest claims are being made for the unifying power of metaphor, these very images rely in fact on the deceptive use of semi-automatic grammatical patterns." And again: "Such a reading puts into question a whole series of concepts that underlie the value judgments of our critical discourse: the metaphors of primacy, of genetic history, and, most notably, of the autonomous power to will of the self" (both passages *AR*, p. 16). What has changed since *Blindness and Insight* is not the ethically charged character of de Man's readings but the fact that they are conducted now in a language of much greater restraint and analytical precision. This results in part from de Man's clearly having taken lessons from Nietzsche in the application of tropological models to the genealogy of concepts and ethical truth-claims. But it also reflects his increasingly Kantian emphasis on the need for such techniques to be practiced in the light of their own conceptual genealogy, their place within that structure of articulated forms of knowledge that constitutes critical reason. For otherwise there is always the danger that one or another of these "faculties" will overstep its limits of accountability and thus create some form of ideological illusion.

De Man finds this question raised most acutely in the various passages of Kant's third *Critique* where he discusses the relationship between mind, nature, and aesthetic judgment. What these passages seek is a clear understanding of that faculty's powers and limits, with regard not only to the specialized sphere of artistic production and taste, but also in relation to epistemology on the one hand and ethical reason on the other. For it is evident throughout Kant's writings that the aesthetic cannot be simply cordoned off within a separate discussion of art and its objects. The *Critique of Pure Reason* effectively begins — starts out, that is to say, on its critical path, once over the merely schematic preliminaries — with a section entitled the "Transcendental Aesthetic." As John Sallis points out, there is something decidedly paradoxical about this phrase, since the aesthetic by definition has to do with "aesthesis, sensibility, a capacity for reception from without."[26] Transcendental judgments, on the other hand, are those that derive *not* from any kind of external impression but strictly from within the thinking subject, by a mode of *a priori* knowledge independent of sensory experience. Kant responds to this apparent impasse at the outset of his labors by distinguishing "pure" from "empirical" intuition — the latter turned wholly toward the realm of sensuous cognition, while the former is indeed given *a priori* and thus provides a hold for conceptual understanding. But clearly there is a sense in which this strategy does nothing more than push the whole argument back a stage. Kant still has to show how the forms of *a priori* knowledge can claim to legislate for experiences whose ultimate source is in the realm of empirical or intuitive sense-certainty. And this claim is of course crucial to his whole enterprise — since epistemology can be saved from the toils of "metaphysical" abstraction only in so far as it has some demonstrable grounding in the way that experience actually makes sense for us, aside from all abstract determinations. "Intuitions without concepts are blind; concepts without intuitions are empty." But Kant's dictum can have only a prescriptive or *de jure* force — can belong, that is to say, only on the side of "inward" intelligibility — if he fails to offer more cogent argumentative grounds for this intimate involvement of sensuous experience with the concepts of pure understanding. And it is here that the aesthetic plays its crucial mediating role, as a source of analogies that Kant will summon up repeatedly throughout the three *Critiques* wherever it is a question of bridging the gap between these otherwise disparate orders of knowledge.

The beautiful and the sublime are the two main categories through which the critique of aesthetic judgment hopes to achieve this ultimate reconciliation. Again, we are mistaken — according to Kant — if we seek for some determinate properties in or of the object that would constitute the beautiful as something that preceded the act of reflective judgment. For then we would be confusing *theoretical* knowledge — that which brings sensuous intuitions under concepts in order to establish their objective validity — with the quite different realm of aesthetic understanding. What the latter involves is a "judgment of taste [which], since it is to be possible without presupposing a definite concept, can refer to nothing else than the state of mind in the free play of the Imagination and the Understanding (so far as they agree with each other, as is requisite *for cognition in general*)" (*KS*, p. 390). Thus the beautiful (whether in artifacts or natural phenomena) is defined in terms of the response it provokes, a response which enables the mind to enjoy a uniquely heightened sense of its own cognitive powers. Those powers are here found in a state of "free play" because there is no determinate concept that binds them to the object in question. But such judgments are nonetheless "valid for everyone" in so far as they reflect the "universal subjective validity of the satisfaction bound up by us with the representation of the object that we call beautiful" (*KS*, p. 390). The knowledge they provide is not, therefore, a knowledge of the object itself, but a grasp of the faculties that come into play when that object is perceived under the aspect of aesthetic judgment. Only by way of this detour, so to speak, through the form-giving powers of subjective response does the artwork take on those "harmonious" or "purposive" attributes that make it an object of beauty. And this comes about through Imagination's power to conjure up experiences "as if" in accord with the way that Understanding normally works to bring intuitions under concepts.

The beautiful thus stands in a strictly *analogical* relation to that process of combined conceptual and intuitive grasp by which we obtain true knowledge of the world. And it is the special gift of genius to raise this analogy to a point where it surpasses all previous manifestations of the kind. In Kant's words,

> the unsought, undesigned subjective purposiveness in the free accord-
> ance of the Imagination with the legality of the Understanding
> presupposes such a proportion and disposition of these faculties as no
> following of rules . . . can bring about, but which only the nature of the
> subject can produce. (*KS*, p. 430)

In the case of beauty, therefore, the analogy holds between Imagination and Understanding, or the faculty that normally legislates in questions of epistemological import. With the Sublime, it points in a different direction, since here the mind is brought up against the limits of phenomenal cognition by its encounter with strange, overwhelming, or mysterious kinds of experience for which no adequate object can possibly be found. If the beautiful is that which evokes a state of harmonious balance between the faculties, the Sublime on the contrary forces us to acknowledge the limits placed upon Understanding by its need to represent experience in the form of intelligible concepts. Thus Kant paradoxically describes the Sublime (in a passage cited by de Man) as "an object (of nature) the representation of which determines consciousness to think the unattainability of nature as a sensory representation" (*KS*, p. 411).

Such moments are typically experienced — as so often in Romantic and post-Romantic poetry — with a sense of the mind's abjection in the presence of natural forces or phenomena that quite overwhelm its powers of recuperative grasp. But there is also, for Kant as indeed for the poets, a redeeming aspect to this experience, a way in which it points beyond ' the limitations of natural or phenomenal cognition to a realm of knowledge that exists for us only as rational, reflective subjects. As the mind fails in its striving to discover some objective correlative, some adequate means of *representing* such moments by recourse to the natural world, so it is driven to reflect on its own "supersensible" nature, that which cannot be determined according to empirical laws of any kind. The Sublime is therefore distinguished from the Beautiful by the fact that it surpasses everything expressible in terms borrowed from the realm of sensuous intuition. It relates not to Understanding but to Reason, the source of all ideas that lead beyond knowledge in its cognitive, epistemological mode to knowledge of man's authentically inward (moral and ethical) nature. As Sallis describes it:

> The Sublime, withdrawn into the subject, becomes a feeling whose essential function is to disclose within man the opposition between sensible and supersensible while, in and through that very disclosure, orienting man toward the supersensible as his genuine destination. (Sallis, p. 14).

So the Sublime, even more than the Beautiful, serves Kant as a kind of categorical touchstone for determining the powers and the limits of aesthetic judgment. In one sense it marks the supersession of epistemological concerns by informing us of that which lies beyond the grasp of any knowledge grounded in the union of concepts with sensuous intuitions. To this extent it indicates a convergence between aesthetics and ethics (or Practical Reason), a convergence at the limit-point where thought finds nothing in the outside world that could match or objectify its own "supersensible" nature. But in so far as the Sublime is still treated as in some sense an *aesthetic* category, it cannot be wholly divorced from the order of phenomenal cognition. In de Man's words, "morality and the aesthetic are both disinterested, but this disinterestedness becomes necessarily polluted in aesthetic representation: the persuasion that [such] judgments are capable of achieving is linked, in the case of the aesthetic, with positively valorized sensory experiences" (PMK, pp. 137–38). Once again, the aesthetic is in danger of overstepping its limits, this time by a move that would seek to accord it all the dignity of Practical Reason by invoking the Sublime as a passage beyond mere sensuous experience. But — and this is de Man's central point — there can really be no such passage "beyond" so long as we remain, with Kant, in the sphere of an aesthetic understanding whose terms are ultimately borrowed from precisely that phenomenalist realm. If the Sublime appears to break with such ideas — if it seems to force reflection to the point of acknowledging the inadequacy of all phenomenalist models — it does so by way of argumentative strategies that cover their own rhetorical tracks. And here the stakes are proportionately higher since the Sublime, unlike the Beautiful, lays claim to insights of a transcendental order close to those of Practical Reason.

Now de Man is *not* suggesting that Kant is simply a dupe of these "ideological" themes and motifs that subsist throughout the progress of the three *Critiques*. On the contrary, he finds them everywhere thrown into question by the rigor of Kant's argumentation, its resistance to that seductive power of the aesthetic that nonetheless continues to exert a powerful hold on his thinking. This resistance is there to be read in the *letter* of Kant's texts, in various problematic turns of metaphor and analogy that don't make their point with quite the intended force. "The critique of the aesthetic ends up, in Kant, in a formal materialism that runs counter to all values and characteristics associated with aesthetic experience, including the aesthetic categories of the beautiful and the sublime" (PMK, p. 136). As in his reading of Proust, de Man finds fault not so much with Kant — whose text, after all, provides every means for its own deconstruction — but with those other, less critical or circumspect readings which take its claims at face value. And this applies especially to Kant since his entire project is devoted to distinguishing valid from invalid orders of truth-claim, those that respect the operative boundary-conditions from those that ignore them and thus create all manner of confusion. De Man starts out in his essay on Kant by reminding us of one such distinction, that which separates "metaphysical" from "transcenden-tal" arguments. The former take for granted the existence of real-world objects or natural phenomena which answer to our commonsense, "pre-critical" view of reality. The latter have to do with that reflective or strictly philosophical attitude that questions commonsense knowledge in order to mark off empirical intuitions from *a priori* concepts. Thus "the objects of transcendental principles are always critical judgments that take metaphysical knowledge for their target. Transcendental philosophy is always the critical philosophy of metaphysics" (PMK, p. 122). And this means furthermore that critique in the distinctively Kantian sense of that term has implications that connect with Marxist and other, more overtly political forms of *Ideologiekritik*. For ideologies, "to the extent that they contain empirical moments, and are directed toward what lies outside the realm of pure concepts, are on the side of metaphysics rather than critical philosophy" (PMK, p. 122). The crucial significance of aesthetics in the Kantian system is the fact that it offers (or appears to offer) a means of articulating these two principles. What chiefly interests de Man is the way that Kant both depends upon a massively extended notion of the aesthetic in order to make good his own philosophical claims, and at the same time subjects that aesthetic ideology to a form of immanent critique.

This is why, as he argues, "ideological and critical thought are interdependent and any attempt to separate them collapses ideology into mere error and critical thought into idealism" (PMK, p. 122). There is no escaping that investment in "metaphysical," phenomenalist, or common-sense assumptions which provides the only possible link between concepts and intuitions, *a priori* knowledge and empirical experience. This is why the aesthetic, in its widest sense, is a constant source of analogies and metaphors as Kant builds up his "architectonic" of interrelated faculties and truth-claims. But it is also why aesthetics has become such an arena of competing ideologies that disguise their motives behind the standard (post-Kantian) rhetoric of "disinterest" and the autonomy of art. "The investment in the aesthetic is therefore considerable," de Man writes, "since the possibility of philosophy itself, as the articulation of a metaphysical with a transcendental discourse, depends on it" (PMK, p. 124). Hence Kant's recourse to phenomenalist language and assumptions, even while insisting that the Beautiful and the Sublime — especially the latter — belong on the side of subjective universality and not to the order of phenomenal cognition. But there is also (as de Man most effectively demonstrates) a subtext of argument in Kant that resists this aestheticizing drive, maintains the distinction between orders of judgment, and thus holds out against ideological confusion. The very title of his essay announces this theme by pointedly contrasting the "phenomenal" and the "material" as disjunct modes of understanding. And the theme is taken up in his closing sentence, which effectively condenses the entire critical project of de Man's late writings. "The bottom line, in Kant as well as Hegel, is the prosaic materiality of the letter and no degree of obfuscation or ideology can transform this materiality into the phenomenal cognition of aesthetic judgment" (PMK, p. 144).

The idea of genius is closely bound up with that complex of "metaphysical" themes and motifs that de Man contrasts with the labors of enlightened or demystifying thought. Genius, like the Sublime, is a category that transcends all categorization; that "gives the rule just as nature does" but cannot itself be reduced to any rule; whose hallmarks are, on the one hand, its power to tease philosophy almost out of thought, and on the other its kinship with the highest ("supersensible") faculties of human reason. To theorize the nature of genius is an impossible undertaking from the start — although this has not prevented Kant and subsequent aesthetic philosophers from making the attempt. We can now return to de Man's essay on Hegel, where he finds early signs of that persistent misreading of Kant that has characterized the discourse of aesthetic ideology down to this day. De Man singles out two propositions in Hegel which between them — as he argues — exemplify the impossible predicament of theory *vis-à-vis* the Romantic ideology of art. One is Hegel's statement that "the Beautiful is the sensory manifestation of the Idea," a claim that clearly represents, for de Man, a considerable slackening of philosophic rigor when compared with Kant's more complex, circuitous, and endlessly self-qualifying treatment of cognate themes. The other is his dictum that "Art is for us a thing of the past," by which Hegel means that philosophy (or Reason in its all-embracing reflective and historical mode) has usurped the privileged role once occupied by the highest forms of aesthetic experience. De Man's point is that these two propositions should be taken together and read as symptomatic of the errors and confusions that overtake aesthetic theory after Kant. What makes art a "thing of the past" for Hegel is not, as he would have us think, its belonging to an earlier, relatively undeveloped stage in the history of culture and thought. Rather, it results from the impossible demand that Hegel himself places upon art, his retreat into a form of aesthetic ideology which seeks to bypass the antinomies of critical reason. It is Hegel's great project in this work "to bring together, under the aegis of the aesthetic, a historical causality with a linguistic structure, an experiential and empirical event in time with a given, non-phenomenal fact of language" (SS, p. 763). Such would be the nature of the Symbol — the highest manifestation of artistic genius — if Hegel could indeed make good his claims. But on a closer reading it is language itself that turns out to frustrate this project, language that undoes the *a priori* valuation of Symbol over other, more pedestrian tropes like allegory.

De Man cites a number of critics — among them Peter Szondi — who register a certain disappointment with Hegel's performance at crucial points in the *Aesthetics*. More specifically, he gives little sign of having responded with genuine insight and sympathy to those achievements in the high Romantic mode which *in theory* his arguments resoundingly endorse. It is, Szondi writes, "his inadequate conception of the essence of language which is the cause of his failure."[27] Or as de Man puts it, condensing various details of the general charge: "Hegel . . . is a theoretician of the symbol who fails to respond to symbolic language" (SS, p. 765). But where Szondi sees this as evidence of Hegel's not living up to his own best insights — as a sign, that is to say, of philosophy's failure in coming to terms with the highest art forms of its age — de Man on the contrary locates the problem in precisely that overvaluation of the symbol that theory cannot fail to put in question. For Szondi, Hegel's shortcomings don't allow us to reject the *Aesthetics* entirely, since they show him to have been "at least on the right track." But they do give warrant for a sharply limiting judgment, to the extent that we (and indeed some of Hegel's contemporaries) have "traveled so much further along the same road." For de Man, by contrast, it is precisely at those moments when Hegel's text falls short of its promise that he reveals those delusions that still exert their hold over modern (post-Romantic) critical thinking.

It may indeed be the case that hermeneutic theory of the kind espoused by critics like Szondi has today advanced "further along the road" marked out by Hegel's aesthetic philosophy. But this is not to say that the road has either an upward course or an endpoint in genuine truth and understanding. What de Man reads in Hegel is the opposite message: that truth resides in those problematic details of the text which work to undermine its more grandiose claims. And this is to reverse the tropological order of priorities in Hegel: to treat his text *not* as a failed exercise in symbolist aesthetics, but rather as a clear-sighted allegory of the reasons for precisely that inevitable failure.

De Man's closing paragraph in the Hegel essay can stand as a summary statement of how deconstruction — on his understanding of that term — relates to the Romantic ideology of genius as manifest in the discourse on Symbol and metaphor. "We would have to conclude," he writes,

> that Hegel's philosophy which, like his *Aesthetics*, is a philosophy of history (and of aesthetics) as well as a history of philosophy (and of aesthetics) — and the Hegelian corpus indeed contains texts that bear these two symmetrical titles — is in fact an allegory of the disjunction between philosophy and history, or, in our more restricted concern, between literature and aesthetics, or, more narrowly still, between literary experience and literary theory. (SS, p. 775)

It is this conviction that gives de Man's writing its singular austerity and rigor, its refusal to countenance what he regards as the easy satisfactions of naive, uncritical reading. T.W. Adorno is another of those modern theorists whom de Man cites as responding very warily to the totalizing claims of Hegel's *Aesthetics*. And if one wanted to find a parallel for de Man's hermeneutics of suspicion, his thoroughgoing principled mistrust of all aesthetic ideologies, then Adorno provides the most striking instance.[28] Deconstruction is indeed a form of negative dialectics, an activity that carries on the project of immanent or self-reflective critique developed by Hegel out of Kant, but which turns this project against its own desire for such premature endpoints as Symbol or Absolute Reason. That de Man pursues these problems by way of their textual or rhetorical manifestation — rather than taking the "philosophic" path of self-assuredly conceptual exegesis — should by now not blind us to the truly philosophical character of his work.

The kinship with Adorno comes out most clearly on those rare occasions in his later writing when de Man allows himself to generalize briefly on what deconstruction "is" or "does." One such occasion is the passage on Rousseau from *Allegories of Reading* where he offers the following programmatic statement:

> Since a deconstruction always has for its target to reveal the existence of hidden articulations and fragmentations within assumedly monadic totalities, nature turns out to be a self-deconstructive term . . . Far from denoting a homogeneous mode of being, "nature" connotes a process of deconstruction redoubled by its own fallacious retotalization. (*AR*, p.249)

In a sense, this passage recapitulates everything that we have seen so far of de Man's engagement with aesthetic ideology, his critique of prematurely "totalizing" truth-claims, and his will to deconstruct the powers of rhetorical mystification vested in privileged tropes like metaphor and symbol. For it is always through the appeal to *nature* — nature as the ultimate source and analogue for human creativity or genius — that aesthetic ideology most strongly asserts its hold. For Kant, we may recall, genius "does not describe or indicate scientifically how it brings about its products, but it gives the rule just as nature does" (*KS*, p. 418). And again: "Nature by the medium of genius does not prescribe rules to Science, but to Art; and to it only in so far as it is to be beautiful Art" (*KS*, p. 419). The legacy of these and other such statements can be read everywhere in the Romantic discourse on art, imagination, genius, and the reconciling power of aesthetic experience. In particular, they generate that single most persistent and seductive of Romantic tropes: the organicist idea of art as a kind of second nature, a "heterocosm" where all bad antinomies fall away and imagination achieves a perfect union of subject and object, inward and outward worlds.

What is disguised in this idealizing movement of thought, so de Man argues, is the autocratic power and potential violence by which imagination may seek to secure its claims. These possibilities are spelled out most clearly when de Man turns to Schiller and the idea of "aesthetic education" as a kind of utopian promise, a passage beyond the various conflicts — the symptoms of "dissociated" thought and sensibility — that currently prevail. For de Man, this promise is more in the nature of a subdued threat, a vision of the faculties as existing *apparently* in a state of harmonious freedom and grace, but *in fact* as constrained by an imperative power of "aesthetic formalization." His remarks about Schiller appear in the course of an essay on Kleist's remarkable text "Uber das Marionettentheater" ("On the Puppet Theater").[29] His point in juxtaposing the two authors is to bring out the essential kinship between Schiller's ideal of aesthetic education and Kleist's disturbing allegory of human perfection (bodily and spiritual) as a kind of mechanical, puppetlike capacity to transcend all forms of disabling self-consciousness or inward division. For Kleist as for Schiller, this perfection is imagined in terms of an ideal *choreography*, a dance in which (as Schiller writes) "everything fits so skillfully, yet so spontaneously, that everyone seems to be following his own lead, without ever getting in anyone's way."[30] And the corresponding stage of aesthetic education is the point at which we glimpse "a wisdom that lies somehow beyond cognition and self-knowledge, yet can only be reached by ways of the process it is said to overcome" (*RR*, p. 265). Thus dance takes on all the attributes of that transcendent, synthesizing power of imaginative vision that Hegel and his followers ascribe to language in its highest creative forms.

De Man sees good reason — on political grounds chiefly — to mistrust this apparently benign promise of an end to our present, self-divided condition. What emerges from the intertextual reading of Schiller and Kleist is "the trap of an aesthetic education which inevitably confuses dismemberment of language by the power of the letter with the gracefulness of a dance" (*RR*, p. 290). So seductive is the promise of aesthetic formalization that it can easily overcome that other, more critical mode of reading which allows for the resistance that language puts up to any forced or premature merging of the faculties. "The 'state' that is here being advocated [in Schiller's *Letters on Aesthetic Education*] is not just a state of mind or of soul, but a principle of political value and authority that has its own claims on the shape and the limits of our freedom" (*RR*, p. 264). As with his reading of Proust, de Man is here concerned to detect that movement of conceptual overreaching where aesthetics — or a certain prevalent form of aesthetic ideology — seeks to legislate in realms beyond its proper epistemological grasp. These are the realms of ethics and politics, the domain of practical reason where Kant found room for *analogies* drawn from aesthetic understanding, but always and only on terms laid down by a rigorous critique of their powers and limits. What distinguishes Kantian aesthetics from the subsequent misreading of Kant by Schiller and others is the blurring of these properly critical lines of demarcation between art, epistemology, history, and ethics. And the fact that such errors may have worldly consequences beyond the specialized sphere of textual hermeneutics is exemplified plainly enough by the aftermath of German idealist metaphysics. "The point," de Man says, "is not that the dance fails and that Schiller's idyllic description of a graceful but confined freedom is aberrant. Aesthetic education by no means fails; it succeeds all too well, to the point of hiding the violence that makes it possible" (*RR*, p. 289)

To deconstruct the ideology of genius is to see just how such notions have carried across into other, potentially more dangerous spheres. It reveals the ideological charge conserved in the word's very etymology — that is to say, its relation to the *genius loci*, the tutelary spirit of homegrounds and origins, a figure that translates readily enough into forms of nationalist mystique. And indeed there were those, like Herder, who found no difficulty in revising Kant's doctrines so as to give them a Romantic-nationalist appeal totally at odds with their enlightenment character. In "The Rhetoric of Temporality" de Man refers to Herder's debate with Johann Georg Hamann — a debate on hermeneutics and the origin of language — as one that brought out the main points at issue between symbolic and allegorical modes of understanding. In Herder, the desire to assimilate language to a mystified ontology of nationalist spirit goes along with the swerve from a Kantian rigor of epistemological critique. And this attitude encounters in Hamann "a resistance that reveals the complexity of the intellectual climate in which the debate between symbol and allegory will take place" (*BI*, p. 189). The ideology of genius is very much a part of this Romantic drive to naturalize art and language in terms of their authentic national provenance and destiny. Kant himself might appear to invite such a reading when he remarks that the notion of genius probably derived from "that peculiar guiding and guardian spirit given to a man at his birth, from whose suggestion these original Ideas proceed" (*KS*, p. 419). But this passage is untypical and goes clean against the most basic precepts of Kantian critical reason. That the aesthetic can exert such a mystifying hold upon the "faculties" of enlightened thought is a theme that continually preoccupied de Man in the writings of his last decade. We are mistaken, he warns, if we treat these as marginal or ultra-specialized problems, of interest only to a handful of philosophers or literary theorists. For "the political power of the aesthetic, the measure of its impact on reality, necessarily travels by ways of its didactic manifestations" (*RR*, p. 273). It is hardly surprising, in light of these claims, that de Man's work continues to generate such widespread hostility and resistance.

3

Deconstruction and Philosophy:
Some Analytic Bearings

I

In his late essay "The Resistance to Theory," de Man sets out to specify the relationship between deconstruction and philosophy of language in its other, more commonly practiced forms and varieties.[1] He does so in terms of the classical *trivium*, the discipline that insisted on separating logic, grammar, and rhetoric in order to prevent any confusion between their distinct areas of applicability. For de Man, this attempt to draw boundary lines is beset with all manner of difficulties, though it is also a necessary attempt if thinking — especially philosophical thinking — is to proceed with any confidence in its own powers. There are two main assumptions that underpin the discourse of philosophic reason, at least in so far as that tradition has been grounded — from Plato to Descartes, Kant and their successors — in the quest for epistemological certainty and truth. These assumptions are 1) that language can be put to the service of logical arguments, concepts, and categories, since these in some way precede and articulate language itself; and 2) that any swerve from this desirable condition can always be detected and brought into line by an effort of conceptual clarification. This is why rhetoric needs to be cordoned off as a realm of merely persuasive figures or tropes whose presence is a threat to the interests of logic and truth, but a threat which can nonetheless be safely contained so long as its effects are clearly recognized.

Thus Plato puts rhetoric firmly on the side of fiction, poetry, sophistics, and other such nonphilosophical activities. Its province is mere opinion or *doxa* (as opposed to answerable truth), and its adepts are able to pass themselves off as experts on this or that topic only by appealing to ignorant or credulous minds. This hostility to rhetoric is carried on by thinkers like Locke and Kant, those who seek to purge philosophy of the errors and delusions that language is prone to when released from the proper self-discipline enjoined by reason. Locke's animadversions on rhetoric occur in a well-known passage from book 3 of the *Essay Concerning Human Understanding*. "It is evident," he writes, "how much men love to deceive and be deceived, since rhetoric, that powerful instrument of error and deceit, has its established professors, is publicly taught, and has always been had in great reputation."[2] So much so, indeed, that anyone who speaks out against it must expect their counsel to fall on deaf ears, at least among the great majority of those habitually seduced by figural language. "Eloquence, like the fair sex, has too prevailing beauties in it to suffer itself ever to be spoken against." This sentence echoes the passage from Dr. Johnson's *Preface to Shakespeare* where metaphor — or Shakespeare's inordinate fondness for the effects of multiplied metaphor — is denounced in a language whose own extravagantly figural character comes back, so to speak, like a boomerang. Thus a "quibble" for Shakespeare "is what luminous vapours are to the traveller . . . it has some malignant power over his mind . . . A quibble was to him the fatal *Cleopatra* for which he lost the world, and was content to lose it."[3] Locke and Johnson both treat metaphor as exerting a wayward, seductive power over thought, a power that is capable of leading it astray from the paths of logical consistency and truth. It is through the will to resist these distinctly *female* blandishments that philosophers (or sturdy commonsense critics like Johnson) can best hang on to their masculine values of propriety, dignity, and truth. And yet, as Locke ruefully concedes, "it is in vain to find fault with those arts of deceiving wherein men find pleasure to be deceived."

Dr. Johnson's attitude to Shakespearean metaphor is mostly considered a peculiar blind spot, an aberration in the history of literary-critical dealings with figural language. It is put down to various factors, among them the eighteenth-century desire for a stable, one-to-one economy of meaning and reference that would ensure a proper correspondence between words, concepts, and real-world objects of experience. And this desire may well have been related in turn — as Johnson often implies in his *Lives of the Poets* — to that widespread anxiety in the wake of the Civil War period that tended to identify any license in language with the forces of looming civil unrest and disruption. For receptiveness to metaphor is, after all, one of the points on which literary criticism (like the discipline of rhetoric in earlier times) has marked its distance from philosophy. If this seemed a reason for philosophers — from Plato to the logical positivists — to hold rhetoric and criticism in scant regard, their attitude could always be turned around by claiming that language was in fact metaphorical through and through;

that every great advance in human understanding had come about through the radically creative powers vested in metaphor; and that philosophers could see nothing of this so long as they persisted in a narrowly referential or hard-line positivist view of language. These arguments are familiar from the various "defenses" mounted against Plato and other such detractors by poet-critics from Sidney to Shelley, and thence from I.A. Richards to the present day. They assume a more technical, sophisticated guise in the Formalist idea of poetic language as a means of renewing our everyday, routine habits of perception through the "defamiliarizing" power of poetic devices; or again, in the rhetoric of "irony" and "paradox" which — according to the American New Critics — distinguishes poetry from straightforward (logical or referential) language. What unites these otherwise diverse creeds is also what sets them against philosophy, or at least against a certain self-image of philosophy created in large part by its old quarrel with the poets and rhetoricians. That is to say, they all agree in promoting figural language, and metaphor in particular, above whatever philosophy takes as the basis of its own claims-to-truth.

In one (fairly moderate) version of this belief, poetic language exists alongside the language of science and conceptual logic, provides us with a different, more expansive sense of human creative potential, but doesn't essentially contest what science or logic have to say about the world. In the other, more radical version — a line of thought that runs from Nietzsche to at least one variety of deconstructionist thinking — science and logic are not only denied any absolute epistemological privilege but are seen as the most self-deluding forms of discourse precisely on account of their failure to reckon with their own, inescapably rhetorical character. Thus Nietzsche reviews the whole history of philosophic truth-claims, from Plato to Kant and Hegel, and finds them to rest on the trick whereby metaphors are raised into concepts — or ideas of reason — which are then accepted as absolute truths by forgetting their metaphorical origins. Hence the now famous passage from Nietzsche's essay "Of Truth and Falsehood in an Extra-Moral Sense," a passage that begins with the question "What is truth?" and replies:

> A moving army of metaphors, metonymies and anthropomorphisms, in short a summa of human relationships that are being poetically and rhetorically sublimated, transposed and beautified until, after long and repeated use, a people considers them as solid, canonical and unavoidable. Truths are illusions whose illusionary nature has been forgotten . . . [4]

In *Allegories of Reading* de Man follows out the furthest implications of this extreme epistemological scepticism. In the end, as we shall see, he questions the possibility of maintaining such an attitude, not because Nietzsche's arguments fail in the sense of lacking "philosophical" force or rigor, but because they work only too well, and thereby undermine the authority of passages (like the one cited above) which do advance truth-claims, albeit to the effect that, in truth, all truths are varieties of fiction and all concepts merely sublimated metaphors.

Thus Nietzsche denies the most basic premises of logical thought — like the law of non-contradiction — but does so, inevitably, in a language that *asserts* their nonbinding or arbitrary character, and thus, in so far as this excludes the opposite possibility (that they might, after all, be universally valid) ends up by subverting his own claim. In the same way, he argues that the "truths" of philosophy are always dependent on their power to persuade, despite what philosophers would have us regard as their absolute, categorical, or *a priori* character. But here again, Nietzsche cannot maintain this position without stating it as a matter of demonstrable fact that all such claims will show up, on closer inspection, as partaking of a generalized persuasive (or rhetorical) dimension. This complication de Man finds characteristic of all deconstructive discourse: "the deconstruction states the fallacy of reference in a necessarily referential mode" (*AR*, p. 125). But to point out such ultimate aporias in Nietzsche's argument — or, for that matter, in de Man's — is not to locate some basic mistake that would finally dispose of deconstruction as a species of sophistical unreason. Rather, it involves the recognition that philosophy is always caught up in this double-bind predicament, always (that is to say) revealing the extent of its own rhetorical construction while unable explicitly to state or acknowledge that fact without falling into manifest inconsistency. This is why de Man can claim that Nietzsche "advocates the use of epistemologically rigorous methods as the only possible means to reflect on the limitations of those methods" (*AR*, p. 86). It is also his warrant for turning back the charge that any semblance of logic in a deconstructive argument is enough to convict that argument of appealing to values, grounds, or criteria which, on its own submission, should not be available. "One cannot hold against him [Nietzsche] the apparent contradiction of using a rational mode of discourse — which he, in fact, never abandoned — in order to prove the inadequacy of this discourse" (*AR*, p. 86). And the same can indeed be said of de Man, whose more striking pronouncements, when taken out of context, appear to defy all the standards of logical self-evidence and truth, yet whose arguments when followed step by step through the text have a character of extreme analytical precision.

So de Man is not suggesting that we should henceforth read philosophical texts *just as if* they were works of literature. No more is he arguing that all concepts reduce without remainder to a play of rhetorical tropes and substitutions that would expose philosophy as merely the dupe of its own inveterate will-to-truth. For "when literature seduces us with the freedom of its figural combinations, so much airier and lighter than the labored constructs of concepts, it is not the less deceitful because it asserts its own deceitful properties" (*AR*, p. 115). In other words, we miss the point of de Man's entire project if we suppose — on the basis of isolated passages — that philosophy for him is just another "kind of writing," a body of texts whose only distinguishing feature is their attachment to self-deluded notions of truth and method, and hence their unwillingness to accept the fact of their own rhetorical constitution. It may be the case, as de Man writes in one such potentially misleading passage, that "philosophy turns out to be an endless reflection on its own destruction at the hands of literature" (*AR*, p. 115). But the word "reflection" has at least as much weight in this sentence as the idea that literature somehow undoes the truth-claims of philosophy by showing up its subtext of concealed tropological swerves and substitutions. This is why de Man lays such stress on the rigorously consequential character of Nietzsche's reasoning, the fact that he "earns the right" to his sceptical pronouncements only by dint of the "considerable labor of deconstruction that makes up the bulk of his more analytical writings" (*AR*, p. 131).

So it is a falsification of de Man's argument to read him as simply turning the tables on that old Platonic prejudice that equates philosophy with truth-seeking virtue and literature with rhetoric, sophistry, and the powers of unreason. What he seeks to bring out is certainly on the one hand the extent of philosophy's involvement with rhetoric, its subjection to forces which it cannot control through any form of *a priori* conceptual legislation. But this goes along with an equal (and by no means opposite) insistence that rhetoric cannot be divorced from the interests of epistemological critique; that even where its claims are pushed to the limit (as in Nietzsche's genealogy of philosophic reason) they can exert a genuinely *critical* force only to the extent that they work within and against that tradition. So it cannot be the case that one moves in any sense "beyond" philosophy by thinking to level the genre distinction between philosophy and literature. If carried through consistently, this project would entail a complete disregard for those issues in the province of knowledge, meaning, and representation that have so preoccupied thinkers in the modern (post-Kantian) tradition.[5] And for de Man such questions are absolutely central, even if — as he argues — they have often been posed in a form that fails to take account of their own rhetorical character. In short, the real choice is *not* between "philosophy" (which prizes the virtues of conceptual cogency and rigor) and "literature" (where those standards simply don't apply, since its texts are rhetorical through and through). On the contrary: it is only because rhetoric has so often been treated by philosophers as a study of language in its merely persuasive, poetic, or demagogic uses that philosophy has managed to avoid examining its own rhetorical resources.

What de Man undertakes is therefore an applied genealogy of concepts in the Nietzschean sense: one that deploys a "rhetoric of tropes" for the purpose of reading philosophical texts with a rigor unfamiliar but not antithetical to the practice of conceptual critique. This is why he describes Nietzsche as "one of those figures . . . whose work straddles the two activities of the human intellect that are both the closest and the most impenetrable to each other — literature and philosophy" (*AR*, p. 103). "Impenetrable" because, despite their common grounding in rhetorical structures, philosophy has always defined its interests in opposition to literature, and literary criticism has tended to reciprocate by acknowledging the difference but reversing the evaluative order of priorities. Thus critics have developed techniques of close reading which possess great rhetorical sophistication but scarcely engage with — indeed, make a virtue of ignoring — issues of epistemological import. And philosophers, from Kant to the present-day analytical tradition, have been inclined to dispense with textual close reading, and thus to bypass such "literary" questions, in the assurance that conceptual analysis was the proper business of philosophy, and rhetoric at most an ancillary study concerned with matters of philosophic "style." De Man rejects both of these presumptions. On the one hand he states often enough that close reading is indispensable, and that philosophers must therefore be deluded in so far as they think to bracket all questions of rhetorical language and thus go straight to the conceptual heart of an argument. For this reason, "the critical deconstruction that leads to the discovery of the literary, rhetorical nature of the philosophical claim to truth is genuine enough and cannot be refuted: literature turns out to be the main topic of philosophy and the model for the kind of truth to which it aspires" (*AR*, p. 115). The apodictic tone of this and other sentences like it might suggest that de Man is indeed simply out to promote "literature" at the expense of "philosophy." But he moves on directly to the above-quoted passage that warns us specifically *against* being "seduced" by the "freedom of its [literature's] figural combinations, so much airier and lighter than the labored constructs of concepts" (*AR*, p. 115). From which it would appear that de Man is equally concerned to close off that other line of least resistance that leads from philosophy to the notion of an all-encompassing general rhetoric that would give no hold for critique of any kind.

What is in question here is not "literature" as such but a certain prevalent notion of literature, one that would treat it as a realm apart, an aesthetically privileged realm where language is released from any kind of referential or epistemological constraints. And it is precisely this parceling out of discursive domains that is called into question by de Man's deconstructing all commonplace ideas of the difference between literature and philosophy. If philosophy has ignored those rhetorical problems that would tend to undermine its absolute privilege in matters of knowledge and truth, criticism has equally devalued literature by treating it in strictly noncognitive terms, as a discourse to which questions of truth and falsehood, referentiality, logical consistency, and so forth, simply don't apply. De Man rejects this view most explicitly in a late interview with Robert Moynihan. It is a false distinction, he argues, "to say that literary texts are aesthetic and therefore do not raise epistemological questions, whereas philosophical texts are scientific and [do] address epistemological questions . . . Aesthetics is not independent of epistemology. If there is a priority, that is, if there has to be one, it certainly is epistemological."[6] What results from the "literary" reading of philosophic texts is therefore by no means a retreat from argumentative cogency and rigor. It requires that analysis should not stop short at the point of confirming its own deep-seated suppositions about language and thought, that it should always be prepared to find those suppositions disturbed or undermined by what actually occurs in the process of reading. When de Man talks of the stubborn "materiality" of language, what he means is precisely this resistance to received or canonical forms of understanding, those which effectively *know in advance* what the text has to say, and which therefore tend to repress or simply bypass any details that get in their way.

The issue is raised most explicitly in a letter of response to Raymond Geuss, a philosopher who had objected to de Man's line of argument in his essay "Sign and Symbol in Hegel's *Aesthetics*."[7] De Man finds evidence of a marked discrepancy between what Hegel says — at the level of detailed textual explication — and what he has most often been taken to say by Hegelian scholars, critics, and philosophers who seek to maintain the coherence and integrity of his work. This discrepancy has to do with his high claims for a certain form of art (the symbolic) which Hegel promotes at the expense of other forms — like allegory — whose working he regards as merely mechanical, artificial, or lacking in "organic" beauty and truth. According to de Man, Hegel's text is unable to articulate this wished-for union of mind, nature, and language in the name of symbolist aesthetics. In fact that text provides all the materials for its own deconstruction by allowing us to see how intent and meaning fail to coincide; how the assumed correspondence between thought and perception (the very basis of Hegel's argument) breaks down at crucial points and invites an *allegorical*, rather than a symbolist, reading. To

Geuss, this appears a perverse way of treating the text, one that deliberately seeks out discrepancies or problematic details while ignoring other, more truly representative passages that would help to resolve such (in any case marginal) issues.

De Man's response is scarcely an effective rejoinder — if by this one understands a counterargument that addresses the same issues but shows the opponent to have reasoned confusedly, missed the whole point, or fallen into manifest error. He makes allowance (though perhaps not sufficient allowance) for the fact that Geuss represents a tradition — by no means exclusively Hegelian — in whose terms the raising of linguistic difficulties must always be subordinate to the process of resolving such problems through conceptual analysis. And this attitude translates, as de Man reads it, into a will to preserve the truth-claims of philosophy against any challenge from unauthorized, heterodox, or "unphilosophical" lines of approach. Thus "Geuss's stance, throughout his commentary, is to shelter the canonical reading of what Hegel actually thought and proclaimed from readings which allow themselves, for whatever reason, to tamper with the canon."[8] I am not concerned here to adjudicate the question between Geuss and de Man, except by pointing out that Geuss's arguments have their own, quite specific kind of rigor, one that is by no means programed in advance by Hegel's concepts and categories, but which does take its bearings from the history of dialectical or enlightened critique descending from Kant, through Hegel, to Theodor Adorno and the Frankfurt theorists. What his response brings out is *not* (as de Man would have it) a desire to save Hegel at all costs from the charge of conceptual error or confusion. Rather, it is the assumption that arguments make sense (or sometimes fail to make sense) according to a logic whose articulations are there to be read in what the text explicitly states, and states moreover in those passages that clearly represent its intended, manifest meaning. "Hegel's views may be unintelligible, unenlightening, implausible, or just plain wrong, but I don't see that de Man has made the case that in his aesthetics Hegel vacillates between two incompatible positions."[9]

So it is not the "canonical" reading of Hegel that Geuss is out to preserve, if by that we understand a reading faithful to every last claim of Hegelian method and logic. In fact his position belongs just as much to that line of strongly dissident or counter-Hegelian readings, works like Adorno's *Negative Dialectics* where thought turns its powers of immanent critique specifically against such premature forms of dialectical mastery or "totalization." What Geuss *does* resist is de Man's use of certain discrepant details in the text — certain tropes; turns of phrase; seemingly casual, even random analogies — to suggest that Hegel "unknowingly vacillates between two incompatible positions." For this would indicate that philosophy can never be fully in charge of its own conceptual resources, that language can always exert a disruptive influence even on those forms of philosophical activity that reflect most intently on their own methods and truth-claims. So it is that de Man can remark of Geuss's objections that they "have to do with the manner of reading philosophical writings prior to the substance that such a reading reveals."[10] In other words, they take for granted the priority of concepts or logical articulations over everything that belongs to the province of language, rhetoric, or so-called philosophic "style." And this attitude in turn presupposes a grasp of the essential difference between logic and rhetoric that would treat the former (on a model that again goes back to the classical *trivium*) as the privileged source of knowledge and truth.

II

We can now see more clearly why de Man rejects any form of the typecast opposition between "philosophy" and "literature." The alternative pairing "philosophy"/"rhetoric" is perhaps nearer the mark, although only to the extent that rhetoric is conceived in distinctly philosophical terms, as continuing the critique of language, concepts, and representations that has occupied philosophers since Kant. De Man credits Nietzsche as the first modern thinker to have pressed this critique to the limit, and thus to have broken with the old, prejudicial idea of rhetoric as concerned with language in its merely suasive, duplicitous, or attention-seeking forms. For Nietzsche, rhetoric is a discipline inseparable from the critique of philosophic reason, a discipline whose peculiar character it is to problematize the terms of such critique. According to de Man, Nietzsche's final insight

> may well concern rhetoric itself, the discovery that what is called "rhetoric" is precisely the gap that becomes apparent in the pedagogical and philosophical history of the term. Considered as persuasion, rhetoric is performative but when considered as a system of tropes, it deconstructs its own performance. (*AR*, p. 131)

This is why de Man insists that rhetoric cannot be decoupled from the interests of critical or epistemological reason; that it belongs on the side of literature only to the extent that "literature" itself resists assimilation to some separate realm of purely aesthetic or noncognitive values.

Hence that otherwise puzzling sentence where he opposes the "labored" conceptualizations of philosophy to the seductive freedoms ("so much airier and lighter") of literary form and style. One could make the point from a slightly different angle by remarking that de Man paid small attention — at least in his published work — to those kinds of literary texts that would seem most actively to solicit a deconstructive reading. Apart from a review-essay on Jorge Luis Borges (dating from 1964)[11] he preserved a near-silence on the topic of postmodernism or on the various forms of *avant-garde* and experimental fiction that are commonly thought of as creative analogues to current (poststructuralist) critical theory. This question came up in a late interview, when de Man commented that the whole idea of a "postmodern approach" struck him as based upon a "naively historical" paradigm of reading and interpretation which reduced the idea of postmodernism to a mere "parody of the notion of modernity."[12] And then, in response to the question whether he would *want* to write more on contemporary authors: "this applies more to the theoreticians of literature who feel the need to align their work with contemporary work in fiction. . . . I don't know if now the innovation of writers in the States or in France or elsewhere is closer or similar to whatever is being done by literary theorists. And in a fairly categorical way the question does not interest me" (*RT*, p. 120). As the context of discussion makes clear, de Man interprets this need for "alignment" between creative and critical writing as essentially a negative symptom, evidence that criticism lacks (so to speak) the courage of its own principles. And he implies also that this has come about through a failure to maintain the more crucial link between criticism and philosophy, or textual close reading on the one hand and on the other those issues of language, truth, and representation that have characterized philosophy in its modern (post-Kantian) form.

Thus de Man makes a point of distancing his own activity from the work of critics who apparently feel a "slight intimidation" *vis-à-vis* creative work, or who wish (more self-assertively) "to 'cash in,' so to speak, on the certain innovative freedom that a writer can have" (*RT*, p. 120). It is not hard to make out the coded reference here to those of de Man's deconstructionist colleagues, like Geoffrey Hartman, who make no secret of their aim to produce a criticism just as inventive, stylish, or "creative" as the literary texts they write about.[13] For de Man, on the contrary, there is no question of the critic's "trying to pattern himself or trying to catch what's going on for this moment in so-called creative fiction as opposed to criticism." This latter distinction may be misconceived to the extent that "so-called" creative writing cannot or should not be treated apart from those issues raised by critical reflection on language in its wider (rhetorical and epistemological) context. Such is indeed the main thrust of all de Man's arguments. But to keep this aim in view is also to insist that criticism not be seduced by the prospect of simply "crossing over" (in Hartman's phrase) from the role of subordinate commentary to that of a writing that would claim to be "creative" in some ultimately privileged sense. For this would amount to nothing more than a kind of opportunist reversal, a move to secure for criticism exactly the same value that has traditionally accrued to writing under its "so-called" creative aspect. It would thus run counter to de Man's reiterated claim: that criticism is best, most productively engaged in exposing the delusions of aesthetic ideology, especially where these take the form of an appeal to language in its distinctively "poetic" or "literary" aspects.

In the same interview de Man offers the example of Maurice Blanchot as a writer of fiction *and* criticism who could none the less carry on these two activities without wanting to sink the difference between them. For de Man, "a model like that of Blanchot remains very revealing because he was a critic who was also a writer, and who was not concerned at all as a critic to justify himself as a writer, or as a writer to concern himself as a critic" (*RT*, p. 120). What distinguishes de Man's work from (let us say) the creative ambitions of a writer like Hartman is the fact that de Man thinks of criticism *not* as in any sense a rival claimant for "literary" honors, but as a quite specific form of intellectual activity that brings about a mutual interrogative exchange between the languages of literature, philosophy, and applied rhetoric. This is why he rejects any premature conflation of realms, or any move to assimilate philosophy to literature in terms of a promiscuously generalized rhetoric of tropes. For the result of such a move could only be to deprive criticism of its genuinely *critical* force, that is to say, its power of revealing the errors and delusions that ensue when an ill-defined notion of the "literary" works to promote an aesthetic ideology devoid of epistemological grasp.

I take it that these are some of the issues at stake in de Man's response to the interview question. "Certainly I would be at any time ready to write on Borges, certainly on the fiction of Blanchot, but if you ask me on what contemporary French authors . . . I could possibly think of myself writing on Calvino, though I might be wrong . . ." (*RT*, p. 120). One wouldn't want to base too many large conjectures on what is, after all, distinctly a piece of ad hoc, improvised musing. But it does suggest several likely reasons for de Man's not having engaged with just the kind of writing that would seem to represent the closest creative or literary equivalent to his own work. The "postmodern," whether in fiction or philosophy, is identified with a stance of extreme epistemological scepticism, a willingness to dispense with every last form of foundationalist argument or truth-claim. In fictional terms, this amounts to a programmatic break with the realist conventions that purportedly held sway over novelists in the nineteenth-century tradition; a desire to expose such ideas as nothing more than the product of an ideological drive to naturalize one kind of writing at the expense of other, less acceptable kinds.[14] Poststructuralist criticism — as practiced most strikingly in a text like Roland Barthes's *S/Z* — likewise grows out of a revolt against the norms and constraints of high-bourgeois or "classic" realism.[15] From this point of view, the realist fallacy — the mistake of reading novels as if they represented anything in the outside world — is merely one aspect of the larger confusion that takes language, *any* kind of language, as possessing referential validity or truth. Such beliefs are supposedly demolished by a poststructuralist critique of language and representation which starts out from Saussure's doctrine of the "arbitrary" sign, and then goes on to argue that realist conventions are ideological precisely in so far as they *conceal* that arbitrary character by maintaining the illusion of a "natural" tie between signifier and signified.

Clearly this position has a strong affinity with the kinds of postmodernist fiction — Borges and Italo Calvino, to take two of de Man's own examples — where any attempt to ground one's reading in a sense of "real-world" actions and events is effectively played off the field. Such writing works against the realist illusion, the idea that there exists some straightforward style of descriptive or narrative discourse where language would serve as a window on reality, or (to vary the metaphor slightly) a mirror held up to nature. It serves to remind us that we can have access to the world only through the various cultural codes, conventions, and forms of linguistic representation that make up the structure of our lived experience. Where realism seeks to efface this knowledge by appealing to a "natural" language, a style degree zero of narrative verisimilitude, postmodern fiction does just the opposite; it works to undermine such naturalizing tendencies by constantly drawing attention to its own stylistic and narrative devices. And this lesson extends beyond texts of an overtly radical or postmodern character since, as Barthes argues in *S/Z*, we can now go back to the classics of bourgeois realism and read them more productively against the grain by suspending belief in their coded reality-effects. It will then appear that the realist illusion depends — and has always depended — on essentially *passive* habits of reading; that even those texts (like Balzac) which invest most heavily in its ideological effects can still be opened up to a plural, disruptive, or "writerly" approach that breaks the conventional mold.

Such at least is the alignment commonly perceived between postmodern fiction and poststructuralist criticism. Both have this capacity to show us how the real is a product of coded meanings and representations whose appeal to our "commonsense," naturalized habits of response is merely the result of cultural conditioning. And for theorists of the postmodern such as Jean-François Lyotard this message extends far beyond the sphere of fictional representation.[16] According to Lyotard, we have moved into an epoch that must witness the final, irreversible demise of all "enlightenment" ideas and values. Historical developments have made it impossible to believe any longer in those great "metanarratives" of progress, freedom, and a universal truth at the end of all inquiry which once sustained the thinking of philosophers from Kant to Hegel, Marx, and their successors. In the absence of such totalizing narratives we must now fall back on a humbler, more pragmatic, or context-specific kind of storytelling, one that lays no claim to ultimate truth but enables us to make at least provisional sense of ourselves and our historical predicament. Reason and truth are shown up as mere fictions — ideas that once possessed a certain emancipating force, but only so long as they were able to exert a suasive or "performative" power. And since this power rested on a root delusion — on the belief that they belonged to a separate order of authentic, *a priori*, or otherwise privileged truth-claims — the enlightenment project was bound to collapse at last under the weight of its accumulated problems and aporias.

The process was carried forward by epistemological sceptics like Nietzsche who rejected every last form of foundationalist argument; who declared that all concepts came down to metaphors in the end; and who denounced the philosophic will-to-truth as merely a species of legitimizing myth, a disguise for the ubiquitous will-to-power that has always been the driving force of "enlightened" reason. Foucault is among the present-day heirs to this Nietzschean tradition, as are neopragmatist thinkers such as Richard Rorty and postmodernists like Lyotard who would have us dispense with all the outworn concepts and categories of rational critique. And the argument is backed up, in Lyotard's case, by the view that historical events have falsified those confident values and beliefs once vested in Kantian, Hegelian, or Marxist forms of metanarrative theory. In short, we are now living in a postmodern epoch where all claims to truth have been finally discredited, where language games circulate without any kind of epistemological warrant, and where "performativity" — or the power of those language games to get themselves accepted on a short-term, provisional basis — becomes the sole criterion for deciding what is rational in any given context of debate.

Now I think that all this has a definite bearing on de Man's reluctance to align his work with postmodernism in its various literary forms. Clearly the term is capable of many definitions, and it would be a mistake to extrapolate directly from the fictional practice of writers like Borges and Calvino to Lyotard's wholesale rejection of post-Kantian enlightenment values. But there is none the less an elective affinity between these two lines of development, a connection reinforced by those literary critics who raise the postmodern (or the idea of a writing that would break with all naive realist assumptions) into a high point of radical theory. For de Man, such ideas can only be self-deluding, since it is quite impossible to conceive of language without taking account of its cognitive or referential aspects. To say that the relation between logic, language, and phenomenal cognition is more problematic than traditional thinking allowed is *not* by any means to reject such thinking as groundless, deluded, or (as Lyotard would have it) now quite simply obsolescent. This is why de Man has tended to engage with texts, whether literary or philosophical, which do indeed resist any simplified account of their referential status or truth-claims, but which nevertheless pose such questions in a form that allows of no premature appeal to rhetoric as a means of escape from epistemological issues. It is also his reason for suggesting that criticism revert to the model of the *trivium* in order to clarify its proper scope and interests. For it is here — in the zone where theory attempts to reconcile the claims of logic, grammar, and rhetoric — that he finds the most productive way forward for critical inquiry.

We can now look more closely at the implications of this model as de Man understands them. Traditionally, he writes, "grammar stands in the service of logic which, in turn, allows for the passage to the knowledge of the world" (*RT*, p. 14). That is to say, grammatical structures are assumed to exist in a close relationship to the forms of articulated thought, and thus to provide a reliable link between language and the way that we conceptualize reality or bring it under the concepts and categories of reason. Such is the enabling assumption of philosophy from Plato and Aristotle to Kant and the modern analytical tradition. It offers, according to de Man, "a clear instance of the interconnection between a science of the phenomenal world and a science of language conceived as definitional logic, the precondition for a correct axiomatic-deductive, synthetic reasoning" (*RT*, p. 13). Thus for Kant, the precondition of all understanding is that concepts should properly match up with phenomenal intuitions; that knowledge of the world comes about through the mind's *a priori* grasp of those intelligible forms of experience (time, space, causality, etc.) which we, as rational creatures, are inherently equipped to comprehend. Hence what Kant considered the great step forward in his philosophy, the argument that there existed self-evidently true propositions that were yet not purely analytic (i.e. whose predicates were not already implicit or contained in their subjects). For there were also, as he claimed, "synthetic *a priori*" propositions which did — unlike their analytic counterparts — contain some information about the world or some appeal to the facts of our experience, but which were none the less known to be true without need for empirical verification. It is this aspect of Kant's thinking that aligns it with the model laid down by the classical *trivium*. For there can be no guarantee that our concepts correspond to the order of phenomenal experience unless we can also be certain that language articulates the logic of thought and thus "stands in the service" of epistemological reason. Otherwise the paradigm would simply break down, since thinking would be subject to a generalized undecidability as regards the passage from language to logic, truth, and the certitudes of synthetic *a priori* knowledge.

De Man thus raises some far-reaching questions about the way that philosophy has worked to establish its foundational truth-claims. He is suggesting, in short, that those claims have always rested on a failure — or a strong disinclination — to read its own texts with sufficient regard to their linguistic or rhetorical aspects. Philosophy takes it for granted that language gives access to a realm of phenomenal cognition which can then be joined up with those concepts and categories that organize our knowledge of the world. This was the point at which the disciplines of the *trivium* were supposed to lead on to those other, more properly scientific forms of knowledge — arithmetic, geometry, astronomy, and music — that made up the classical *quadrivium*. "In the history of philosophy," de Man writes, "this link is traditionally . . . accomplished by way of logic, the area where the rigor of the linguistic discourse about itself matches up with the rigor of the mathematical discourse about the world" (*RT*, p. 13). Here again, the root assumption that enables this passage from one discursive order to another is the idea that language can be brought under the rule of grammar, and that logic can thereby make good its claim to legislate not only over the realm of *a priori* concepts but also over that of phenomenal experience. De Man sees this as a crucial argumentative turn, especially for seventeenth-century thinkers like Pascal, those to whom mathematical knowledge — or the notion of reasoning *more geometrico* — stood as the paradigm of all rigorous intellectual activity. "This articulation of the sciences of language with the mathematical sciences represents a particularly compelling version of a continuity between a theory of language, as logic, and the knowledge of the phenomenal world to which mathematics gives access" (*RT*, p. 13).

Of course there is a long history of debate around this question of the status of mathematical truth: whether its propositions are purely ideal, intuitively self-evident, or derived from our experiential knowledge of the world. But de Man has a more specific interest to pursue, namely the role of language (or rhetoric) in this distribution of cognitive powers. For it is his contention that rhetoric has always been the suppressed problematic term — the aspect of language that could not be reduced either to logic (via grammar) on the one hand, or to the order of phenomenal cognition on the other. This is the burden of his opening chapter in *Allegories of Reading*, where de Man looks at various attempts (by A.J. Greimas, Gérard Genette, and Tzvetan Todorov among others) to arrive at a more or less systematic way of classifying figures and tropes. These thinkers are engaged in the same activity that required the subordination of rhetoric to grammar in terms of the *trivium* model. That is to say, they assume that rhetorical effects must obey some kind of organizing logic that prevents them (so to speak) from getting out of hand and thus subverting the whole critical enterprise. De Man offers the instance of Genette's work on Proust,[17] a study that "shows the combined presence, in a wide and astute selection of passages, of paradigmatic, metaphorical figures with syntagmatic, metonymic structures" (*AR*, p. 7). But, unlike de Man in his own chapter on Proust, Genette sees these figures as simply *coexisting* within the text, each producing its own specific range of stylistic and semantic effects, but with no suggestion that their workings might ultimately get into conflict. "The combination of both is treated descriptively and nondialectically without considering the possibility of logical tensions" (*AR*, p. 7). For de Man, on the contrary, there *is* such a conflict, one that emerges from his reading of Proust in the way that metonymic figures tend to disrupt, subvert, or "undo" the high imaginative claims vested in metaphor. Genette seeks to bring some order to the otherwise unruly forces of rhetorical language by assimilating rhetoric to a systematic "grammar" of tropes. De Man thinks this project admirable up to a point, but impossible to carry through consistently since rhetoric cannot in the end be reduced to any logic or system based upon grammatical models.

This presumption de Man finds characteristic of just about every modern school of critical thinking. It emerges even in the writings of those who identify "literary" language precisely in terms of its *difference* from the language of straightforward (referential or cognitive) discourse. Thus:

> We . . . think of the relationship between grammar and logic, the passage from grammar to propositions, as being relatively unproblematic: no true propositions are conceivable in the absence of grammatical consistency or of controlled deviation from a system of consistency no matter how complex. (*AR*, p. 7)

"Controlled deviation" from a grammatical or referential norm is indeed the basis for most versions of formalist criticism. The best-known example is Jakobson's powerfully condensed statement that the "poetic function" in language "projects the principle of equivalence from the axis of selection onto the axis of combination."[18] That is to say, poetry gives concrete or phenomenal form to those otherwise purely *structural* properties of language — contrasts, resemblances, parallelisms, patternings of sound and sense — that normally exist only at the level of abstract, unrealized elements in the system. Thus it deviates significantly from the language of straightforward prose communication, where such devices could only attract notice to themselves, and would hence interfere with the business of effectively conveying facts or ideas.

An obvious difficulty with Jakobson's model is the problem of maintaining this notional difference between aesthetic and nonaesthetic kinds of language. On the one hand poets have often made a point of rejecting the prevalent stylistic conventions of their day, declaring (like Wordsworth) that "poetic diction" was merely a kind of decadent artifice, or demanding (like Pound) that poetry school itself in the discipline of honest, craftsmanlike prose. On the other, there is always the borderline instance of so-called "prose-poetry," writing that displays none of the formal attributes of verse but which none the less exploits the full range of poetic devices like symbol and metaphor. Jakobson meets this objection by arguing that it rests on a basic misunderstanding; that literary texts (and other art forms) cannot be identified in terms of any *single* prevailing figure or trope, but should rather be distinguished generically according to their various predominating styles. Thus metaphor would still be the hallmark — the most distinctive structural trait — of poems, especially lyric poems, that belonged to that particular mode. But we should not be misled, Jakobson argues, by the high privilege that has always been attached to metaphor by critics and literary theorists from Aristotle to the present. For this attitude engenders a corresponding bias against metonymy, a tendency to treat it as a merely pedestrian, prosaic, or uncreative trope whose workings scarcely require detailed attention. In fact, according to Jakobson, metonymy is not only a structuring principle basic to language, but also a distinctive artistic resource which often escapes notice for precisely that reason. To treat it as the poor relation of metaphor — or simply as a "literal" mode of describing or representing the way things are — is to suggest that criticism can have nothing very useful to say on the subject. The effect would thus be to marginalize, devalue, or count as non-"literary" all those forms of writing whose governing principle is metonymy and which thus tend toward the documentary-realist mode.[19]

Jakobson sees an answer to this problem in his bipolar model of linguistic structure, based on the twin axes of metaphor and metonymy. But this model still relies on the idea of literature as an essentially *deviant* form of language, one that effectively "foregrounds" or exploits to the maximum those properties intrinsic to language-in-general. For it is a central claim of Jakobsonian linguistics that every signifying system can be grasped in terms of the same fundamental opposition: that is to say, as exhibiting two distinct aspects, the one having to do with *selection* of items from a paradigm of available choices or alternatives, the other involving the *combination* of those items at the level of syntagmatic order. These dimensions in turn correspond to the metaphorical and metonymic axes, since metaphor is precisely a substitution of one term for another selected from the same paradigm, while metonymy works by constructing a chain or succession of significant details that exist in some contiguous or proximate real-world relationship one to another, and thus give the impression of directly representing objects and events. From which it follows, 1) that *literary* texts in the metonymic mode will be marked by a more intensive or systematic use of such commonplace devices; and 2) that metaphor still retains something of its old privilege, in so far as it involves a very striking departure from the referential norm. Metaphor requires that we shift linguistic gear, so to speak, and attend to those creative substitutions of figural for literal meaning, rather than looking for a certain degree of correspondence between language and the world of everyday perceptual experience.

This rather lengthy excursion into Jakobson's poetics should help us to grasp what is at stake when de Man questions the presumed continuity between "grammatical" and "rhetorical" models of understanding. His point is that rhetoric cannot be reduced to the compass of a generalized "grammar" of tropes without in the process ignoring, repressing, or systematically misreading all the signs of its power to disturb that same project. De Man makes the point most simply with regard to the class of rhetorical questions, such as asking "What's the difference?" without the least desire to receive any answer. In such cases, he writes, "the same grammatical pattern engenders two meanings that are mutually exclusive: the literal meaning asks for the concept (difference) whose existence is denied by the figurative meaning" (*AR*, p. 9). Or, expressed in slightly different terms: "a perfectly clear syntactical paradigm (the question) engenders a sentence that has at least two meanings, of which the one asserts and the other denies its own illocutionary mode" (*AR*, p. 10). Rhetorical questions thus figure as a lead into the subsequent, more complex chapters of argument that make up *Allegories of Reading*.

For de Man, large consequences flow from this simple lesson in the disjunct properties of grammar and rhetoric. It indicates one reason why theorists like Jakobson start out by rejecting the high claims of metaphor — by asserting, that is, the equal status of metonymy as a trope with its own distinctive powers — but end up by covertly restoring metaphor to its original, privileged position. This comes about through that same persistent habit of thought that de Man finds entrenched in the classical *trivium*. It involves a threefold order of assumptions: that grammar reliably articulates the forms of logical reasoning; that language gives access to the world through its power to communicate phenomenal experience; and that therefore reality can be grasped in thought by way of the link between logic and language. But there are, as de Man points out, two questions left open within this otherwise perfectly circular and self-validating system of ideas. One is whether language — language in all its aspects and dimensions — can indeed be brought under the governing terms of a purely *grammatical* account. The other is the question whether language can indeed provide that passage to a real-world, phenomenal order of experience that would guarantee such perfect correspondence between thought and reality. And these two problems are closely interlinked, since the articulation of logic with our knowledge of the external world can be achieved only through the ordering of language on essentially grammatical terms. So any suggestion that there might be elements in language that escape this general rule is perceived as an affront both to reason itself and to the notion that we do have reliable epistemic access to the world.

Hence de Man's argument that *rhetoric* is the aspect of language that philosophy has never been able to accommodate except on reductive terms of its own devising. "Only if the sign engendered meaning in the same way that the object engenders the sign, that is, by representation, would there be no need to distinguish between grammar and rhetoric" (*AR*, p. 9). And meaning cannot be engendered in this way since language is never simply, purely, or unproblematically a product of phenomenal cognition. The desire to think otherwise — to believe that language, especially the language of poetry, can achieve such intimacy with the world of natural processes and forms that all distinctions at last fall away — is a delusion that de Man finds characteristic of "aesthetic ideology" in its various guises.[20] One example from *Allegories* has a special pertinence here since it approaches this topic again by way of a rhetorical question. His text is Yeats's "Among School Children," and specifically the closing stanza:

> O chestnut tree, great-rooted blossomer,
> Are you the leaf, the blossom or the bole?
> O body swayed to music, O brightening glance,
> How can we know the dancer from the dance?

Most readings assume that this last line is indeed a rhetorical question; that it doesn't seek an answer in terms of how the two things *might* after all be distinguished, but instead celebrates their hypostatic union in a metaphor of consummate organic form. The image of the dance thus follows on naturally from that of the tree since both suggest that art has a power to transcend those antinomies (subject and object, content and form, sensuous and intellectual modes of apprehension) that plague human understanding in its other, more prosaic forms. What the poem thus seems to provide is a powerfully naturalized example of "the continuity from part to whole that makes synecdoche into the most seductive of metaphors." And this effect is achieved through its appeal to "the organic beauty of the tree, stated in the parallel syntax of a similar rhetorical question, or the convergence, in the dance, of erotic desire with musical form" (*AR*, p. 11).

There are various factors that contribute to the persuasive force of this reading. One is the post-Romantic or Symbolist assumption that art in its highest forms can indeed bring about the reconciliation of mind and nature through a synthesis achieved by the power of creative imagining. This goes along with a corresponding notion of Yeats's poetic develop- ment: his progress, that is to say, from an "early" phase of elaborate mythological and verbal artifice, through a "middle" period of increasing stylistic maturity, to a "late" stage where his poetry is at last in full possession of its powers and there is simply no distinguishing form and content, style and substance, art and its sources in living experience.[21] So there is a strong inducement to read this poem as a kind of triumphal manifesto, a vindication of the Symbolist aesthetic as borne out in Yeatsian practice. But, de Man argues, this reading has to ignore the other possible sense of the poem's last line, the sense in which it *could* be taken literally to demand some answer to its question, rather than giving us notice in advance that no such response is called for. The poem would then seem to address that question "with some urgency," precisely *not* asserting that "sign and referent are so exquisitely fitted to each other that all difference between them is at times blotted out," but asking rather: "since the two essentially different elements, sign and meaning, are so intricately intertwined in the imagined 'presence' that the poem addresses, how can we possibly make the distinctions that would shelter us from the error of identifying what cannot be identified?" (*AR*, p. 11). The rhetorical question cannot exclude this other reading, no matter how strong the appeal of that aesthetic ontology which invites us to set such doubts aside and enjoy the poem on what are, after all, its most "natural" terms of understanding.

De Man concedes that his paraphrase is awkward, syntactically and logically complex to the point of near-incoherence. And indeed, it stands in marked contrast to the gracefulness, assurance, and sense of spontaneous natural grasp that is achieved by readings in the high Symbolist mode. But this is no reason to reject the "literal" reading as merely perverse, beside the point, or pedantic. If anything, it is the *figurative* reading of this line — the interpretation of it as purely and simply a rhetorical question — that would seem the more culpably naive. On this account the poem resolves easily enough into a mood of elevated reverie, a sense of its having transcended every form of conflict, doubt, and self-division. It is the "literal" reading that effectively resists such aesthetic seductions, and so brings out (as in de Man's tortuous paraphrase) problems evaded by its "figural" counterpart. And this is because the treatment of Yeats's line as a straightforward rhetorical question is itself not so much a rhetorical as a grammatical treatment. That is to say, the figural reading assumes that the sentence means one thing only — the sheer *impossibility* of knowing the dancer from the dance — and that its grammar is therefore perspicuous enough to exclude interference from other potential readings. For de Man, on the contrary, this example clearly shows "that two entirely coherent but entirely incompatible readings can be made to hinge on one line, whose grammatical structure is devoid of ambiguity, but whose rhetorical mode turns the mood as well as the mode of the entire poem upside down" (*AR*, p. 12). Nor can this tension be accommodated on terms like those developed by the American New Critics: by declaring that poetry just *is* paradoxical, that it involves structures of multiple meaning that exist in a kind of aesthetic equilibrium and therefore cannot get into logical conflict, since poetry belongs to an order of language quite separate from that of logic or assertoric statement. De Man very firmly closes off this escape route when he says of the line from Yeats that "the two readings have to engage each other in direct confrontation, for the one reading is precisely the error denounced by the other and has to be undone by it" (*AR*, p. 12). In short, the interpretation that reads the line simply as a rhetorical question is evading both its real rhetorical complexity *and* those problems of a philosophic order which criticism habitually tends to evade or foreclose.

III

We can now see more clearly why de Man associates the "grammatization of rhetoric" with a certain form of *aesthetic* ideology that has affected the discourse of philosophy and literary criticism. He spells out this connection at greater length in "The Resistance to Theory," where his main object is to examine the order of epistemic necessity that holds logic and grammar securely in control over rhetoric, and thus ensures the stability of language as a representational medium. "In such a system, the place of aesthetics is preordained and by no means alien, provided the priority of logic, in the model of the *trivium*, is not being questioned" (*RT*, p. 13). In Jakobson's case — though de Man doesn't pursue this point — the link is by way of a grammar of tropes (more specifically, of metaphor and metonymy) which seeks to provide criticism with a basis of orderly, systematic method. And it also involves the claim that poetic language has a power to refresh or to sensitize our routine, jaded habits of perception by presenting the world anew through its various devices of creative "defamiliarization." Hence the frequent assumption, as de Man writes, that "literariness is another word for, or another mode of, aesthetic response" (*RT*, p. 9). For aesthetics is traditionally the subject-domain where thought and perception are supposed to coexist in a peculiarly close and intimate relation. Hence the reiterated formalist appeal to terms like "foregrounding" and "concretization," metaphors that effectively assimilate language to the order of sensory perception or phenomenal experience.

This is why aesthetics plays such a crucial role in Kantian epistemology and in the various post-Kantian attempts, from Hegel on down, to provide a full-scale articulated system of human knowledge. For it is precisely in terms borrowed from aesthetics — terms like the Kantian "productive imagination" — that philosophy seeks to overcome the ontological gulf between sensuous intuitions and concepts of the pure understanding.[22] This may go against the more usual understanding of Kantian aesthetics, that which holds the Beautiful and the Sublime to consist *not* in any determinate attributes of the object itself, but in the "free play" of our appreciative faculties which thereby discover their own highest powers of self-governing, harmonious coexistence. Thus Kant describes the Sublime (in a passage cited by de Man) as "an object (of nature) the representation of which determines consciousness to think the unattainability of nature as a sensory representation."[23] But de Man's central point in this late essay is that Kant's entire philosophy depends on the aesthetic as a bridge between orders of knowledge and experience that would otherwise exist in isolation. Hence, he writes,

> the need for a phenomenalized, empirically manifest principle of cognition on whose existence the possibility of such an articulation depends. This phenomenalized principle is what Kant calls the aesthetic. The investment in the aesthetic is therefore considerable, since the possibility of philosophy itself, as the articulation of a transcendental with a metaphysical discourse, depends on it. (PMK, p. 124).

De Man is here using the terms "transcendental" and "metaphysical" in a strictly Kantian sense. The "metaphysical" is that which has to do with knowledge at the stage of empirical self-evidence, that is to say, as falling under laws (like those of gravity or causation) that are not yet subject to the scrutiny of critical reason. The "transcendental," by contrast, is the order of reflection that takes such laws as its starting point and then looks beyond them to establish their *a priori* grounds in the structure of human understanding. Thus "transcendental principles contain no knowledge of the world or anything else, except for the knowledge that metaphysical principles . . . are themselves in need of critical analysis, since they take for granted an objectivity that, for the transcendental principles, is not *a priori* available" (PMK, p. 122).

Aesthetics plays a crucial mediating role in the Kantian system because it occupies precisely that contested zone where these two kinds of knowledge seemingly converge. That is to say, it holds out the prospect of reconciling thought and sensory perception in a moment of ideally unified grasp where such distinctions would no longer apply. But it also gives a lead to critical or deconstructive readings, those which (like de Man's essay on Kant) attend more closely to the signs of disruption or ambivalence where language holds out *against* the drive to reduce it to the order of phenomenal cognition. Indeed, he goes so far as to equate "the controlling principle of rigorous philosophical discourse" with the effort to articulate these two dimensions (the metaphysical and the transcendental) without, in the process, simply collapsing the difference between them. Thus de Man asserts that all criticism (including the critique of ideology) must take rise from those points of resistance where language obstructs the ideal reciprocity of concepts and phenomenal intuitions. Metaphysical philosophies are exactly those whose "conditions and modalities of occurrence are determined by critical analyses to which they have no access" (PMK, p. 122). Transcendental philosophies, on the other hand, have no possible object save those metaphysical beliefs and convictions which alone provide the promise of a link between concepts and the order of phenomenal (pre-reflective) knowledge. In short, "philosophies that succumb to ideology lose their epistemological sense, whereas philosophies that try to bypass or repress ideology lose all critical thrust and risk being repossessed by what they foreclose" (PMK, p. 123).

It should now be evident how far from the truth is that widespread idea of deconstruction that sees it as a bid on the part of literary critics to play philosophy clean off the field by reducing it to a handful of rhetorical tropes. De Man does indeed make out a case for regarding rhetoric as the aspect of language that philosophy has always, for reasons of its own, sought to hold stringently in check. But this by no means amounts to a license for deconstructive readings to make what they will of philosophical texts, or to disregard the protocols of logical consistency and truth. On the contrary, as we have seen with the passage on Yeats, it is de Man's purpose to alert literary criticism to problems — distinctly *philosophical* problems — that are kept out of sight by other, less taxing forms of interpretative grasp. This is what leads to his recasting of the poem's rhetorical question as a plea for more adequate conceptual understanding ("how can we possibly make the distinctions that would shelter us from the error of identifying what cannot be identified?"), rather than as a means of escaping such problems by recourse to a realm of mystified aesthetic values. It is also the burden of his essay on Kant, a reading none the less rigorous or consequent for the fact that de Man finds significant tensions between what Kant *says*, at the level of overt, declarative statement, and how his text *performs*, at the level of analogy, metaphor, and other such enabling rhetorical devices. For it is exactly de Man's point that these devices are intrinsic to the discourse of Kantian reason; that they function within that discourse not merely as persuasive or illustrative figures but as the means of articulating crucial passages of argument.

This is why de Man insists — here as in his writings on Nietzsche — that rhetoric should be taken as belonging to the field of critical or epistemological analysis, and not to some separate dimension of language where performative effects are the only criterion. He therefore objects to those recent neo-pragmatist or speech-act versions of literary theory that think to resolve various issues (like the problem of fictional reference) by declaring literature a special kind of language, one that merely *simulates* our normal, everyday kinds of linguistic behavior, and which thus carries none of their regular entailments.[24] For de Man, this move amounts to an "equation of rhetoric with psychology rather than with epistemology," and threatens to open up "dreary prospects of pragmatic banality" (*RT*, p. 19). That is to say, thinking loses all critical force — in literary studies as well as in philosophy — if it simply overrides theoretical problems by declaring them irrelevant from a speech-act or performative viewpoint. In de Man's words,

> to empty rhetoric of its epistemological impact is possible only because its tropological, figural functions are being bypassed. It is as if, to return for a moment to the model of the *trivium*, rhetoric could be isolated from the generality that grammar and logic have in common and considered as a mere correlative of an illocutionary power. (*RT*, pp. 18–19)

So it is clearly a mistake to read de Man's essays as attempting to discredit or to undermine philosophy by means of a rhetoric which "deconstructs" the very logic of reasoned inquiry. Certainly it is possible to convey this impression by taking his pronouncements out of context and ignoring what he calls (with reference to Nietzsche) the "considerable labor of deconstruction" that has led up to them. But on a closer reading these passages should leave no doubt of de Man's commitment to a rigorously critical approach which excludes any recourse to rhetoric as a means of avoiding philosophical problems. It may be, as he says, that rhetoric brings about a "disturbance of the stable cognitive field," the order of epistemological assurance that "extends from grammar to logic to a general science of man and of the phenomenal world" (*RT*, p. 17).

But this "undoing of theory" can be achieved only through a rhetoric that engages closely with those unresolved problems of knowledge and representation that have set the main terms for post-Kantian philosophical inquiry.

What de Man proposes is therefore "a theoretical project of rhetorical analysis that will reveal the inadequacy of grammatical models of non-reading" (*RT*, p. 17). Each word in this sentence has a weight of implication that needs unpacking very carefully. "Grammatical models" may become models of "non-reading" to the extent that they offer a self-assured method for coping with problems of textual understanding, problems that would otherwise complicate the link between logic, grammar, and method itself. "Rhetorical analysis" reveals their inadequacy by pointing to those moments of self-induced "blindness" in the critical or philosophic text where figural language exceeds or subverts the compass of methodical thought. But this remains a strictly *theoretical* project in so far as the rhetoric in question can find its model and its field of application only in the problems thrown up by that same tradition of epistemological critique. Any claim that thinking has now moved on into a "post-philosophical" culture — as argued by proponents of neo-pragmatism in its various currently fashionable forms — must therefore seem both self-deluding and devoid of all genuine critical force. "Difficulties occur," as de Man writes, "only when it is no longer possible to ignore the epistemological thrust of the rhetorical dimension of discourse" (*RT*, p. 14). And those difficulties are such as to permit no resort to a simplified or undifferentiating rhetoric that would treat all language as possessing merely suasive or performative force.

The point can be made by comparing de Man's approach to these issues with that adopted by a thoroughgoing epistemological sceptic like Michel Foucault. For Foucault, the Kantian "revolution" in philosophy was nothing more than a momentary paradigm-shift, a "fold" in the fabric of knowledge and representation which happened to produce the idea of man as transcendental subject or privileged source of his own epistemological truth-claims. There is absolutely no reason to treat those claims as possessing any greater validity than the previous systems of thought whose shortcomings Kant set out to diagnose and remedy. The enlightenment turn toward forms of self-legitimizing knowledge, truth, and critique was merely one episode — one short-lived mutation — in the history of shifting discursive regimes. And this despite the fact that it purported to transcend such limiting cultural factors, to provide philosophy with a groundwork of *a priori* concepts and categories that would hold good for every possible exercise of human critical reason. So where Kant poses the transcendental question: what are the *conditions of possibility*, the aspects under which experience presents itself as intelligible according to our conceptual powers and capacities, Foucault entirely dismisses this question and asks instead: what were the historical conditions that led to the emergence, at a certain point in time, of exactly this epistemological drive to ground truth and reason in a universal order of intersubjective validity.[25] Hence Foucault's aim, as described in *The Archaeology of Knowledge*,

> to analyze history in the discontinuity that no teleology would reduce in advance . . . to allow it to be deployed in an anonymity on which no transcendental constitution would impose the form of the subject; to open it up to a temporality that would not promise the return of any dawn. My aim was to cleanse it of all transcendental narcissism.[26]

From this perspective, the truth-claims of Kantian reason appear as just one more transient example of the epistemic will-to-power whose various ruses and configurations make up the narrative of Western intellectual history. What therefore needs explaining is not so much how knowledge is possible, or how best to provide it with cognitive foundations, but why it should ever have come about that the question got posed in this particular form.

For Foucault, the answer lay first in a full-scale applied "archaeology" of concepts and categories, and then — as Nietzsche's influence came through more strongly — in a critical "genealogy" of power/knowledge that related every discourse to tis role in maintaining the forms of socio-political surveillance and control.[27] Hence the downright *impossibility*, as Foucault reads it, of the Kantian attempt to offer rational grounds for the critique of knowledge and representation. To Kant's way of thinking, "man . . . is a strange empirico-transcendental doublet, since he is a being such that knowledge will be attained in him of what renders all knowledge attainable.[28] At a certain historical point — around the end of the eighteenth century — there occurred (according to Foucault) a decisive shift in the currency of the human sciences, one that effectively opened the way for "man" to become both the transcendental subject and the problematic locus of all critical inquiry. Knowledge had previously been ordered on the model of a "general science," a universal system of identities, differences, and classifying terms whose validity was taken to extend across all disciplines. Thus for seventeenth-century thinkers like Descartes and Leibniz, it was possible to envisage every kind of intellectual activity as proceeding in some sense *more geometrico*, by analogy (that is) with those forms of classificatory and rational-deductive method whose validity had been proven in the realm of mathematics. So it was that these disciplines "all expressed, on the visible surface of events or texts, the profound unity that the Classical Age had established by positing the analysis of identities and differences, and the universal possibility of tabulated order, as the archaeological basis of knowledge" (*OT*, p. 247). But with Kant — or rather, in the period that was marked by the inception of Kantian philosophy, but also across a whole range of related disciplines and subject areas — there occurred that shift toward a critique of human truth-claims and knowledge-constitutive interests that henceforth characterized the discourse of reason. Knowledge, in short, withdrew from the space of ordered correspondences, analogies, and representations, and attempted to ground itself in the very nature of human *a priori* cognitive powers. "That space is brought into question in its foundation, its origin, and its limits: and by this fact, the unlimited field of representations which Classical thought had established . . . now appears as a metaphysics" (*OT*, pp. 242–43).

So truth-claims can be assessed henceforth only through a mode of "enlightened" critique which posits man as the transcendental subject of knowledge and thus as both source and ultimate judge of his own cognitive powers. To Foucault, this appears just a self-deluding enterprise, one that thinks to escape the relativity of *all* human knowledge — the fact of its dependence on ideas of truth that are solely the product of discursive formations — by appealing to a realm of absolute, disinterested reason. And he finds evidence enough for this claim in the subsequent (post-Kantian) history of thought, where philosophy shuttles endlessly between various forms of "subjective" and "objective" idealism. Thus:

> If man is indeed, in the world, the locus of an empirico-transcendental doublet, if he is that paradoxical figure in which the empirical contents of knowledge necessarily release, of themselves, the conditions that have made them possible, then man cannot posit himself in the immediate and transparent sovereignty of a *cogito*; nor, on the other hand, can he inhabit the objective inertia of something that, by right, does not and never can lead to self-consciousness. (*OT*, p. 322)

So the Kantian project is deluded at source, and along with it those subsequent episodes in the history of thought — from Hegel and Marx down to the present — that likewise involve the quest for veridical knowledge, and hence the desire to distinguish true from false (or "ideological") representations. For they all presuppose an activity of mind in which truth would stand out as distinct from the various discourses, modalities, or forms of knowledge-production that make up the received idea of truth for some presently existing community. And this, Foucault argues, is simply an impossible dream, an idea that took hold two centuries ago and soon achieved hegemonic status, but has now

— on his own reading of the signs — reached a point of virtual dissolution. What we are currently witnessing in various forms is the shift to an alternative paradigm, one in which *language*, rather than reason, is the model for all understanding. Linguistics, semiology, information theory, the structuralist "sciences of man," and the texts of avant-garde or post modernist literary practice — these are aspects of a widespread cultural mutation whose effects extend yet further into the field of (say) genetics as a study of the codes and quasi-semiotic structures that replicate living forms. Everywhere we are faced with the multiplying evidence that language now constitutes the very condition and horizon of human knowledge.

From here Foucault moves to his dramatic peroration: that "as the archaeology of our thought easily shows, man is an invention of recent date . . . and one perhaps nearing its end" (*OT*, p. 387). "Man," more precisely, as the figure whose being was first composed "in the interstices of language," at a time when the all-embracing Classical order of signs, correspondences, and representations gave way to the *epistemological* quest for self-grounded knowledge and truth. "From within language experienced and traversed as language, in the play of its possibilities extended to their furthest point, . . . [man] arrives not at the very heart of himself but at the brink of that which limits him . . . " (*OT*, p. 383). Thus for Foucault the project of enlightened critique has run its historical course, and can now be seen for what it always was: the product of a certain configuration in the discourse of post-Classical reason which could lay claim to absolute truth only so long as its linguistic or rhetorical modalities were not examined too closely. With the advent of a new paradigm — one that takes language as its very model — this claim becomes merely a transient episode in the history of Western post-Renaissance discursive regimes. In which case, Foucault rhetorically demands, "ought we not to admit that, since language is here once more, man will return to that serene non-existence in which he was formerly maintained by the imperious unity of Discourse?" (*OT*, p. 386).

IV

I have allowed myself this detour into Foucault's "archaeology of knowledge" in order to emphasize the very different character of de Man's approach to such questions. Up to a point their two projects clearly have much in common. Both are concerned to analyze the relation between different orders of truth-claim, and the ways in which certain privileged models — like that of the classical *trivium* — have worked to impose their terms of understanding. Both have a particular interest in the structure of priorities that obtains between logic, grammar, and rhetoric — since it is here that various disciplines construct their methodological self-image, as well as marking their distance from adjacent subject domains. Foucault, like de Man, sees the link between logic and grammar as that which assures the stability of representation by connecting language on the one hand to the analysis of concepts, and on the other to the realm of empirical knowledge where objects are named and classified. "Around the privileged position occupied by the name in the Classical period, the theoretical segments (proposition, articulation, designation, and derivation) constitute the frontiers of what the experience of language was at that time" (*OT*, p. 119). Hence the various seventeenth-century programs for a unified "general grammar" that would serve as the basis for a taxonomic science not only of language but of every branch of human intellectual inquiry. Such, Foucault writes, is "the nexus of the entire Classical experience of language: the reversible character of grammatical analysis, which is at one and the same time science and prescription, a study of words and a rule for constructing them, employing them, and remolding them into their representative function" (*OT*, p. 117). Thus grammar acts as a kind of inbuilt guarantee that language will serve to articulate the forms of logical thought and also to ensure their exact correspondence with the forms and classifications of empirical phenomena.

Foucault and de Man are likewise agreed in viewing rhetoric as the aberrant dimension of language where this model comes up against the limits of its own intelligibility and grasp. According to Foucault, rhetoric is what enables the Classical discourse to continue in its work of ceaselessly transcribing, comparing, and analogizing the various objects of its investigation, without finally arriving at the point where those objects could be specified once and for all, and thus rendering further discourse wholly redundant.

> This is why it [the Classical *episteme*] is linked with rhetoric, that is, with all the space that surrounds the name, causes it to oscillate around what it represents, and reveals the elements, or the adjacency, or the analogies of what it names. The figures through which discourse passes act as a deterrent to the name, which then arrives at the last moment to fulfill and abolish them. (*OT*, pp. 117–18)

Rhetoric is therefore the enabling condition of all articulate thought, but only in the sense that it keeps these discourses talking, as it were, and prevents them from being entirely absorbed into the mute, nonsignifying "language" of pure nomination. (One recalls, in this context, Swift's satire upon the sages of Lagado who succeeded so perfectly in reducing the rhetorical complexities of language that they dispensed with words altogether and simply carried around with them any object they might have need to refer to.) There is no question here of rhetoric's possessing any genuine critical or *epistemological* force, any function beyond this power of maintaining language in a state of productive suspension. For Foucault, the relationship between logic, grammar, and rhetoric is a force-field of constantly shifting values and priorities where everything reduces to the power of some particular "discourse" to impose its own privileged mode of understanding.

So when the Classical paradigm gives way to the regime of Kantian enlightened reason, that change comes about for reasons that remain profoundly obscure — and which certainly cannot be accounted for in terms of any rational or immanent critique. Thus "criticism brings out the metaphysical dimension that eighteenth-century philosophy had attempted to reduce solely by means of the analysis of representation" (*OT*, p. 243). But we are mistaken, according to Foucault, if we interpret the signs of this "epistemological break" as betokening more than a transient shift in the order of discursive forms and relations. The Kantian "revolution" in philosophy is one that "opens up at the same time another metaphysics, one whose purpose will be to question, apart from representation, all that is the source and origin of representation" (*OT*, p. 243). In other words, the Classical order breaks down at that point where man, or the transcendental subject of knowledge, becomes the sole legitimizing ground of appeal for truth-claims of every kind. But to Foucault such claims are neither more nor less deluded than the paradigm they managed so effectively to displace. For there is simply no comparing these disparate orders of knowledge in point of their critical accountability or the reasons advanced in their support. What force they possess comes entirely from their power to reorganize some existing field of representations in accordance with a dominant set of discursive or rhetorical constraints. And rhetoric is here conceived as the active *antithesis* of knowledge and truth — a disruptive force within language that lays bare the ruses of that will-to-power concealed behind the claims of pure, disinterested reason.

For de Man, the relation between logic, grammar, and rhetoric cannot be reduced to any such straightforward reversal of the standard order of priorities. Rhetoric may figure as the problematic term, the aspect of language that complicates the move from phenomenal perception to concepts of pure understanding. But it can exert this deconstructive leverage only in so far as it remains an activity of thought closely in touch with epistemology and critical reason. I have tried to show how this affects de Man's readings of Kant, Nietzsche, and various texts in the modern and presumptively "postmodern" lines of philosophical descent. In each case he resists any move to circumvent such problems by simply declaring them outmoded, redundant, or (like Foucault) reducing them to figments of an all-encompassing rhetorical domain. And the same applies to that earlier, "Classical" order of representations, the seventeenth-century discursive regime where logic and grammar supposedly combine to articulate the ultimate truth of things without recourse to the synthesizing powers of a Kantian transcendental subject. The most significant text here is de Man's late essay "Pascal's Allegory of Persuasion." I don't propose to offer anything like an adequately detailed account of this essay since it resists paraphrase to the degree that such treatment would have to take the form of a line-by-line critical exegesis. Indeed, this is one of de Man's most exacting and concentrated pieces of argument, to which might be applied his own remark on Pascal, that "for all the somber felicity of their aphoristic condensation, the *Pensées* are also very systematically schematized texts."[29] But it may provide a useful focus for what I have said so far about the relation in his work between criticism, epistemology, and the deconstructive rhetoric of tropes.

De Man's chief concern, here as elsewhere, is with the different orders of truth-claim that characterize philosophical and other forms of discourse. More specifically, it is with Pascal's appeal to mathematics, to that sovereign mode of reasoning *more geometrico* whose power of intuitive and rational self-evidence might then be extended, via philosophy to the conduct of all human inquiry. He begins by considering a relatively little-known text whose title — *Réflexions sur la géométrie en générale: de l'esprit géométrique et de l'Art de persuader* — de Man finds highly suggestive in this regard.[30] For Pascal, the kind of certainty attained by mathematical proofs should properly have nothing to do with the arts of mere persuasion or rhetorical plausibility. Or rather, such reasoning should close the gap between these two orders of discourse, since mathematical arguments must carry the kind of *de facto* persuasive power that convinces by virtue of its own indubitable truth. "Persuasion and proof should not, in principle, be distinct from each other, and it would not occur to a mathematician to call his proofs allegories" (PAP, p. 2). For it is precisely the hallmark of allegory that it doesn't allow for a straightforward passage from the level of sequential (or narrative) exposition to the level of achieved, demonstrative grasp. Allegory involves a perpetual suspension of meaning, a detour through the various tropes, figures, and modes of oblique signification where language can never reach the point of simply saying what it sets out to say. Thus it poses the question: "why is it that the furthest reaching truths about ourselves and the world have to be stated in such a lopsided, referentially indirect mode?" Or again, in more specifically deconstructive form: "why is it that texts that attempt the articulation of epistemology with persuasion turn out to be inconclusive about their own intelligibility in the same manner and for the same reasons that produce allegory?" (PAP, p. 2).

For de Man, these issues are nowhere resolved but everywhere forced upon the reader's attention in the detailed unfolding of Pascal's arguments. Moreover, they cut across conventional distinctions between one kind of writing and another — in Pascal's case, between those texts that argue their way in a logical, demonstrative, or rational-deductive mode, and those that have to do with questions of a moral or ethico-religious import. On the contrary, de Man asserts: these two aspects of Pascal's thinking are in fact both marked by the same paradoxical strains and tensions, the same aporetic structures of argument that signal the need for a strictly allegorical reading. This is indeed the chief interest of a text like the *Réflexions*: that it spells out in epistemological terms those problems that are otherwise "so often expressed, in Pascal himself and in his interpreters, in a tonality of existential pathos" (PAP, p. 7). One might recall here the influence on the early de Man of Heidegger, Sartre, and that whole way of thinking to which "existential pathos" in some sense figures as the mark of authentic philosophical truth. As we have seen, hostile commentators — Frank Lentricchia among them — advert to this fact as if thereby to prove (and discredit) de Man's lingering attachment to a Heideggerian mystique of origins and long-lost primordial Being.[31] Certainly this strain persists into many of the essays collected in *Blindness and Insight* (1971).[32] But by the time of *Allegories of Reading* — published some eight years later — it has given way to a language for the most part meticulously purged of such existentialist residues. And with the essay on Pascal, de Man arrives at a stage where epistemological questions of truth and falsehood have clearly come to dominate his thinking — or at least to provide a more secure point of access to questions of an ethical or religious character. This text (the *Réflexions*) may "help to undo the tendentious and simplistic opposition between knowledge and faith which is often forced upon Pascal" (PAP, p. 7). But it does so, in de Man's reading, precisely by virtue of its first having raised the question of what (if anything) distinguishes the discourse of logical "proof" from that of allegorical persuasion. "What is it, in a rigorous epistemology, that makes it impossible to decide whether its exposition is a proof or an allegory?" (PAP, p. 5). This question is rhetorical in the sense that de Man will work round to the conclusion that no such difference exists, that "proofs" in the mode of reasoning *more geometrico* themselves depend in the last analysis on figures of thought that cannot be accounted for in strictly logical terms. But the only way of making this point is through a labor of critical exegesis which respects the force and the logical precision of Pascal's argumentation.

Pascal lays it down as a starting requirement that we distinguish between "nominal" and "real" definitions — that is, between terms to which has been assigned some specific sense or logical function, and terms which belong to natural language and thus carry with them all manner of referential doubts and ambiguities. Nominal definitions are "entirely free and never open to contradiction." They are postulates within a well-defined system of purely *analytical* terms and equivalents, concepts which admit of no possible ambiguity on account of their having been constructed with a view to eliminating just such sources of extrasystemic confusion. Real definitions, by contrast, "are a great deal more coercive and dangerous: they are actually not definitions, but axioms or, even more frequently, propositions that need to be proven" (PAP, pp. 5–6). But Pascal is unable to maintain this distinction when it comes to explaining how the logic of concepts can possibly relate to the evidence of "natural reason," or to the kind of intuitive "commonsense" apprehension that enables us to make sense of those concepts. At this point the text "glides almost imperceptively [sic]" from nominal to real definitions.

> These terms (which include the basic topoi of geometrical discourse, such as motion, number, and extension) represent the natural language element that Descartes scornfully rejected from scientific discourse, but which reappear here as the natural light that guarantees the intelligibility of primitive terms despite their undefinability. (PAP, p. 6)

This turn away from nominal definition is also a "turn" in the rhetorical sense, a movement that abandons the claim to straightforward, literal signification in so far as it involves meanings that cannot be accounted for on purely analytical or stipulative terms. The word no longer functions "as a sign or a name," but performs rather "as a vector, a directional motion that is manifest only as a turn, since the target toward which it turns remains unknown" (PAP, pp. 6–7).

So language achieves a purchase on the world of phenomenal experience — of number, time, space, motion, etc. — but only at the cost of giving up its claim to exist as a perfect, self-regulating system of internal terms and definitions. At this stage "the sign has become a trope, a substitutive relationship that has to posit a meaning whose existence cannot be verified, but that confers upon the sign an unavoidable signifying function" (PAP, p. 7). Nominal definitions cannot be maintained without a certain admixture of "primitive terms" whose signification exceeds the grasp of any purely analytic understanding. And this ambivalence in Pascal's language affects not only his thinking on topics of mathematical and scientific truth, but also the very supposition of a difference between "nominal" and "real" orders of equivalence. For "the nominal definition of primitive terms always turns into a proposition that has to, but cannot, be proven." From which it follows that "since definition is now itself a primitive term . . . the definition of the nominal definition is itself a real, and not a nominal, definition" (PAP, p. 7). Any attempt to make intelligible sense of this distinction will have to depend at some point on the positing of entities which cannot be defined analytically on terms laid down by that same distinction. This produces a kind of generalized aporia, or something like Gödel's paradoxical theorem as applied to formal systems of mathematics: namely, that there will always be at least one proposition whose truth must be taken as axiomatic, but which cannot be either proved or disproved within the terms of its own system.[33] The effect is to destabilize Pascal's model of language and representation at precisely the point where he needs to establish a firm methodological base.

De Man pursues this argument into the so-called principle of "double infinity," the idea of the infinitely large and infinitely small as concepts which (in Pascal's words) "open up the mind to the greatest marvels in nature." Here he detects a similar vacillating movement between ideas that seem to have their ground in some purely nominal definition and ideas that appeal outside the system to aspects of phenomenal or intuitive self-evidence. Pascal's arguments "move between spatial and numerical dimensions by means of simple computation (as in the instance of the irrational number for the square root of two), or by experimental representations in space, without the intervention of discursive language" (PAP, p. 8). What de Man finds especially revealing here is the way that Pascal has to separate concepts of number from spatial intuitions, but at the same time needs periodically to suspend that separation, since "the underlying homology of space and number, the ground of the system, should never be fundamentally in question" (PAP, p. 10). When Pascal reflects on the properties of number he does so in a transcendental mode of reasoning where the system requires an introduction of ideal entities (like the unit and the zero) which exist purely for the purpose of maintaining its coherence and explanatory power. Thus the concept of infinity is arrived at on the basis of a "synecdochal totalization" which starts out from "the unit of number, the *one*," and proceeds by way of simply postulating "N+1" to a notional infinity. And the infinitesimal can likewise be conceived on the model of an infinite divisibility which supposes the zero as its vanishing point. This procedure has its analogues at the level of phenomenal or "intra-worldly" experience, since the zero corresponds to the ideas of "instant" and "stasis" in the realms of time and motion respectively.

Thus Pascal might appear to have succeeded in establishing the "necessary and reciprocal link" that would enable the extension of such reasoning *more geometrico* to regions of phenomenal or real-world cognitive grasp. His cosmological arguments would then have a grounding in principles of *a priori* knowledge whose validity was purely analytic and hence beyond reach of sceptical objections. But, according to de Man, "this has happened at a price," since "the coherence of the system is now seen to be entirely dependent on the introduction of an element — the zero and its equivalences in time and motion — that is itself entirely heterogeneous with regard to the system" (PAP, p. 10). For the zero and its spatio-temporal correlates are the product of real, not nominal definition; they derive from the need to homogenize the order of phenomenal cognition on the model of purely numerical concepts. And the same applies to the unit (one), whose paradoxical status was recognized by Euclid: a term which, while serving as the basis of all numerical calculation, cannot be truly called a number since of course it excludes plurality. It may appear, at the end of Pascal's demonstration, that "the homogeneity of the universe is recovered, and the principle of infinitesimal symmetry is well established." But this appearance depends on the reversibility of that passage between concepts and analogues (or tropes) which can always be turned back against the claim to have grounded all knowledge in a prior analysis of absolute mathematical certainties. What signals the presence of this double operation in Pascal's text is the "systematic effacement of the zero and its reconversion into a name." That is to say, the nominal concept must always have assumed a certain "intra-worldly" or phenomenal extension if it is to serve the purpose required of it. "The continuous universe held together by the double wings of the two infinites is interrupted, disrupted *at all points* by a principle of radical heterogeneity without which it cannot come into being" (de Man's italics; PAP, p. 10).

This is the central argument of de Man's essay, and his reason for deploying the term "allegory" as a kind of deconstructive master trope in the reading of Pascal's text. For it is, to repeat, the characterizing mark of allegory that it prevents or defers any punctual grasp of the relation between word and concept, and instead points the way to a mode of reading that tracks the course of an argument through all its self-imposed problems and resistances. This is why Pascal provides a model instance of the fact that epistemological rigor may indeed go along with a strictly allegorical form of understanding. Pascal's discourse is marked through-out by a tension between the orders of nominal and real definition which cannot be reduced to concept or system but only sustained as his argument unfolds by various forms of tropological displacement. As de Man writes in a crucial passage, this rupture of the infinitesimal and the homogeneous does not occur on the transcendental level, but on the level of language, in the inability of a theory of language as sign or as name (nominal definition) to ground this homogeneity without having recourse to the signifying function, the real definition, that makes the zero of signification the necessary condition for grounded knowledge. (PAP, p. 10)

To read the *Réflexions* allegorically is not, therefore, to treat it as a "literary" text with no claims to truth save those engendered by its own delusive "philosophical" aspirations. Rather, it is to acknowledge that "allegory is the purveyor of demanding truths," and that the only way to meet such demands is to read with an adequate attentiveness to language in its more oblique or figural aspects.

In the second part of his essay de Man goes on to read some sections of the *Pensées* as likewise exhibiting a double articulation of logic and rhetoric that cannot be resolved in straightforwardly dialectical terms. These passages include Pascal's reflections on nature and custom, on truth and justice, and on knowledge (*episteme*) as opposed to mere opinion or popular prejudice (*doxa*). In each case the characteristic movement of thought is what Pascal himself describes as a "continual reversal from pro to contra," and de Man as "an endless set of variations on chiasmic crossings of binary oppositions" (PAP, p. 20). Here it might seem that we have moved into a different realm of thought, one where ethical values of right and wrong predominate over purely epistemological issues of truth and falsehood. But de Man (as we have seen) very firmly rejects this compartmentalized approach. He argues that Pascal's thinking on questions of ethics, politics, and religion in fact follows the same pattern of aporetic reasoning established in the earlier *Réflexions*. That is to say, he is always at the point of setting up conceptual terms and distinctions which then turn out to controvert the very grounds of their own oppositional logic. Again, it is in the name of allegory that this process is best understood: as a "pattern of reasoning . . . in which oppositions are, if not reconciled, at least pursued toward a totalization that may be infinitely postponed, but that remains operative as the sole principle of intelligibility" (PAP, p. 20). In short, any reading of Pascal that chooses to expound his "existential" concerns while ignoring this epistemological dimension — any reading, that is, on the commonplace thematic or literary-critical model — will thereby be deprived of genuine insight and validity.

I have argued that de Man's own work should be treated with the same degree of analytical care and attentiveness that he brings to this essay on Pascal. That work remains squarely within the tradition of philosophical thinking about language, logic, and truth, even if it must appear — at least to mainstream philosophers — as respecting none of the rules laid down for serious debate on such matters. This is why I have emphasized de Man's distance from those varieties of "advanced" poststructuralist and postmodernist thinking that would simply collapse the difference between philosophy and literature. For the upshot of such counterdisciplinary gestures is first to reduce every discourse to an undifferentiating general rhetoric, and then to deprive rhetoric itself of any critical or epistemological force. Hence the importance of de Man's return to the classical *trivium*, to the distinction between logic, grammar, and rhetoric as a model that needs to be preserved, however unstable its presumptive order of priorities. Hence also his resistance to that postmodern turn (in philosophy and criticism alike) which treats such paradigms as merely the products of a shifting order of "knowledge" and "discourse" detached from all considerations of validity or truth. The most relevant contexts for assessing his work are those provided by the various modern forms of analytical philosophy of language. Though he addresses their problems in a different register, this fact should not prevent — as it has so far — any serious engagement with de Man's texts by thinkers in that "other" tradition.

4

Aesthetic Ideology and the Ethics of Reading: Miller and de Man

I

What are the constraints that govern our reading of texts, in particular those texts that implicitly thematize or foreground the activity of reading? Could one spell out any kind of *ethical* imperative that would lay down rules for this activity and thereby establish a generalized code for the practice of responsible criticism? And if so, what relationship could possibly obtain between the absolute, categorical nature of any such claim and the detailed business of applying it to this or that text? These are some of the questions that J. Hillis Miller raises in a series of essays first delivered as the Wellek Library Lectures at Irvine, California in 1985.[1] As he remarks, there was a certain irony in this situation, since René Wellek is prominent among those who have condemned "deconstruction" in general — and Miller's recent work in particular — as a species of last-ditch nihilism bent upon destroying the ethical and humanistic bases of literary study.[2] These critics tend to compromise their own declared values by giving little sign of having carefully *read* the texts in question, or by conducting their polemics mainly at the level of unargued imputation. So when Miller takes the "ethics of reading" as his theme it is with a view to turning back these ill-founded charges by engaging his opponents very much on their own chosen ground.

This involves the claim that deconstruction is not only responsive to the demands of close reading but also, inescapably, compelled to raise problems of an ethical character. There are two main strands to Miller's argument — roughly speaking, "philosophical" and "literary" — though he wants us to see, by the end of his book, that in fact they are inseparably linked. The one starts out from the Kantian principle that "our respect for a text is like our respect for a person," that is, an attitude which shows due regard for their autonomy or independent selfhood, and which doesn't treat them as the means to some further, exploitative end of one's own. But how could such a precept be workably translated into terms of literary-critical practice? More specifically, what is the nature of that "law" which, according to Kant, should be binding on the subject regardless of private or self-interested motives, and yet be entered into by an act of freely willed autonomous choice? In this case, Miller writes, "the act of reading would lead the reader voluntarily to impose the ethical law embodied in that text on himself" (*ER*, p. 35). The ethical moment in criticism would then involve something decidedly more complex and obscure than talk about the various specific moral *themes* ("thou shalt not commit adultery," "always tell the truth," and so forth) to be found in novels or poems. It would open onto questions of a philosophic import beyond the usual interests — or assumed competence — of literary studies.

But it is precisely this commonplace division of realms that Miller sets out to challenge. He does so by returning to a passage in Kant — a footnote to the *Foundations of the Metaphysics of Morals* — where philosophy is forced up against its own conceptual limits in confronting the antinomies of ethical reason. Here Kant argues that the "highest and unconditional good" can only be located in the "pure will of a rational being directed out of respect to what he [Kant] calls the 'law in itself'" (*ER*, p. 19).[3] Such a law necessarily stands above and beyond any particular instance or rule that might be followed in detailed, practical terms. It is the precondition of ethical knowledge, but, for that very reason, incapable of summary statement or direct exemplification. Miller sees a parallel with Kafka here, notably with that cryptic allegorical episode from *The Trial* entitled "Before The Law." In this parable, a bewildered "man from the country" respectfully requests (and of course fails to get) a face-to-face audience with the Law.[4] Like the *deus absconditus* of Jansenist theology, the Law is that which refuses any sign or token of its visible presence, all the more effectively to command assent through a pure, unconditional act of faith on the subject's part. For Kant likewise, the source and authority of ethical injunctions can never be encountered, so to speak, in person but only by analogy or oblique inference from this or that specific case in hand. The law in itself is that which categorically compels respect aside from all mere relativities of time and circumstance.

So what happens, Miller asks, when we apply this lesson to the reading of Kant's problematical footnote? For one thing, we find that Kant has recourse to parables and fictions of his own, forms of analogical thinking that effectively substitute for conceptual argument. "If Kant cannot tell you exactly what the law is, where it is, or where it comes from, he can nevertheless tell you to what it is analogous" (*ER*, p. 20). Rhetorically, Kant's procedure involves the tropes of *catachresis* or *hypotyposis*, defined by Miller (who here takes a lead from de Man) as the "naming by figures of speech what cannot be named literally because it cannot be faced directly" (*ER*, p. 21). Thus Kant denies that our respect for the law — for law in its pure, categorical form — can possibly be based on fear, inclination, or any such merely self-interested motive. But he then goes on to say that fear and inclination are indeed the best analogies or terms by which to grasp the nature of that absolute ethical demand. "Since there is no proper word for what it is based on, he is forced to say it is like just those two feelings, fear and inclination, he has said it is *not* like" (*ER*, p. 21). Kant himself, in the *Critique of Judgment*, warns of the dangerous influence exerted by figures like catachresis, "abusive" tropes for which no literal meaning exists and which can therefore thoroughly bewilder thought by substituting rhetoric for reason. In fact, Miller argues, this is precisely what happens at the crucial point in Kant's own thinking on the nature of ethical law. His rhetorical procedure can best be read as "an example of the forced or abusive transfer of terms from an alien realm to name something which has no proper name in itself" (*ER*, p. 21). And the fact that this maneuver takes place in a footnote — as if by way of casual afterthought — is likewise indicative of the problems it creates for Kant's more overt line of argument.

There is also, according to Miller, a fictive or narrative dimension bound up with Kant's ethical philosophy. The categorical imperative demands that we behave *as if* the private maxim that governs our action were to be made a universal law binding on all mankind for all time. It would then be wrong to tell lies under any circumstances — even to avoid causing hurt to others — since, if everyone adopted this maxim, it would undermine the very foundations of trust in each other's word. So how should we determine what this law amounts to in the absence of more explicit guidelines? By acting, Kant suggests, "as if" the categorical imperative applied in each case, and further by imagining various kinds of hypothetical predicament by which to try out its implications. Thus ethical reason has to fall back in the end upon a certain irreducible storytelling interest. In Miller's words, "the power to make fictions . . . serves for Kant as the absolutely necessary bridge without which there would be no connection between the law as such and any particular ethical law of behavior" (*ER*, p. 28). And this despite Kant's explicit desire to ground the dictates of moral conscience in a law transcending all accidents of circumstantial time and place. For at last he is forced to acknowledge — nowhere directly, but everywhere through ruses and strategic turns of analogy — that the ethical domain is *linguistic* through and through, brought into existence by the performative power of words and maintained by necessary fictions adopted "as if" in accordance with absolute law.

Will this have been a faithful, responsible reading of Kant — one that respects the categorical imperative to treat the text as an end in itself, and not as a means for impressive displays of critical ingenuity? Many readers would doubtless return a negative answer, especially those for whom "deconstruction" is synonymous with just such an attitude of feckless, self-delighting interpretive "freeplay." Miller denies very strongly that this is the case. If his chapter has gone against what Kant means to say about the nature of ethical obligation, then it has done so by reason of "an inevitable necessity" which may yet turn out to be "the true ethics of reading" (*ER*, p. 39). For Miller, this comes down to the need for close reading of problematic passages *despite* all the powerful, traditional inducements to make sense of texts on their own preferred terms. So strong is the desire to go along with Kant — to ignore whatever complicates a "faithful," recognizably Kantian reading — that Miller can present the deconstructionist case as a well-nigh heroic struggle against the bewitchment of our intelligence by language.

This is why he next turns to de Man as an exemplar of the kind of criticism that holds out to the limit against such bewitchment. Miller does not underrate the sheer resistance, the affront to all normative values and assumptions that we encounter in de Man's readings. Here, after all, is a critic who declares reading itself to be in some sense an "impossible" activity; who asserts the aberrant or error-prone nature of all understanding; and who argues (notoriously) that *every* form of knowledge — from primitive sense-certainty to pure reason, from ethics to history and politics — is somehow contingent on the radically figural character of language. Hence the extreme hostility to de Man among critics who mistake his sceptical rigor for a "nihilist" indifference to meaning, value, and truth. Miller contests these criticisms, and also rebuts the absurdly inaccurate (but widespread) charge that deconstruction, as practiced by a critic like de Man, comes down to an attitude of "anything goes" with respect to textual meaning. On the contrary, de Man insists: whatever the problems, temptations, or obstacles in the way of critical reading, they nonetheless occur as a matter of strict necessity and not as the result of some ultimate freedom to make what one will of an indeterminate text. Hence the distinction — crucial to de Man — between *errors* of reading induced by perplexities genuinely there in the text and *mistakes* which come about through lapses of attention or mere inability to read.[5] Aberrations of the former kind are in some sense "bound to take place," even though this occurs "against the grain of the reader's or the author's wishes" (*ER*, p. 51).

Thus Miller can enlist de Man on the side of a readerly ethics whose imperative is that of cleaving always to the letter of the text and holding out against the premature seductions of coherent sense. His point is made concisely in the following passage which aims at the mistaken (*not* erroneous) idea of deconstruction put about by its current opponents.

> Far from being "indeterminate" or "nihilistic", however, or a matter of wanton free play or arbitrary choice, each reading is, strictly speaking, ethical, in the sense that it *has* to take place, by an implacable necessity, as the response to a categorical demand, and in the sense that the reader *must* take responsibility for it and for its consequences in the personal, social, and political worlds. (*ER*, p. 59)

So it is that de Man's radically antinomian stance on questions of meaning and interpretation is equated by Miller with the Kantian antinomies of freewill and ethical law. It is a bold (some would say an utterly perverse) stroke of argument, and one that marks a clear transition in his book from broadly "philosophical" questions to the reading of several exemplary narrative texts.

The chosen novelists are George Eliot, Anthony Trollope, and Henry James, and Miller's chief interest is in passages that more or less explicitly reflect on the activities of writing and reading. For Eliot, famously, the purpose of art is to capture the realities of inward and outward experience with a straightforward devotion to truth which carries its own ethical authority. Thus Miller cites the well-known Chapter 17 of *Adam Bede*, "In Which the Story Pauses a Little" while George Eliot (or the implied author — here referred to rather oddly as "he") takes time off to develop this commonsense-mimetic theory.[6] In fact, Miller argues, the passages in question are a good deal more complex than might be supposed on a reading that "faithfully" accepted their express ontological claims. Though Eliot wants to think — and indeed plainly believes — that "the language of realism is a proper language functioning like a photograph," she is unable to present it in this light without her own language implicitly revealing the problems with any such simplified account. This produces, as de Man might say, an "allegory of reading" (or of unreadability) whereby Eliot's text "dissociates the cognition from the act," showing up the tensions that develop between what the passage *says* and what it is effectively *constrained to mean*. And in George Eliot this tension arises chiefly from the conflict of epistemological and ethical truth-claims — that is to say, from the problem of reconciling narrative realism with a will to do justice to human motives and passions through a power of heightened sympathetic insight. It is a version, Miller argues, of the Kantian dilemma which demands unconditional adherence to a law whose terms or conditions necessarily elude any form of adequate statement or exemplification.

On her own account, George Eliot seems squarely opposed to the kind of high-toned visionary rhetoric adopted by poets and critics in the wake of Kant's philosophical revolution. In particular she rejects the idea of creative activity as a bringing forth of imaginary worlds beyond the grasp of commonplace, quotidian perception. "I turn, without shrinking, from cloud-borne angels, from prophets, sibyls, and heroic warriors, to an old woman bending over her flower-pot . . . ."[7] The Romantic Sublime is thus connected, for Eliot, with a failure to respect the needs and realities of everyday mortal experience. It involves — most explicitly in Kant — a turning aside from the objects of commonsense perception to a realm of heightened self-knowledge where the mind momentarily exults in a sense of its own imaginative powers. True genius, in Miller's paraphrase of Kant, "imitates nature not by copying it, but by duplicating its manner of production . . . As God spoke nature into existence by means of the divine word . . . [so genius] speaks into existence a heterocosm which adds something hitherto unheard-of to nature" (*ER*, p. 67). It is against this overweening Romantic ideology that George Eliot asserts the straightforward claims of a humble documentary realism. Her model will therefore be those Dutch genre paintings that abjure the temptation of religious, mythological, or other such high-flown themes, and which stick to the patient recording of life in its commonplace, humdrum detail.

But there is a problem in squaring this basically Aristotelian mimetic doctrine with George Eliot's desire to present her characters in the light of an inward, imaginative grasp that would somehow redeem or transform their everyday lives. It is a problem most aptly figured, Miller thinks, in the way that Adam himself oscillates between a "too hard-headed and clear-seeing power of judgment" and a willingness to suspend all such habits where Hetty Sorrel is concerned. Thus Adam, in Eliot's words, "created the mind he believed in out of his own, which was large, unselfish, tender" (cited by Miller, *ER*, p. 80). And this leaves us undecided as to whether such illusions are the basis of all sympathetic understanding or the cause of much error and confusion. There is a curious echo of the Kantian sublime in the principle of unbounded charity that operates in Adam's feelings for Hetty and in Eliot's reflections on the novelist's art. If love of one's neighbor is indeed the prerequisite of moral and social goodness, then clearly it demands something more than a "hard-headed," realist view of persons and motives. This is what makes all the difference between a "baseless cynicism" devoid of human charity and those equally baseless but necessary fictions which provide the only possible alternative view. It is a choice, Miller writes, like the "plus or minus sign placed before a zero," since both these attitudes — the positive and the negative, idealism and cynicism — follow from the willed imposition of values on an otherwise neutral reality.

In the end George Eliot is compelled to believe in that "fictive plus value" that transforms the commonplace (as seen by Mr. Gedge the innkeeper: "A poor lot, Sir, big and little") into fit subjects for the novelist's redemptive art. But this requires precisely that one go beyond the real-life evidence and interpret human actions, motives, and feelings in a manner more akin to what Kant describes as the moment of Sublime imagining. George Eliot holds out explicitly for a realist mode which avoids falling prey to either of these opposed temptations. For it is, she remarks, often to be observed that those who "pant after the ideal," who "find nothing in pantaloons and petticoats great enough to command their reverence and love," are those same people who, when faced with some unpalatable truth, take refuge in an equally unreal and exaggerated cynicism. She will therefore stick to the true path of wisdom, novelistic and moral, which consists in taking characters pretty much as they are and not as the idealist (or his disenchanted counterpart, the cynic) would have them. But her writing is unable to achieve this happy mean, since it constantly affirms the need for a charitable vision — a power of redemptive insight — which can bring out the best in characters who are "*in fact*" ugly, stupid, inconsistent, or otherwise flawed.

What the chapter tries to do is differentiate clearly between three attitudes: "baseless cynicism," an equally baseless idealism, and the realist mode (mimetic and ethical) which avoids these acutely disabling extremes. What it actually presents is the stark impossibility of drawing and maintaining any such firm distinction. In Miller's words, "there is more than simple opposition in the relation between the closed circuit economy of realism, on the one hand, the ugly mirroring the ugly and returning the ugly to the ugly, and, on the other hand, the infinite economy of genius, the beautiful (angels and Madonnas, prophets, sibyls) mirroring nothing but the inventive soul of its creator, flying off into the inane ideal without possibility of return" (*ER*, p. 79). The opposition is not "simple" but strictly *undecidable*, since Eliot's version of mimesis, as she herself expounds it, necessarily partakes of that same oscillating movement between idealism and cynicism which she hopes to avoid by sticking to the plain, unvarnished facts of human nature. She is, Miller suggests, too good and too faithful a reader of her own writing to suppress altogether these complicating signs of a discrepancy between meaning and intent, between what her analogies actually *say* and what she would preferably have them mean.

This argument is pursued in the chapter on Trollope, where Miller detects a similar pattern of divergent implications at work. On the face of it Trollope seems largely immune from the problems that beset more self-conscious or "sophisticated" writers. He believes in the straightforward storytelling virtues of a narrative that poses questions of ethical choice for characters with whom we are irresistibly led to identify by reason of our everyday shared humanity. There is — or so we might think — absolutely no sign in Trollope of that ambivalent attitude to language and representation that complicates the picture even in a piece of "classic" provincial realism like *Adam Bede*. Thus Miller quotes some passages from the *Autobiography* which show Trollope not only espousing this simplified aesthetic creed but taking great pleasure in the way it has gained him an entry to the best, most fashionable circles of Victorian society. Such is presumably the fit reward for novelists who hold up a mirror to the current self-images of the age.

But on a closer reading it appears that Trollope is by no means so confident in the power of his writing to present moral choices and truths of experience in a straightforward, uncomplicated way. His predicament is more like that of Mr. Harding in *The Warden*, obliged to give up his sinecure *as if* by an absolute moral obligation but scarcely understanding what the law might be that compels him to act as he does. "I am thought in the wrong by all those I have consulted in the matter," he writes in his letter of resignation, going on to confess that "I have very little but an inward and unguided conviction of my own to bring me to this step."[8] Like the countryman in Kafka's parable, Harding comes up against the ultimate elusiveness of a law that can be known only through its instances in this or that complex situation, and not in any form capable of clearcut ethical statement. The result is a kind of contagious ambivalence, a generalized doubt that affects Trollope's fiction not only in its ethical but also in its mimetic or representational aspect. "Instead of showing that these decisions, and others like them, are solidly grounded, Trollope demonstrates again and again that the sought-for solid ground slips away and vanishes. Moral decision may therefore be an ungrounded act of self-affection like Trollope's act of creating characters out of nothing but his unaided 'moral consciousness'" (*ER*, p. 97). Once again we are in the presence of those Kantian antinomies which might have been thought quite irrelevant to the sober, industrious, truth-telling narratives of a writer like Trollope.

II

With Henry James — the subject of Miller's final chapter — it is no longer a case of discovering complications that the narrative attempts, unsuccessfully, to hide from view. Of all modern novelists James is the most insistently aware of those problems, ethical and otherwise, that attend the very acts of writing and reading — especially when reading one's own texts from a distance of time and self-imposed critical detachment. Understandably, Miller chooses to focus on *The Art of the Novel*, the collection of prefaces to the New York edition of his work where James casts a coolly appreciative eye over his major achievements to date. What so fascinates Miller in this scene of deferred self-reckoning is the way that James's essays acknowledge their peculiar temporal predicament — the inescapable gap between past intentions and present understanding — while also, as a matter of principle, accepting full *responsibility* for whatever is there, set down in the text. This seemingly unique "special case" is after all not so special, perhaps, but an object lesson in the ethics of reading as practiced by a novelist-critic of uncommonly rigorous standards.

Thus Miller looks to the prefaces for an account of what it means to read such texts — whether novels or criticism — with a sense of their elusive but exacting demands upon the reader's ethical intelligence. His guideline here is the well-known sentence from the Preface to *Roderick Hudson* where James declares that "really, universally, relations stop nowhere."[9] If this is indeed the case, Miller argues, then it places an immense responsibility on those — including Henry James himself — who want their readings to respect something genuinely "there" in the text, and not to serve merely as a useful means toward their own interpretative ends. At this point the argument again takes a Kantian turn as Miller draws out the paradoxical entailments of freedom and necessity involved in this ethics of reading. On the one hand, it is always possible for an author to disown what he or she once wrote — thinking it perhaps ill-judged, wrongheaded, or simply out of keeping with their present views. One obvious example would be Auden's attempt to rewrite or censor those overtly political passages in his youthful work (especially the great poem "Spain") which later gave him cause for embarrassment. In such cases, there is a simple desire to repudiate the earlier writing in the name of some different, presently more binding sense of ethical obligation. Disavowals of this kind, Miller says, are like promises we ultimately decide not to keep. They are commitments made in good faith at the time but now — for whatever reason — felt to be no longer valid or relevant. Yet even then (as the Auden example makes clear) there is a lingering tie between author and text which cannot be dissolved by any subsequent act of negation, principled or otherwise. "Our literary acts," as James says, "enjoy this marked advantage over many of our acts, that, though they go forth into the world and stray even in the desert, they don't to the same extent lose themselves; their attachment and reference to us, however strained, needn't necessarily lapse — while of the tie that binds us to them we may make almost anything we like."[10] The freedom to discover new relations, new terms for analysis — even (or especially) when revisiting one's own earlier work — goes along with the law which decrees that what is written is written; that the text may spring great surprises on the novelist-critic who comes to it, supposedly, as a privileged self-reader in the wisdom of creative hindsight.

Hence the frequent air of bemused admiration in James's prefaces, the sense of his having only now perceived, from a distance of time and altered understanding, what the novels were properly *about* in the first place. The pleasure of discovering such unlooked-for subtleties is mixed with a feeling that they don't in any special sense belong to the present writer who is really in much the same position as any other decently qualified critic. This business of reviewing one's own productions is therefore a kind of object lesson in the need to let texts speak for themselves, or lay down the law of their own best reading. But this law is emphatically *not* of a kind that could ever be spelled out explicitly in terms of some generalized reader-response theory or hermeneutic method. On the contrary, it is always liable to take new forms or appear under different guises as the reader comes up against unforeseen complexities in this or that narrative situation. In Paul de Man's words (quoted by Miller), "reading is an argument . . . because it has to go against the grain of what one would expect to happen in the name of what has to happen."[11] Such is indeed the "ethics of reading" as Miller understands it: a willingness to stick with the letter of the text, to follow out its formal or rhetorical complexities wherever these may lead. One is reminded of the way that certain characters in James (especially in his short stories "The Lesson of the Master" and "The Figure in the Carpet") reveal their inadequate capacity as readers by attempting to go straight to the truth of a complex narrative structure. What these interpreters miss in the grip of their single-minded hermeneutic quest is everything that belongs to the order of style, rhetoric, and form. In short, they sacrifice the problems and the pleasures of *reading* for the sake of imposing their own tidy narrative solutions.

So when de Man writes of the "resistance to theory" his phrase must be taken in two distinct senses.[12] Most obviously it refers to that widespread institutional resistance which comes of treating "theory" as a threat to all humanistic values, and which often goes along with a failure to read what the theorists have actually written. It is this resistance that Miller has chiefly in mind when he sets out to analyze the causes and motives of such a curious compulsion not to read. But there is also, as de Man acknowledges, a temptation for theory to become so attached to its own ruling preconceptions that it passes clean over those checks and resistances properly encountered in the reading of texts. This is why de

Man so often made a point of defending the "old" New Criticism against those who believed — partly on the evidence of his own writings — that its methods and assumptions had been somehow totally discredited. Whatever their dubious doctrinal adherences, at least the New Critics were habitual and disciplined close readers whose exemplary practice in this regard was apt to subvert their more programmatic claims. Such was the argument of an early essay (reprinted in *Blindness and Insight*), and such is de Man's steady conviction in the writings of his final decade.[13] "Mere reading, it turns out, prior to any theory, is able to transform critical discourse in a manner that would appear deeply subversive to those who think of the teaching of literature as a substitute for the teaching of theology, ethics, psychology, or intellectual history" (*RT*, p. 24). So the "resistance to theory" is not simply a matter of that deep-grained critical prejudice that refuses a reading to anything that goes under the name of literary theory. It is also, more importantly, the kind of immanent or self-induced resistance that theory encounters when put to work in the reading of particular texts. And this it accomplishes, according to de Man, "very often in spite of itself because it cannot fail to respond to structures of language which it is the more or less secret aim of literary teaching to keep hidden. (*RT*, p. 24).

Miller's reading of James is conducted very much in the spirit of these remarks by de Man. It fastens unerringly on moments in the Prefaces where James has to recognize the sheer *impossibility* of thinking his way back — as if by a movement of inward, sympathetic recall — into the motives, the psychology, or the structural genesis of his own fictions. One might remark here that the progress of Miller's criticism since the mid-1960s has been, broadly speaking, from a phenomenological to a deconstructionist standpoint. That is to say, he started out (in books like *Poets of Reality* and *The Disappearance of God*) from the conviction that it was indeed possible to establish a degree of intimate rapport with an author's deepest, most distinctive qualities of mind, perception, or experience.[14] It was here that Miller parted company with the "old" New Critics, those who believed — often, like W.K. Wimsatt, as a high point of principle — that the poem should be treated as a "verbal icon," an inwrought structure of meaning whose formal characteristics ("irony," "paradox," "tension," etc.) set it absolutely apart from the language of mere prose commentary. Thus when Wimsatt takes issue with Miller — in a rearguard defense of New Critical methods and precepts — it is mainly on the grounds that Miller has embraced a subjectivist approach that obliterates these crucial distinctions and thinks to gain access to the poet's mind by an act of privileged, intuitive insight.[15] For Wimsatt, this amounts to a kind of willful and backsliding heresy, a neglect of ontological boundaries (between poetry and criticism, meaning and intent, objective and impressionistic modes of reading) that threatens to destroy the very basis of critical judgment. And equally, when Miller (along with Geoffrey Hartman) looks "beyond formalism" for a larger sense of hermeneutic openness and freedom, he does so by annulling those same distinctions that Wimsatt is so anxious to keep in place. Reading is now aimed toward a reflective communion of mind with mind, an act of sympathetic recreation where all such differences fall away in the moment of achieved understanding.

Such is the phenomenological approach that Miller so admired in the work of Georges Poulet and the Geneva school of critics.[16] But his subsequent writings — from the early 1970s — bear witness to a growing sense of the difficulties that stand in the way of any such perfect, unimpeded meeting of minds. These problems have to do with the resistance put up by chains of problematic (as de Man would say, "aberrant") signification that begin to register as soon as one abandons the reassuring notion that a text must ultimately mean what its author intended it to mean. Thus the "turn" in Miller's work comes about through his perceiving — not without a measure of nostalgic regret — that a genuine, sustained attentiveness to textual detail may point criticism away from that dream of achieved communication. Hence the insistence, first signaled in essays like "Ariadne's Thread" (1976), on the sheer *impossibility* of resolving those textual complications to a point where meaning would at last coincide with a sense of organic wholeness in the work, or of authorial presence as something that can always be restored by an act of inward identification on the critic's part.[17] Hence also Miller's running argument with those — especially Romantic scholar-critics like M.H. Abrams — who stake their whole enterprise on the power of poetry, at moments of high visionary pathos, to transcend all the commonplace antinomies of subject and object, mind and nature, language and the world of immediate sensory experience.[18]

This belief goes deep in Romantic tradition, from its origins in the symbolist-organicist aesthetic of thinkers like Coleridge to its latter-day expression in the work of mainstream academic interpreters. In a sense, as Miller well knows, it defines the very nature of that tradition and offers the readiest line of defense against those — like T.S. Eliot and the New Critics — who on principle rejected the entire ideology of Romanticism, and who set out to create an alternative, classicist line of descent. What Abrams defends in the name of "High Romantic Argument" is precisely what these critics deplore (after T.E. Hulme) as a species of "spilt religion": the idea that poetry can achieve states of mind transcending the limits of commonplace perceptual experience. So Miller, himself a devoted interpreter of Romantic texts, is far from treating such visionary claims as naive illusions to be "deconstructed" from a standpoint of superior cognitive grasp. On the contrary, his argument is that we can do justice to these texts — read them aright — only by to some extent going *against the grain* of their overt meaning or intention. That is to say, we must suspend belief in their manifest truth-claims, the better to grasp how complex and refractory are the ways of language when forced up against the limits of intelligible sense. Such is the powerful revaluative impulse behind Miller's, Hartman's, and de Man's reading of Romantic poetry: a reading that discloses how language may fail to achieve its wished-for effects, but fail (so to speak) in exemplary fashion, by pointing to signs of incoherence at the heart of more orthodox idealist accounts.[19]

It is here, in de Man's work especially, that a connection is forged between the poetics of English Romanticism and the discourse of German "aesthetic ideology" from Kant, through Hegel and Schiller to the interests of contemporary criticism. For it is precisely by refusing to address such problems — by adopting a mystified "organicist" aesthetic dependent on those high Romantic claims for metaphor, symbol, and other such privileged tropes — that criticism avoids that strenuous "labor of the negative" involved in all authentic thinking about language and representation. When de Man reads Kant, he typically fastens on those moments where the text has resort to analogies or figural expressions at odds with its own purported argument, and where consequently there is a choice to be made between fidelity to Kant's known ideas on a given topic and fidelity to the letter of his text.[20] In opting for this second alternative, de Man also proposes an "ethics of reading" that considerably complicates the standard hermeneutic view. With Kant, as we saw, it amounts to a rejection of that simplified organicist way of thinking which attempts to transcend ontological difference, or to naturalize the language of poetry, by collapsing the two distinct orders of *sensuous perception* on the one hand and *linguistic representation* on the other. And this leads on to a questioning of that wholesale aesthetic ideology which has managed to impose its terms upon successive generations of (otherwise very diverse) critics, philosophers, and theorists. It is, de Man argues, a repeated misreading of specific passages in Kant that has enabled this widespread mystification to gain such a hold on the discourse of aesthetics. And the same applies to those canonical readings of Romantic poetry which accept its high claims for metaphor and symbol — its rhetoric of unmediated vision — as a matter of revealed truth.

It is understandable, therefore, that Miller should take such a keen interest in James's *The Art of the Novel*. For the Prefaces indeed make an ethical point of not claiming privileged access to the author's mind or original intentions. They propose to take a law always from the text in hand, not least when this transports criticism into regions of productive ambivalence and doubt which offer their own reward. "What could be more delightful," James asks, "than to enjoy a sense of the absolute in such easy conditions? The deviations and differences might of course not have broken out at all, but from the moment they began so naturally to multiply they became, as I say, my very terms of cognition.[21] This last could well be taken for a phrase of de Man's, with its way of insisting categorically that *the text* is what compels our response, even where the terms of that response appear to go against the express meaning of the text. But there is also the sense — quite foreign to de Man — of a delighted receptiveness to novel possibilities of reading which open up beyond the confines of a narrower, more strictly self-regulating hermeneutic creed. And this is no doubt one reason why the Prefaces possess such compulsive interest for a critic of Miller's highly speculative bent. With de Man one always feels the opposite, negative compulsion at work — as if the entire effort of that singular intelligence were devoted to foreclosing, regretfully but firmly, whatever new dimensions of sense the adventurous reader might hope to find.

One could make the point briefly by remarking that a work like *Allegories of Reading* is utterly different, in its aims and effects, from one like William Empson's exuberantly inventive *Seven Types of Ambiguity*. With Hillis Miller, this inventiveness is still very much in evidence, despite his resolve in the present book not to yield hostages to those foes of deconstruction who regard it as a species of mere irresponsible "freeplay". So on the one hand, as he writes, "I want to make James's text my law, . . . to follow what he says with entire fidelity and obedience, to see whether what he says about the ethics of reading may be made the basis of a universal legislation" (*ER*, p. 102). But on the other he is just as much taken with that reverse side of the Jamesian paradox which finds the critic delightedly enjoying "a sense of the absolute in such easy conditions." Miller remains characteristically a brilliant and ingenious close reader of texts, neither of which epithets would really hit the mark if applied to de Man.

In the end one feels that Miller's pleasure in these paradoxes has more to do with their *aesthetic* yield — with what they enable him to say, strikingly afresh, about literary texts — than with anything strictly pertaining to the Kantian antinomies of freewill and necessity. Not that he fails to make good his case for deconstruction as a principled activity with its own distinct standards for what may and what may not be said about texts. But these standards again have more to do with a sense of extended interpretative scope than with the kind of rigorous, argumentative drive that powers the writings of de Man. If one wanted to construct a genealogy for Miller's criticism it would begin with Kant, to be sure, but then run down through Schiller's idea of "aesthetic education" to the modern emphasis on textual close reading as a means to liberate the sheer multiplicity of meaning contained in poetic language. For de Man, on the contrary, Schiller represents one of those highly seductive "aberrations," or modes of misreading, in the wake of Kantian aesthetics.[22] His philosophy is based on the idea that art can bring about an ultimate harmony or reconciliation between the various, otherwise disparate orders of human knowledge and experience. "Aesthetic education" is the process of learning how the mind can and should take pleasure in a jointly sensuous and intellectual exercise which brings the various faculties into a state of ideally reciprocal interdependence. In other words, it takes for granted that organic continuity of perceptual, cognitive, and linguistic structures which Kant (according to de Man) attempted but significantly failed to articulate. And the same seductive notion is at work, he argues, in those modern critics (like I.A. Richards) who identify the value of poetic language with its power to evoke a rich and complex experience, a sense of organic "unity in multiplicity" which brings the reader into privileged contact with a mind at full creative stretch.[23] Such ideas — and their extension into various kinds of formalist poetic — exert their potent appeal only by ignoring (as de Man would argue) the very real problems bequeathed by Kant to any project that seeks to reconcile the claims of aesthetic and ethical judgment.

III

In the essays of his last decade, de Man set out to argue the political consequences of this widespread aesthetic ideology. His chief contention was that the discourse on aesthetic values after Kant had been kidnapped, so to speak, by a mode of premature organicist or totalizing thought which collapsed certain crucial distinctions in the Kantian enterprise. "What gives the aesthetic its power and hence its practical, political impact, is its intimate link with knowledge, the epistemological implications that are always in play when the aesthetic appears over the horizon of discourse."[24] But this power can take effect in two very different ways: as a *critique* of aesthetic ideology, directed toward those persistent confusions of linguistic and phenomenal reality, or as a means to further mystify thought by claiming a knowledge on the far side of all such bad antinomies. This is the paradox embraced by most versions of aesthetic understanding, of "a wisdom that lies somehow beyond cognition and self-knowledge, yet that can only be reached by ways of the process it is said to overcome" (AF, p. 265). Such is (for instance) the high Romantic faith, carried on by modern critics like Abrams, in the power of language to transcend the opposition between sensuous and intellectual modes of apprehension. What tends to be ignored in this will to reconcile disjunct or opposing truth-claims is the element of coercive mystification that always, implicitly, goes along with it.

So when de Man argues against this aestheticizing drift in post-Kantian idealist thought, his reasons have as much to do with politics — with questions of power and authority — as with issues of purely epistemological import. For there is, he argues, a sinister aspect to the claims for "aesthetic education" put forward by thinkers from Schiller to the present day. The state of mind these thinkers envisage is one in which the various faculties (sensuous, cognitive, emotive, and ethical) would be subject to an overriding harmony of interests achieved through aesthetic contemplation. Its utopian appeal comes from the promise of a perfect *equilibrium* of forces, a condition that would ultimately point the way beyond all forms of conflict, inward and outward. It is not, de Man writes, simply a state of mind but "a principle of political value and authority that has its own claims on the shape and the limits of our freedom" (AF, p. 264). One obvious example here would be T.S. Eliot's massively influential myth of a "dissociation of sensibility," an event that occurred (so we are given to believe) around the mid-seventeenth century, and which subsequently left its debilitating mark on the history of English poetry, language, and culture.[25] Before that time — especially in the age of Shakespeare, Donne, and their contemporaries — thought and emotion supposedly existed in a balanced, harmonious state whose outward manifestation was the ordered, hierarchical structure of society at large. With the Civil War period there came about a fall into religious difference, class division, political and ideological conflict. The signs of this collapse (so Eliot argued) are there to be read in the poetry of Milton, a style whose sheer remoteness from the living energies of Shakespearean English serves to enforce the diagnostic point. What emerges from Eliot's account is precisely the linkage that de Man perceives between a certain, highly simplified notion of poetic language and an attitude that reduces all history to a species of reactionary myth. For of course it is no coincidence that Milton — preëminently the voice and conscience of Civil War republican politics — should figure as the poet whose stylistic influence Eliot in some sense blames for this process of long-drawn secular decline. From a given aesthetic standpoint (one that equates the chief good of poetry with a straightforward match between language, thought, and perception) Eliot develops his mythical account of English cultural history.

This example helps to explain why de Man should attribute such political importance to these seemingly ultra-specialized issues of aesthetic theory and principle. "For it is," he writes, "as a political force that the aesthetic still concerns us as one of the most powerful ideological drives to act upon the reality of history." And again: "what is then called, in conscious reference to Kant and to the questionable version of Kant that is found in Schiller, the *aesthetic*, is not a separate category but a principle of articulation between various known faculties, activities, and modes of cognition" (AF, pp. 264–65). It is in the will to transcend these articulate distinctions — to overcome them in the name of a mythical state exceeding the grasp of mere reason — that aesthetic ideology most strongly asserts its hold. In Schiller, this state is expressly represented in terms of a liberating movement, a passage that leads through and beyond the oppressive antinomies of present-day thought. It can thus appear as a utopian ideal, fixing its sights on a future stage of perfected human development when the faculties would be free to develop in harmonious coexistence, and society at large would give back an image of this inward state of grace. For de Man, on the contrary, such thinking leads to a kind of aesthetic imperialism, an authoritarian drive whose signs may be read in the subsequent uses of organicist myths and metaphors. Thus in Eliot, for instance, the idea of "tradition" goes along with that of a imaginary, long-lost cultural order when thought and sensibility were as yet untouched by the dislocating forces of secular history and politics. We should therefore be on guard, de Man writes, against the "potentially violent streak in Schiller's own aesthetic theory," the ease with which its utopian values can always be converted into a backward-looking, mystified vision of cultural order. "If the aesthetic model is itself flawed or, worse, if it covers up this lesion by a self-serving idealization, then the classical concept of aesthetic education is open to suspicion" (AF, p. 280).

For de Man, then, the ethics of reading is closely bound up with a *political* critique of the powers vested in aesthetic ideology. If his opponents (the Marxists especially) have failed to perceive this dimension of his work, their mistake is symptomatic of a wider misunderstanding, one that ignores the prominent role of aesthetic ideas and analogies in the process of constructing a naturalized, commonsense world of experience. "We think we are at ease in our own language, we feel a coziness, a familiarity, a shelter in the language we call our own, in which we think that we are not alienated" (*RT*, p. 84). But this assurance comes largely from the idea we have that meanings, intentions, and phenomenal cognitions *must* correspond through some preëstablished harmony in the nature of language and experience. As de Man readily admits, such assumptions go deep and may perhaps be indispensable to the conduct of our everyday linguistic and social lives. But they nevertheless have to ignore the evidence — most strikingly offered by problems in the theory and practice of translation — that language may produce anomalous, aberrant, or seemingly random signifying structures that resist all forms of semantic accountability.

These reflections arise in the course of de Man's late essay on Walter Benjamin, more specifically on Benjamin's cryptic text "The Task of the Translator." They make the point that our sense of being "at home" in some particular language is closely related to the naturalizing process by which ideological values appear as simply, self-evidently true. And from this it follows — according to one of de Man's most willfully provocative statements — that those who routinely reproach deconstruction for its indifference to historical realities or its supposed political quietism "are merely stating their fear at having their own ideological mystifications exposed by the tool they are trying to discredit. They are, in short, very poor readers of Marx's *German Ideology*" (*RT*, p. 11). Deconstruction would then be a vigilant practice of textual critique alert to those moments where the drive for aesthetic transcendence creates the kind of timeless, mystified ideal of "tradition" (or "unified sensibility") so potently embodied in Eliot's critical writings.

It is significant in this regard that Hillis Miller devotes his first chapter to a defense of the "ethics of reading" as opposed to other, more expressly political priorities. He does so chiefly by arguing that Marxist and sociological approaches come down to a certain elective *tropology* of reading, their truth-claims reducing to various privileged figures of thought which deconstructive analysis can pinpoint easily enough. Thus "mirroring, reflection, or mimesis is a species of metaphor," while ideology itself is a variant of anamorphosis, a trope which Miller glosses as "the transformation of one form into another which is recognizable as being a distortion of its original only when viewed from a certain angle" (*FR*, pp. 6–7). And again, the notion of context — indispensable to any sociological poetics — reveals itself at last as hovering vaguely "between metonymy in the sense of mere contingent adjacency and synecdoche, part for whole, with an assumption that the part is in some way genuinely like the whole" (*ER*, p. 6). In a couple of pages Miller runs deftly through the gamut of figural themes and variations which he takes to underlie all current — and perhaps all conceivable — versions of the "literature-and-history" paradigm. Hence his claim that the study of texts must always, in the last analysis, come down to a study of language in its various tropological aspects, even where the critic is most firmly committed to a Marxist or cultural-materialist position.[26] Otherwise the search for "grounds" in literary criticism — for some ultimate, privileged explanatory model — must end up by reducing literature to "no more than a minor by-product of history, not something that in any way makes history" (*ER*, p. 8).

Now there is a subtle but crucial difference between Miller's and de Man's way of making this point. For de Man also — as Marxist critics are quick to point out — history is an eminently *textual* domain, a realm of discursive tropes and transformations to which we can have no direct, unmediated access. But of course this would apply equally to those forms of advanced critical thinking which call themselves Marxist or historical-materialist but which likewise acknowledge the nonavailability of any ground — any bedrock of reference or truth — outside the field of representation created by signifying practices. Such acknowledgment may take the form of an Althusserian Marxist "science" convinced that criticism can, after all, distinguish between levels of ideological misrecognition, and thus make good its own claim-to-truth as a discourse immune to those symptomatic blind spots or vagaries. But this position can only be deluded in so far as it arrogates to itself a standpoint of "meta-linguistic" detachment from the languages, discourses, or ideologies it sets out to analyze. If indeed it is the case, as poststructuralists assert — albeit at risk of paradoxically undermining their own argument — that "there is no meta-language," no escaping to the high ground of pure theory, then Althusserian Marxism is clearly open to just such a line of *tu quoque* response.

It is this kind of inconsistency that Miller is well able to exploit when he points to those various rhetorical tropes that (in his view) effectively exhaust the field of Marxist criticism and historiography. One alternative is the path traced out by Terry Eagleton in a sequence of books that move steadily away from the high Althusserian rigor of his *Criticism and Ideology* (1976).[27] Thus one now finds Eagleton advocating a return to rhetoric — or the study of language in its suasive, performative aspects — as a means of preserving the political force of criticism without laying claim to such questionable forms of epistemological certitude.[28] And this pragmatist turn is likewise evident in Frank Lentricchia's recent book *Criticism and Social Change* where he argues the case for political commitment through a sharpened understanding of the power struggles, conflicts, and tensions enacted in the language of ideological exchange.[29] For Eagleton and Lentricchia, both of them writing very much in Althusser's wake, the only way forward at present is one that abjures high theory and pins its faith to an activist rhetoric devoid of ultimate (epistemological) truth-claims.

In Chapter 1 I noted how Lentricchia mounts his polemic partly by means of a running comparison between de Man and Kenneth Burke as chief exemplars of two, radically divergent styles of rhetorical criticism. Burke represents the positive value of a thoroughly "engaged" critical practice, one that seeks constantly to grasp and demystify the powers of manipulative rhetoric and suasion encountered not only in "literary" texts but in all manner of cultural discourses. His writings should be seen, Lentricchia argues, as a fine vindication of criticism's role in the active raising of political awareness and resistance to forms of entrenched ideology. De Man, on the other hand, figures to this way of thinking as a theorist determined to obstruct or undo the potentially liberating work of cultural critique. This he achieves by endlessly directing attention to the gaps, the aporias, and moments of rhetorical "undecidability" that seem to drive a wedge between textual understanding and the real world of sociopolitical powers and interests. De Man's is therefore (so Lentricchia argues) a mystifying practice, a rhetoric whose own deepest motive — however well disguised — is to reinforce the kind of aesthetically sanctioned political quietism which runs all the way from Kant, via the "old" New Critics to this latest, most sophisticated version of textual close reading.[30].

What Lentricchia's argument fails to take into account is that whole dimension of de Man's work concerned with aesthetic ideology, with the power of language (or mystified conceptions of language, symbol, and metaphor among them) to impose false ideas of achieved understanding through the appeal to aesthetic categories. This conviction gives rise to one of the central and undoubtedly most provocative passages of his essay "The Resistance to Theory," "What we call ideology," de Man writes, "is precisely the confusion of linguistic with natural reality, of reference with phenomenalism. It follows that, more than any other mode of inquiry, including economics, the linguistics of literariness is a powerful and indispensable tool in the unmasking of ideological aberrations, as well as a determining factor in accounting for their occurrence" (*RT*, p. 11). Lentricchia mistakes the whole point of passages like this when he charges de Man with having simply fallen in with a long line of philosopher-critics determined to insulate the literary work from everything perceived as a threat to its sovereign, autonomous value. For de Man is not talking about "literature," at least in any sense of that term familiar to the discourses of present-day literary criticism. What he calls the "linguistics of literariness" is precisely the *resistance* to aesthetic sublimation, to the way that theory — "literary theory" — seeks a grounding for its own high claims in various essentialist notions of literary meaning and value. Such is the potent aesthetic ideology that de Man traces down from the Romantics to the New Criticism, from the overvaluation of symbol and metaphor to the Formalist and structuralist emphasis on poetry as a special kind of language, one that transcends the condition of everyday discourse through its power to communicate ideas in vividly "concrete" or sensuous form.

"If the return to the aesthetic is a turning away from the language of allegory and rhetoric, then it is also a turning away from literature, a breaking of the link between poetics and history" (*RT*, p. 68). This sentence (from the essay on Hans-Robert Jauss) brings together all the main points at issue in de Man's critique of aesthetic ideology.

"Literature" may be taken, on the one hand, as a body of texts possessing some unique attribute, some quiddity of style or form that sets them apart from the everyday run of communicative language. But this is to ignore the fact that "literature" is always an essentially contested concept, a term that can only be deployed in such purely self-validating fashion by repressing the knowledge of its own genealogy or historical provenance. What enables this repression to take place is precisely the aesthetic scheme of values that sets up the category "literature" as a term of absolute, transcendent value aside from all merely ideological determinants. It is against this mystified ontology that de Man directs his own, very different idea of the "literary" — namely, as denoting that resistance encountered in the reading of specific texts which prevents them from becoming mere illustrative samples of a preconceived aesthetic creed.

Thus Jauss, as we saw, can be seen to base his whole ambitious program of *Rezeptionsaesthetik* on a question-begging synthesis of poetics with historical method through the mediating term of aesthetic perception.[31] This is, de Man writes, "the very point at which the procedures of a historian such as Jauss and poeticians [such as the Russian and Czech Formalists] converge" (*RT*, p. 64). They both take for granted the existence of aesthetic attributes — "foregrounding," "defamiliarization," etc. — which characterize the literary work of art and which thus, by making it available to repeated acts of assured cognition, enable a critic like Jauss to construct his totalizing version of literary history. It is Jauss's great merit (as de Man puts it in a typically double-edged compliment) to have "perceived and demonstrated the linkage between reception and semiotics . . . The condensation of literary history and structural analysis occurs by ways of the category of the aesthetic and depends for its possibility on the stability of this category" (*RT*, p. 64). Whereas it is the function of de Man's deconstructive counter-terms ("allegory," "metonymy," etc.) to hold out against this powerful aestheticizing drift and assert the stubbornly resistant character of a language that cannot be wholly reduced to such a perfect circularity of values and assumptions. Thus "allegory is material or materialistic, in Benjamin's sense, because its dependence on the letter, on the literalism of the letter, cuts it off sharply from symbolic and aesthetic syntheses" (*RT*, p. 68).

So Lentricchia's critique is distinctly off target in so far as he ignores (or symptomatically misreads) de Man's constant invocation of the "linguistics of literariness." What is in question is *not* some ultimate privilege accruing to the "literary" as a realm of autonomous meaning and value. Rather, it is the way that language effectively undoes such claims through a reading alert to its rhetorical strategies and — inseparably linked with these — its ideological investments. Quite simply, de Man is not practicing "literary criticism" in anything like the current, institutionally accepted sense of that term. There is no ready way to categorize his work, although its arguments may be said to inhabit the endlessly contested zone between linguistic philosophy, rhetoric, epistemology, and *Ideologiekritik*. What gives his writings their critical force is de Man's understanding of the errors and confusions brought about by a failure to observe more precisely where these modes of cognition come up against their own conceptual limits. Hence the mystifying power exerted by those erroneous readings of Kant whose effects, de Man argues, extend to just about every variety of present-day literary theory. "Whenever the aesthetic is invoked as an appeal to clarity and order, whenever, in other words, a symptom is made into a remedy for the disorder that it signals, a great deal of caution is in order" (*RT*, p. 64). In such cases — especially those where some large historical claim is being advanced — "the suspicion arises that aesthetic judgment has trespassed beyond its legitimate epistemological reach."

Miller's approach in *The Ethics of Reading* remains, by contrast, very much on the side of "literary" deconstruction. Thus he moves from an opening chapter on Kant, one that raises issues in the province of ethical reason, to a sequence of essays on the various novelists who allow such issues to be neatly transposed into literary-critical terms. And of course this progression is shrewdly prepared for by Miller's latching onto precisely those passages in Kant that open the way for a diagnostic reading of their fictive, narrative, or figural aspects. Unlike de Man, Miller still makes room for an appeal to the literary, not (to be sure) in the sense of some absolute, transcendent realm of aesthetic value, but at least on account of its *superior* power to unmask — deconstruct — the claims of philosophic reason. His book, after all, has a distinct narrative shape of its own, a storyline that runs from the high moral earnestness of Kantian critique to the complex, ironic, self-delighting play of creative intelligence manifest in James's *Art of The Novel*. The act of reading, as Miller describes it, is "an act which is enlivening and momentous . . . It has import, and it is life-giving . . . Re-reading brings about an influx of spiritual power. In that sense it is exhilarating, 'infinitely interesting and amusing'" (*ER*, p. 116). It would no doubt be oversimple to read this passage — couched as it is in the interpreter's equivalent of free indirect style — as straightforwardly expressing Miller's own attachment to an ethos of so-called interpretative "freeplay," For one thing, he goes straight on (within the next half-paragraph) to cite that most sternly self-denying of de Manian ordinances, that reading is an "argument" precisely in so far as it "has to go against the grain of what one would want to happen in the name of what has to happen" (*ER*, p. 116). But such reminders count for less, to Miller's way of reading, than the sheer sense of open possibilities — of new and "exhilarating" freedoms —

experienced in the reading of literary texts. And this is where his criticism rejoins that line of aesthetic-speculative thought which de Man traces from Schiller to the discourse of current literary theory. Miller's essays can thus be seen as a recapitulation, in summary form, of the change that overtook post-Kantian philosophy when it turned to the aesthetic as the source of its highest values, rather than as a persistently problematic term in the critique of knowledge and representation.

De Man makes this point most clearly in a passage from the essay on Hans-Robert Jauss. "The aesthetic is, by definition, a seductive notion that appeals to the pleasure principle, a eudaemonic judgment that can displace and conceal values of truth and falsehood likely to be more resilient to desire than values of pleasure and pain" (*RT*, p. 64). His own writings hold out against the power of aesthetic seduction in various closely connected ways. They reject the appeal to "literary" values, except in so far as "literature" is construed as a class of texts whose character it is to resist or negate every attempt at self-sufficient (aesthetic) definition. They nowhere achieve the kind of satisfying sequence, the sense of well-made narrative shape, that Miller so strikingly brings off in *The Ethics of Reading*. This no doubt has to do with de Man's mistrust of totalizing arguments and his Nietzschean conviction that truth is to be found — if anywhere — only at a level of intensive engagement with specific textual issues that cannot be treated in large-scale, systematic fashion. So it is that his essays, when collected in book form, signally fail to produce the sort of orderly, sequential pattern that readers most often expect. Here we might recall de Man's rueful observation in his Preface to *The Rhetoric of Romanticism*: "laid out in a roughly chronological sequence, they do not evolve in a manner that easily allows for dialectical progression . . . Rather, it seems that they always start again from scratch and that their conclusions fail to add up to anything. If some secret principle of summation is at work here, I do not feel qualified to articulate it . . . "[32] The totalizing drive goes along with that desire for organic unifying principles which de Man locates at the heart of aesthetic ideology. It is here that his work stands decidedly apart from the project of literary deconstruction, a project that Miller, in *The Ethics of Reading*, carries on at a high level of subtlety and refinement.

5

Against a New Pragmatism:
Law, Deconstruction and the Interests of
Theory

I

There is a simplified polemical response to the case "against theory" which goes roughly as follows. We are all of us doing theory all the time, whether we like it or not. Mostly we get along happily enough without needing to spell out the kind of theory we are working with, or the kinds of justification we might produce if challenged. Still there is this tacit theoretical dimension to everything we do, from the politics of everyday behavior to the business of interpreting literary texts. Those who deny this argument on commonsense or pragmatist grounds are usually (as J.M. Keynes once remarked) in the grip of a bad old theory which has left them blind to their own ruling prejudices and assumptions. So the issue is not, as the anti-theorists would have it, a choice between just getting on with the job or allowing oneself to be distracted by unreal problems. What it comes down to is the question whether or not one is prepared to think at all beyond the limits imposed by received commonsense wisdom. Taking a stand "against theory" — as if such a thing were really possible — is tantamount to rejecting Socrates' claim that the unexamined life is not worth living.

This position has the weakness of most *tu quoque* rejoinders: it can always be turned right around and used to support exactly the opposite conclusion. Perhaps we are doing theory all the time and prevented from seeing it merely by our own stubborn preconceptions. But one could just as well argue — along pragmatist lines — that we are none of us theorists in the strong sense of the word that some of us (the pro-theory lobby) want to maintain. That is to say, the very notion of "theory" rests on a mistake if it claims that one can stand *outside* some existing context (language-game, cultural convention, "interpretive community," or whatever) and theorize from a vantage point of pure, disinterested reason. Stanley Fish has erected this argument into something like a structural *a priori* for literary criticism, legal discourse, and the human sciences in general.[1] There is simply no getting "beyond" interpretation to a level of metalinguistic inquiry where the interests of truth would finally prevail over all those partial motives and interests that distort our everyday pre-critical understanding. And this on the grounds that theory is always already a product of interpretation, a reasoning that proceeds on its own basis of inbuilt values and assumptions, and which wouldn't make sense in default of our willingness to take that context into account. So literary critics are deluded when they think to back up their position on this or that interpretative issue by appealing to some *theory* — hermeneutics, deconstruction, reader response — by way of ultimate authority. Such appeals are always open to the twofold objection 1) that the theory can be nothing more than a rationalization of interpretative interests, and 2) that its relevance to the case in hand must anyway be established by a further act of interpretation.

So theory is everywhere and nowhere. It is what we do all the time (wittingly or not) and what we never succeed in doing, despite our belief to the contrary. And there may not be very much to choose between these rival positions. For if theory is indeed — as the first party claims — an inescapable condition of each and every interpretative act, then what could be the *point* of defending it as if there were something (some distinctive activity) that stood in need of such defense? The knock-down argument that everyone is a theorist would end up by subverting its own major premise. The adversary case looks stronger, since it rests on precisely this argument: that theory is an enterprise inherently deluded on account of its self-promoting separatist claims. But one can still remark of Fish that he arrives at this conclusion through a process of reasoning by no means free from theoretical premises of its own. Steven Knapp and Walter Benn Michaels make this point in an essay that finds just about everyone — Fish included — guilty of lapsing back into one kind of "theory" or another.[2] It is worth looking closely at their argument here since it pushes the current neo-pragmatist line to a point where every possible alternative seems to be played off the field.

Knapp and Michaels take issue with Fish on the question of whether knowledge and true belief amount to the same thing for all practical purposes. If this is the case — if it is just another theoreticist delusion to think of them as two different orders of truth-claim — then clearly the pragmatist wins hands down. For the whole point of theory is to give good reasons for questioning some of our beliefs (those things we merely *hold* to be true) and thus arriving at a better, more enlightened or rational standpoint. Knapp and Michaels agree with Fish that such a standpoint is unattainable since we can never give reasons for not believing what we *do* in fact believe. Or, differently put: any reasons adduced for abandoning previous beliefs would still be offered from a certain point of view, on the basis of alternative convictions. It simply doesn't make sense (Fish argues) to set up this dichotomy between genuine knowledge on the one hand and what we take for genuine knowledge on the other. For the state of belief just *is* the condition of accepting certain truth-claims, ideas, or propositions as warranting rational assent and therefore as standing in no need of further justification. We are unable to doubt what we believe since doubting it would lead us to believe something different. In Wittgensteinian terms, the "logical grammar" of belief includes the necessity of claiming to know — and of being in a good position to know — those things we believe.

Knapp and Michaels have no quarrel with this aspect of Fish's argument. They likewise go along with his view that "progress" is an empty notion when applied to the history of variant readings and interpretative styles. It would only make sense if those readings could finally be assessed against the standard of some ultimate truth accessible to theory or method. And of course this belief is just another form of the same old delusion that holds out for a knowledge transcending all mere relativities of time and place. Knapp and Michaels concede (with Fish) that such ideas may have a basis of purely *psychological* necessity — in the sense that literary critics (or for that matter scientists and philosophers) would hardly have a motive for carrying on without the conviction of advancing toward some kind of truth. Thus in Fish's words, "the idea of progress is inevitable, not, however, because there *is* progress in the sense of a clearer and clearer sight of an independent object but because the *feeling* of having progressed is an inevitable consequence of the firmness with which we hold our beliefs."[3] But it is here that Knapp and Michaels part company with Fish over his further claim that there is really no question of progress having been made; that earlier critical performances which (to us) look so crude and wrong-headed must in fact be seen "not as unsuccessful attempts to approximate our own but as extensions of a literary culture whose assumptions were not inferior but merely different."[4] To which Knapp and Michaels respond by asking what *position*, what epistemological vantage point wuld have to be claimed by anyone who could thus think to discount his or her ruling beliefs. For it is (they remind us) a main plank in Fish's arguments against critical theory that there is no way of separating knowledge and true belief; that the convictions and values we actually work with are all that can be had in the way of legitimizing grounds. So when Fish makes a precept of the relativist case — claiming we can *know* that progress is a myth, despite our constitutive need to think otherwise — Knapp and Michaels are ready with the standard diagnosis. "To imagine that we can see the beliefs we hold as no better than but 'merely different' from opposing beliefs held by others is to imagine a position from which we can see our beliefs without really believing them."[5]

All the same Fish comes closest to satisfying the Knapp-Michaels requirements for a critic untouched by the modern theoreticist taint. If he falls into error, it is by virtue of his wanting — very rightly, they think — to question a certain Enlightenment myth of reason, knowledge, and truth. Fish indeed goes so far in this direction that he winds up briefly in the opposite camp, translating the pragmatist argument (that what is true is what is good in the way of belief) into a kind of theoretical prescription (that *true* pragmatists can and must apply this lesson to their own beliefs). In which case — Knapp and Michaels argue — there would have to exist some higher court of judgment where reason presided over the mere convictions that happen to capture our minds from time to time. But this line of appeal is simply not open, since any verdict handed down by that higher court would also be a choice among rival interpretations — still (that is to say) an item of belief and not the result of applying some presuppositionless abstract rule.

The analogy from law is important for Fish since it is here — especially in current debates about judicial review — that the hankering for "rules" is most apparent. For without such a framework of regulative concepts law would be open (so it is argued) to all manner of corrupting influences from political parties and pressure groups. So there must be some core of settled rules or decision-procedures by which to adjudicate in accordance with law where the issue would otherwise come down to a clash of interests or priorities. The same would apply to those "hard cases" which don't exactly fit the provisions of any existing law, or for which no precedent suffices to determine a verdict one way or the other. Here again, attempts are made to theorize this awkward situation by appealing to rules of interpretative conduct, either in terms of framing intent (what the lawmaker[s] had in mind) or of guidelines for establishing the relevant context. But such arguments just won't work, according to Fish, since they rest on the idea that one can get *beyond* interpretation to some firm procedural ground where all these problems would simply fall away. This ignores the fact that, for any given "rule," there will always be a range of conflicting interpretations which require the addition of further, supplementary rules. And so on, to the point where this whole way of thinking becomes demonstrably absurd. Attempts to put a stop to the infinite regress — as for instance, by appealing to self-entrenched clauses or a primary "rule of recognition" —

must ultimately fail for the same reason. That is to say, the quest for theory reaches a stage where all parties must at last come round to the view that everything is a product of interpretation, rules and theories included.

Then Fish has to ask what *consequences* would flow from this belated understanding that theory was a pointless (or impossible) enterprise. If the pragmatist is right and theory doesn't make any difference — if it is just interpretation under another, more grandiose name — then it should also be the case that giving up theory must leave things pretty much as they were. But Fish thinks there will be a shift in the currency of debate, as people come to realize that motives, principles, and interests — not "theories" — are the bottom line of appeal in every case. Again he instances the "problem" of judicial review, of how it has come about that the Supreme Court — a small group of men and women appointed for life — can determine or contest the validity of laws drawn up by elected representatives of the people. Such practices can be justified (as some would argue) only on the basis of a strictly non-partisan *theory*, an "argument that does not presuppose the interests of any party or the supremacy of any political goal or borrow its terms from the practice it would regulate."[6] Otherwise they are forced to conclude that no such legitimizing grounds exist, and that law must therefore come down to the assertion of straightforward coercive power. Theoretical jurisprudence will continue to flourish so long as the debate is conducted on these terms, just as literary theory remains in business while critics persist in making a problem of matters like meaning, intention, and validity. If all parties could be brought to see that such anxieties were simply misplaced, then the resulting change of view would indeed have consequences, though not — Fish stresses — *theoretical* consequences. Should everyone be persuaded by the case against theory (a most unlikely outcome, he admits) then "the search for certain kinds of justification might very well cease or, at least, be carried on with altered hopes, and that would be a consequence."[7] But it is wrong, he insists, to argue from this negative conclusion (that giving up theory may have practical effects) to the positive claim that theoretical commitments must, after all, have some distinctively theory-based character. In each case the question of "consequences" can only be decided on empirical grounds, by noting how people argue and behave whatever their notional justification according to this or that theory. For the fact that one is persuaded by a given point of view — a position on some issue of law, politics, or interpretative practice — can never be an outcome of theory in the strong consequentialist sense. It can only be a post hoc justification for beliefs that neither require such a theory nor follow inevitably from it. To think otherwise is to fall into the trap that Fish repeatedly springs on the theorists, and which Knapp and Michaels in turn spring on Fish: the delusion (as all these pragmatists would have it) that theory has consequences beyond what is explainable in terms of straightforward belief.

II

This debate goes deep and far back in the history of philosophic thought. For Plato, it is the difference between *doxa* and *episteme*, received opinion on the one hand and knowledge (arrived at through active critical reasoning) on the other. In Kant, it is the claim of an Enlightenment outlook which equates human dignity and truth with the freedom to criticize existing beliefs, institutions, and values. Any hopes of improvement in the moral and social sphere are pinned to this faith in the emancipating power of a reason that is not wholly given over to the currency of orthodox opinion. There is a clear enough connection between Kant's thinking on "technical" problems in the philosophy of mind and his attitude to questions of a wider sociopolitical import. The connection is spelled out in his essay "What is Enlightenment?" where Kant upholds the liberty of each individual to think out his or her considered position with regard to certain dictates of religious and ethical belief.[8] This leads to his contrasting the "private" and "public" uses of reason, the private (paradoxically) having to do with those social or citizenly roles where submission to authority may rightly be required, while the public involves that critical exercise of mind which entitles us to participate, as autonomous individuals, in the enlightened community of thought. Opting out of this community — assenting uncritically in the public as well as the private sphere — is for Kant a dereliction of the duty thus devolved upon all thinking subjects. And this means resisting any attempt by church or state to encroach upon the freedoms legitimately claimed by those thinkers (notably the philosophers) whose role it is to theorize the relations of knowledge and belief. Where authority seeks to annul such distinctions — as by laying down rules and limits for the exercise of critical reason — it is no longer respecting this proper separation of realms.

This whole project must be self-deluding if one accepts the kinds of argument advanced by Knapp and Michaels. According to their diagnosis, it is precisely at the moment when he lapses into a Kantian way of thinking that Fish betrays his own best pragmatist insights. Theory is the name (or one modern name — "philosophy" and "enlightenment" are others) for that recurrent delusion that insists on separating knowledge from true belief. And this applies equally to "positive" and "negative" theories, to the sort that holds out for ultimate solutions and the sort that finds sophisticated reasons for believing that no such solutions are available. Among literary critics the dividing line would fall between exponents of various hermeneutical approaches (like E.D. Hirsch) and those others — notably the deconstructionists — who think to problematize language, meaning, and interpretation by showing that the hermeneutic model just won't work. Where Hirsch goes wrong (Knapp and Michaels argue) is in driving an impossible wedge between meaning and authorial intention. At least, this implication begins to emerge in the course of Hirsch's *theoretical* arguments, although on the face of it nothing could be further from his own express position. Thus Knapp and Michaels wholeheartedly endorse Hirsch's statement that the meaning of a text "is, and can be, nothing other than the author's meaning," which in turn "is determined once and for all by the character of the speaker's intention."[9] But when Hirsch gets onto methodological ground he is somehow induced to separate these terms and so create all manner of unnecessary problems. "He begins by defining textual meaning as the author's intended meaning and then suggests that the best way to find textual meaning is to look for authorial intention. But if meaning and intended meaning are already the same, it's hard to see how looking for one provides an objective method — or any sort of method — for looking for the other; looking for one just *is* looking for the other."[10] And so it goes with all theories which conjure up distinctions (belief/knowledge, meaning/intention) where in truth no such distinctions can ever be consistently maintained. If hermeneutics rests on a mistake, it is one that underpins the entire theoretical enterprise, a constitutive error without which that enterprise would show up as so much pointless, misguided talk. And this — as Knapp and Michaels see it — is indeed a consummation devoutly to be wished.

Negative theorists, like Derrida and de Man, draw opposite conclusions from the same erroneous premise. That is to say, they assume that meaning can be determined (or knowledge arrived at) only on the basis of some deep further fact about language that would leave no room for hermeneutic doubt. So if it turns out that no such deep further fact exists — that neither context nor intention will serve as a grounding rationale — then the way seems open to a deconstructive rhetoric of aberrant tropes and random signification that exceeds all the bounds of interpretative reason. Instead of just accepting (like Knapp and Michaels) that meaning and intention are synonymous terms, these theorists erect a whole negative hermeneutics on the imagined noncoincidence between them. Thus when Derrida takes issue with John R. Searle on the topic of speech-act philosophy his argument is 1) that *intentions* won't do as a test of performative good faith, since speech-acts are conventional ("iterable") forms of address whose effect cannot depend upon the utterer's present intent; and 2) that any appeal to *contextual* factors — the right thing said by the right person in the right place — is likewise doomed to fail, since speech-acts by their very nature can always be cited, taken "out of context," adapted to improbable circumstances and so forth.[11] To Knapp and Michaels this seems nothing more than a species of perverse negative reaction, a last ditch retreat from the hermeneutic quest for determinate meanings and intentions. Only by ignoring one self-evident fact about language — that it *must* possess meaning and intentionality in order to be recognized as such — can Derrida's arguments appear in the least degree plausible.

In de Man also, as we have seen, the breakdown of hermeneutic faith — the way that language seems capable of functioning in a purely machine-like way, devoid of intentionalist guarantees — produces a radical scepticism as regards meaning and interpretative truth. De Man finds a twofold deconstructive process everywhere at work in the texts of Western tradition. On the one hand there is a rhetoric of tropes whose effect is to subvert (or to render "undecidable") any utterance seemingly couched in straightforward constative terms. On the other there is a repetitive, quasi-mechanical "grammar" of figural drives and substitutions which makes it impossible for language — the language of poetry, criticism, and philosophy — to maintain the delusion of authentic, self-present meaning. Rhetoric "undoes" grammar and logic by creating the possibility of utterances (e.g. the rhetorical question) whose meaning can never be pinned down in terms of propositional content. But it is equally the case that grammar "undoes" rhetoric since the tropes have a random, aleatory character, one that seems quite indifferent to meaning and intent. And so it comes about that, for de Man, "there can be no use of language which is not within a certain perspective thus radically formal, i.e. mechanical, no matter how deeply this aspect may be concealed by aesthetic, formalistic delusions."[12] From the pragmatist standpoint espoused by Knapp and Michaels, this "perspective" is wrongheaded or, indeed, simply unavailable.

So hermeneutics and deconstruction come down to the same theoreticist mistake of ignoring the absolute inseparability of meaning and authorial intent. The one says in effect: "when confronted with language, read it as a speech-act;" the other responds: "when confronted with what seems to be a speech-act, read it as language."[12] Such at least is the Knapp-Michaels diagnosis, with varying degrees of support from others in the neo-pragmatist camp. It is an argument whose consequences are even more crucial in the field of legal interpretation. For here it must involve the wholesale rejection of any theory that claimed to criticize existing juridical norms from a different (implicitly more rational or enlightened) position. As Fish remarks, this debate has a special pertinence and force in the context of American law, where a written Constitution is framed (for better or worse) in terms that admit a wide range of competing interpretations. Particularly in the area of "fundamental rights" — racial and sexual equality, freedom of thought and speech, religious education, abortion, and other such issues — the judges are notoriously able to arrive at differing conclusions on the basis of a single, self-identical clause. To Fish this seems a perfectly natural state of affairs, and in any case not a situation that "theory" could hope to clear up. When constitutional lawyers, professors of jurisprudence and suchlike fret about the absence of interpretative ground rules, they are betraying the old desire for a knowledge that transcends mere conviction or belief. Others again, having failed to discover such rules, conclude that "the legal process is political through and through and is therefore a sham."[14] Thus debates on the question of judicial review tend to replicate the kind of drastic antinomy — the all-or-nothing attitude to textual meaning — that characterizes present-day literary theory. They could best be recalled to good sense, Fish argues, if the two contending parties would simply accept 1) that no justifying *theory* will ever be discovered, and 2) that this is nothing to worry about, since debate can still proceed — as it always has — by airing straightforward differences of view. Subtracting the illusory theoretical component will then have the wholly beneficial effect of showing up those differences in a clearer, more searching light.

A survey of the literature (the current law journals) confirms Fish's point that the problems besetting literary theory have migrated into other adjacent fields.[15] One school in particular — the Critical Legal Studies Group — makes a program of questioning received ideas on the basis of arguments derived very largely from "literary" deconstruction.[16] These theorists maintain (like Fish up to a point) that the law in each given case cannot be determined by any rule, protocol, or set form of reasoning; that judgments are arrived at through a process of interpretative *choice* between conflicting positions, and must therefore always be open to challenge or review. Furthermore, there is no appeal to any ultimate authority vested in the documents, the texts, and case histories that make up legal tradition. For the meaning of those texts is likewise subject to endless interpretative argument. Meaning cannot be fixed for all time — as a naive hermeneutics would have it — whether by the framers' original intentions or by ground rules implicit in the nature of judicial reasoning. On these grounds they conclude that neutrality in law is the merest of legitimizing myths — an idea sustained only by the need to disguise political interests and motives. Their favorite epigraph is the celebrated quip of Anatole France: that "the law, in its majestic equality, forbids the rich as well as the poor to sleep under bridges, to beg in the streets, and to steal bread".

So far there would seem to be general agreement between Fish and the Critical Legal Studies position. Both take the line that theory is useless if by "theory" we mean the search for determinate meanings, or for rules and decision-procedures that would henceforth regulate the practice of legal interpretation. Each declares in favor of an open debate on values, priorities, and social interests which could then be argued out directly and not disguised behind a rhetoric of judicial neutrality or disinterest. But this resemblance turns out to have sharp limits when it comes to specifying the *kind* of political argument that would follow from the two positions. For Fish, the appeal to a broad-based consensus (or "interpretive community") is as far as one can get in the quest for justifying principles.[17] That community would consist of a specialized subgroup (judges, professors, constitutional lawyers, experts of various kinds) whose opinions must in turn be endorsed or found convincing by a wider (nonspecialized) public. Arguments make sense only in so far as they are couched in communally acceptable terms, that is, to the extent that they respect what conventionally *counts* as valid judicial reasoning. For the great mistake of theory (we recall) is precisely its belief that grounds exist — theoretical grounds — for getting outside the current consensus of knowledge-constitutive interests. For Fish, this clearly precludes any critique of that consensus which would challenge its validity by pointing to the conflicts, aporias, or illogicalities that are rendered invisible by the norms of prevailing discourse. Such an exercise would be altogether pointless — indeed unintelligible — since its reasoning would fail to strike the relevant "community" as possessing the right kind of argumentative force. Effective argument can only be a matter of appealing to principles whose validity is established by common assent among various (more or less qualified) bodies of opinion. It is therefore inconceivable — according to Fish — that theory could establish some alternative ground, some Archimedean point of critical leverage from which to challenge, subvert, or deconstruct the whole basis of consensual belief.

For the Critical Legal Studies Group, conversely, theoretical activity still has a vital role to play, though not the same reassuring role that it plays in more conservative forms of juridical thinking. Here the main object is to point up the various antinomies that plague the discourse of legal philosophy, among them the conflicts between fact and value, the "letter" and the "spirit" of the law, the duty to interpret what is (notionally) there in the text, and the need to keep faith with changing social and political values. As one commentator describes it, the dilemma comes down to this:

> For a theory to generate answers, it must be mechanical, yet no mechanical theory can render an adequate account of our experience of legitimate moral choice . . . Moreover, the history of legal thought has repeatedly demonstrated that *any* indeterminacy in a theory fatally undermines the appearance of determinacy elsewhere . . . someone who opposes a rule or an outcome within the supposedly determinate, objective core will inevitably use an open-ended standard to reopen an issue that was supposed to have been laid permanently to rest, and the theory will enable her to do this.[18]

These problems are normally kept out of sight by an appeal to one or other of the common techniques for rescuing law — the authority of law — from any hint of political compromise. Thus it may be argued (the "constructionist" position) that judges need only apply their best endeavors to interpret what is written as faithfully as possible according to the framers' intent. Or again, that the text leaves room for variant readings, but only within the limits established by a long and evolving constitutional debate on questions of right interpretation. This second line of argument is found most often in response to attacks on the "myth" of judicial neutrality like those mounted by the current deconstructors. If certain clauses in the Constitution are notoriously apt to generate conflicting views, still there is a good chance that agreement may be reached with the aid of other, more detailed provisions — especially when these are read in the light of constitutional history and precedent. The rule of law would then seem sufficiently proof against the charge that its texts lack determinate meaning and can therefore be twisted to any political end.

Such is the claim of Stephen L. Carter in an essay that sets out specifically to rebut the arguments of the Critical Legal Theorists. To Carter these arguments look like a species of last-ditch "nihilism," an irrationalist drive to destroy the very grounds of judicial debate. Such accusations have indeed a familiar ring, being typical of mainstream humanist responses to literary deconstruction. Thus Carter confronts this Nietzschean threat with a statement of the broad constitutionalist case for law as an ongoing dialogue of principles, conventions, and social practices which, taken altogether, give reason for rejecting the so-called "nihilist" case. For one thing, the framers were a good deal more circumspect in establishing limits to governmental power (on the famous "checks and balances" principle) than in setting out a program of individual rights. This accorded well enough with the purposes of a liberal charter, and still provides a basis — Carter argues — for sound constitutional law. Thus "the more determinate clauses of the political Constitution may provide a comprehensible structure within which adjudication that requires judicial interpretation is a legitimate activity." In which case the integrity of law is saved after all and "the delegitimizers need not carry the day."[19]

But Carter mistakes the deconstructionist position when he treats it as a kind of feckless nihilism bent upon reducing law to a free-for-all of naked political interests. The same misunderstanding is at work when literary critics charge Derrida or de Man with a total disregard for the elementary protocols of reading, a willingness to sacrifice reason and truth to the notion of an infinitized textual "freeplay." This characterization would appear to rest largely on a second-hand acquaintance with the deconstructors' work. It scarcely stands up to a closer reading of those texts where Derrida and de Man pursue the analysis of language, ideology, and representation far beyond the limits of received (consensual) belief. Their object is *not* to create problems with this normative account merely for the sake of it, or in order to establish their own credentials as "strong misreaders" beyond the old textual-legitimist regime. Rather, they are concerned to indicate the very real difficulties that arise when theorists seek to erect whole philosophies of meaning, truth, and interpretation on the basis of our everyday conventional habits of linguistic usage. This is why Derrida chiefly takes issue with Searle — the methodical exponent of speech-act theory — rather than with J.L. Austin, whose arguments, style, and offbeat choice of examples positively invite a deconstructive reading. What is at issue is the problematic move from how we actually, conventionally "do things with words" to the position of deriving a wholesale philosophy — a set of binding juridical norms — from those same speech-act conventions. There is a parallel here with the thinking of those (like H.L.A. Hart) who have sought systematically to explain the peculiar force of legal language in terms of its performative character.[20]

This is also why de Man takes Rousseau's *Social Contract* as a key example of the problems induced by any document that lays down rules for political conduct while remaining necessarily ignorant of the circumstances in which those rules may come to be applied.[21] In de Man's terms, this demonstrates the tension between grammar and rhetoric (or language in its "constative" and "performative" aspects) which to some extent characterizes all kinds of utterance. Its effects are most crucial in matters of law — or in quasi-legislative texts like the *Social Contract* — since everything turns on the implicit claim that these enactments are necessary truths (and therefore good for all time), rather than mere prescriptions issued in the service of this or that short-term political interest. If law provided rules for its own interpretation unaffected by the vagaries of context — *if* it possessed this kind of programmatic power — then disputed cases could never arise. But of course there is always room for divergences of qualified legal opinion, even in the case of statute law, where this "constative" ideal should in theory come closest to being satisfied. And this for the obvious reason that law can only work — only make sense or take effect in particular contexts — so far as its provisions can be stretched to encompass a range of applications which could never be explicitly allowed for within those same provisions. Rousseau's text thus provides de Man with a perfect illustration of the paradoxes that afflict legal reasoning as soon as it attempts to theorize the relation between rules, juridical practice, and actual case histories. Thus it comes to seem

> that the "law of the text" is too devious to allow for such a simple relationship between model and example, and the theory of politics inevitably turns into the history, the allegory of its inability to achieve the status of a science.[22]

This sentence formulates exactly the point that the Critical Legal Theorists are making when they argue against conventional ideas of judicial neutrality or disinterest. For, as Carter somewhat ruefully remarks, "the courts continue to 'discover' fundamental rights in the less determinate provisions of the Constitution, and every fundamental rights decision provides for the delegitimizers another illustration of the value-laden indeterminacy of law."[23]

III

But in this case it might seem that Fish, Knapp, and Michaels were right after all: that the only use for theory (in its "negative" role) is to undermine precisely those deluded beliefs that have hitherto shored up the whole theoretical enterprise. If language is indeed — as de Man argues — "undecidably" suspended between grammar and rhetoric, forever revealing the performative character of its own constative truth-claims, then theory would always self-deconstruct into just another kind of rhetorical assertion. Such is the conclusion arrived at by at least some proponents of Critical Legal Studies. Thus, according to Joseph William Singer, "theories are incoherent when they set impossible tasks for themselves: they purport to give us guidance in deciding what to believe and what to do, yet they are either so vague and ambiguous as to give us no real help, or they are internally contradictory, telling us to do opposite things."[24] On which basis Singer goes on to argue (like Fish) that legal theories are always "indeterminate and open-ended," that they "express controversial political and moral commitments," and that therefore we had best give up theoretical talk and come straight out with these differences of view. In so far as it survived the process, theory would lose (or willingly forego) its superior cognitive claims and consent to play a role as just one more voice in the ongoing dialogue of aims and interests. Singer thus comes round to a thoroughly pragmatist viewpoint, echoing Richard Rorty on the non-availability of justifying "grounds" and the turn toward a new, conversational ethos where exchanging ideas — and *not* giving reasons — would constitute the best kind of move. "Legal theory should 'edify,' that is, it should 'help readers, or society as a whole, break free from outworn vocabularies or attitudes, rather than . . . provide a grounding for the intuitions and customs of the present'."[25]

So it seems there is not much to choose between, on the one hand, those opponents who attack legal deconstruction as a species of intellectual nihilism and, on the other, those theorists who endorse it as a means of discrediting theory itself. Both arguments come down to an ultimate denial that theory can be anything more than a post hoc rationalization of the values, motives, or governing interests that define what will count, within a given community, as valid "theoretical" reasoning. This position has a kind of inbuilt plausibility that explains its currently widespread appeal. It is the same line of argument one finds in philosophers like Hans-Georg Gadamer: namely, that theory is an impossible project except in so far as it acknowledges the "hermeneutic circle," the dimension of tacit preunderstanding that comes of our belonging to a certain cultural tradition.[26] Otherwise — so Gadamer believes — we could never make a start in *understanding* what we set out to criticize, since all understanding arises from a context of shared assumptions and values. In which case the ambitions of critical theory would rest on a single, self-evident mistake, that of thinking to criticize an existing tradition on terms which would not have been supplied in advance by that same all-encompassing tradition. Thus Gadamer takes issue with Jürgen Habermas over the latter's claim to do precisely that: to provide valid grounds (*theoretical* grounds) for challenging the assumptions that currently prevail in what he — Habermas — regards as an irrational or "distorted" form of sociopolitical consensus.[27] Habermas invokes an alternative standard of enlightened rationality, a theory of optimized communicative grasp (the so-called "ideal speech-situation") where a false consensus would no longer be imposed by the interests that maintain an unequal distribution of discourse, knowledge, and power. Gadamer effectively denies that such a standpoint is available, since thinking can proceed — or be recognized as possessing any kind of critical force — only within the shared horizons of a given cultural community.

The implicit conservatism of Gadamer's hermeneutics emerges very sharply in the context of his difference with Habermas. The same issue is raised when followers of Wittgenstein assert that it is impossible to criticize belief-systems other than our own unless such criticism is couched in terms that would carry conviction with members of the community concerned.[28] Otherwise we would not be *understanding* those beliefs — genuinely grasping the reasons why people might have held them — but merely offering "rational" explanations according to our own current wisdom. And by the same token we can only be self-deceived if we think to stand outside that current wisdom and criticize our existing modes of belief from some supposed alternative ground. Such at least is the lesson most commonly drawn from Wittgenstein's appeal to "language-games" (or "forms of life") as the furthest we can get in giving explanations of why people act, think, and talk as they do. This position lines up readily enough with the current neo-pragmatist orthodoxy. It is the same type of argument that Fish deploys against the claims of critical theory, and which then provides Knapp and Michaels with a chance to beat Fish at his own game.

So Singer concedes some vital ground when he argues that the end of all theorizing is simply the belated recognition that theory is and always was a mistaken enterprise. In effect he leaves the door wide open for pragmatists like Fish to deny that legal arguments can possibly *make sense* outside the context of currently held values and beliefs. One would then have to reject as incoherent the idea of enlightened judicial reform through the critique of existing institutions. This is why Singer's understanding of deconstruction scarcely differs from that of his more orthodox opponents who attack it as a last-ditch "nihilist" retreat from all the standards of right reasoning and ethical responsibility. On both sides there is a failure to grasp the very specific kinds of rigor and consequential argument found in the work of Derrida and de Man. In fact — as Derrida is at pains to point out in a number of recent essays — deconstruction is an activity which measures its distance from the Kantian tradition of enlightened critique, but only in order to preserve the force of such thinking against its more reductive or doctrinaire uses. "We cannot and we must not . . . forego the *Aufklärung*, in other words, what imposes itself as the enigmatic desire for vigilance, for the lucid vigil, for elucidation, for critique and truth."[29] That desire is "enigmatic" in the sense that it is forever seeking out rational foundations — justifying grounds — for a knowledge that purports to be purely *a priori*, self-evident to unaided human reason. But such paradoxes cannot be taken as a pretext for rejecting the entire tradition of enlightenment critique. As Derrida writes: "who is more faithful to reason's call, who hears it with a keener ear . . . the one who offers questions in return and tries to think through the possibility of that summons, or the one who does not want to hear any question about the principle of reason?"[30] It is essential to grasp this ambivalent relationship if we are to see more clearly what is wrong with the view of deconstruction that registers only its negative or "nihilistic" aspects.

One can best make the point by looking briefly at Derrida's most recent writings on Kant. In these, he is concerned with the political implications of Kant's idea that philosophy should occupy a particular, well-defined place within the hierarchy of disciplines that make up the modern ("enlightened") university system. Philosophy seeks no executive powers, Kant argues, no involvement in affairs of state or practical politics.[31] Its competence is strictly confined to theoretical matters, if by "theory" is understood a practice of disinterested rational critique which may be brought to bear upon policies enacted in that other, executive sphere. Philosophy is one of the "lower" faculties in so far as it claims no direct or privileged access to the machinery of power. In one sense this puts it at a clear disadvantage compared with those other faculties (law, theology, medicine) whose interests are more closely bound up with the business of state administration. But it is precisely on account of its willingness not to overstep these juridical bounds that philosophy can rightfully exercise its privilege in the domain of pure, disinterested reason. Thus there operates a kind of contractual exchange whereby the state leaves philosophy free to pursue its inquiries without fear of censorship, while philosophy for its part consents not to meddle with affairs of state. In speech-act terms, the discourse of reason should conduct itself on a purely "constative" level, thus preserving its claim to theorize freely where other forms of utterance — those exerting some "performative" force — are legitimately subject to state control.[32]

In this curious late text (*The Conflict of the Faculties*) Kant was defending philosophy's rights against what he saw as the two main threats to its continuing critical role. On the one hand the Prussian state was seeking to tighten up the censorship laws and revoke some of the freedoms that thinkers like Kant had enjoyed under the previous (relatively enlightened) regime. On the other — and to much the same effect — theologians were contesting the competence of philosophy to adjudicate in matters pertaining to religious doctrine and faith. Kant responds by insisting that such boundary disputes can only arise where the lawgivers and theologians have radically mistaken the true nature of philosophical inquiry. The theologians have no cause for concern since philosophy restricts itself to a critique of "rational religion" — of doctrinal arguments in so far as they submit to such treatment — and doesn't presume to dictate on matters of faith or revealed truth. If it did so, the state would be acting quite legitimately in curbing philosophy's pretensions, since church and state have a joint interest in preserving the currency of popular belief. So it is right for governments to assert their prerogative when it comes to religious teaching, just as it is right for theologians — who respect and in some degree share that prerogative — to insist that philosophy not stray beyond the bounds of rational religion. But it is wrong, a determinate abuse of power, if the state or its officials in the ideological sphere (that is, the "higher" faculties, including theologians) should exploit their authority to suppress the kind of thinking that philosophy truly represents.

Again, this line of argument amounts to a form of speech-act classification. The theologians have their place in a performative chain of command which descends from the twofold authority of God and King, and which cannot, by its nature, brook any kind of rational, enlightened dissent. And this authority extends to the interpretation of scripture in so far as God's word is taken to possess an ultimate, self-validating power of revelation beyond mere human reason. Thus "a biblical theologian is, properly speaking, one *versed in the Scriptures* with regard to *ecclesiastical faith*, which is based on statutes — that is, on laws proceeding from another person's act of choice." Whereas conversely the philosopher of rational religion "is one *versed in reason* with regard to *religious* faith, which is based on inner laws that can be developed from every man's own reason" (*CF*, p. 61). So the professors of biblical hermeneutics are justified when they argue (like Gadamer) that true understanding can only come about through acceptance of the authorizing word vouchsafed to those with the competence to judge in such matters. But it is none of their concern — any more than it should be the concern of a proper, well-regulated government — if philosophy raises *theoretical* questions as regards certain items of religious belief. For, according to Kant, it is beneath the dignity of governments to engage in philosophical disputes ("to decide about the intrinsic truth of these tenets and so to play the role of scholar"), while the great mass of people lack time or inclination to take them up. So nobody need worry if philosophers continue to theorize and occasionally come up with arguments that question the established consensus view. Indeed, the state can only benefit in the long run from such localized conflicts of allegiance, since "the insight gained from this freedom" — from the play of disinterested critical reason — will turn out "a better means of achieving its [the government's] ends than its own absolute authority" (*CF*, p. 57).

Let us summarize the Kantian position and then ask what bearing it may have on those issues of law, theory, and the politics of interpretation raised by the current neo-pragmatist trend. The state does not teach, Kant argues, but "commands those who, in accepting its offices, have contracted to teach what it wants (whether true or not)." These authorized delegates have power to decide what kinds of belief are passed on to the people as best conducing to the public good and the stability of state institutions. But there must also exist some further, independent tribunal, one that "having no commands to give, is free to evaluate everything, and concerns itself with the interests of truth" (*CF*, p. 27). Such is philosophy's role, and such are the necessary preconditions if philosophy is to exercise that role in the service of an enlightened liberal regime. Kant is quite clear that this division of intellectual labor will also give rise to political differences; that any increase in the freedom to criticize existing arrangements must place the philosophers at odds with the custodians of received wisdom and truth. Thus when Kant depicts the rival interests at work he does so in terms of the "right"/"left" distinction which — so it seems — first gained political currency as a result of the distribution of seats in the postrevolutionary French National Assembly. In Kant's words: "the rank of the higher faculties (as the right side of the parliament of learning) supports the government's statutes; but in as free a system of government as must exist when it is a question of truth, there must also be an opposition party (the left side), and this is the philosophy faculty's bench" (*CF*, p. 57–59).

So critical reason will most often be found on the side of those dissident voices that question received wisdom as embodied in the dictates of legislative power. But at the same time it is essential to the workings of an enlightened polity that reason should continue in this critical role unhindered by the censorship of church or state. For otherwise (as Kant argues) there is no effective check on the tendency of governments to use all the powers at their command in order to silence reasoned opposition. And in this case they run the more serious risk that their laws will come to seem so devoid of rational warrant that they no longer carry any kind of legitimate force. Thus philosophy remains the final arbiter of political justice and reason, for all its apparently modest desire to be placed among the "lower" faculties. "The reason why this faculty, despite its great prerogative (freedom), is called the lower faculty lies in human nature; for a man who can give commands, even though he is someone else's humble servant, is considered more distinguished than a free man who has no one under his command" (*CF*, p. 29). In fact it seems clear, on the evidence of passages like this, that *The Conflict of the Faculties* has a double-edged argument with one meaning for its orthodox readership and another for those with the wit or the will to perceive its more searching implications. It would thus serve to demonstrate exactly the point Kant is making when he distinguishes the two kinds of reason, conformist and critical. It would also pose a challenge to those adepts of the hermeneutic circle — whether "biblical theologians" or latter-day pragmatists — who deny that theory can take us any further than the authorized canonical sense of things.

IV

In Derrida's reading of Kant these ironies go largely unnoticed, no doubt because Derrida is more concerned with the paradoxes of classic liberal reason, and not so much with Kant's particular attempt to get around the problems of censorship. At a certain level Derrida is out to show how these paradoxes work to problematize the whole undertaking of Kantian enlightened critique. Most crucial here is the notion of philosophy as defined by its essentially "disinterested" character, its belonging to a realm of theoretical inquiry ideally remote from the pressures and distortions of everyday practical discourse. This is why the critique of aesthetic judgment — seemingly a marginal aspect of his enterprise — in fact comes to bear such a weight of argument in Kant's philosophical system. For aesthetic understanding is *par excellence* the mode wherein the cognitive faculties achieve that state of pure, contemplative detachment which lays all their conflicts of interest momentarily to rest. In the *Critique of Pure Reason* (as de Man remarks) it is by way of the "productive imagination" — an eminently aesthetic category — that Kant negotiates the problematic passage from concepts to sensuous intuitions.[33] And he likewise has recourse to aesthetic ideas and analogues at a number of crucial points where the logic of his argument demands the resolution of otherwise conflicting motifs. Thus Kant's doctrine of aesthetic detachment is a proving ground for his idea of philosophy as consisting in the pure, disinterested play of a "faculty" devoted to no further end than that of enlightened self-knowledge.

Derrida reads a history of ideological mystification in this appeal to the aesthetic (and the concept of disinterest) developed in Kant's third Critique.[34] He goes about various ways to "deconstruct" it, partly by attending to stress points revealed in the strategy of argument, partly by remarking how these are engendered by the willed exclusion of political motives and interests. For Derrida, Kant's attempt to insulate the aesthetic domain involves him in repeated metaphors of *framing*, of the artwork as somehow set off against that which effectively delimits or surrounds it. In pictorial terms the frame is what distinguishes the space of aesthetic representation from everything that belongs outside that space and merely serves as a more or less tasteful background. Here it seems scarcely a metaphor at all but a straightforward, natural fact of visual perception. But as Kant reflects on the nature of such frames he is led into regions of undecidability where the fundamental concepts of Kantian aesthetics are successively placed in doubt. On the one hand they can only be outworks, ornaments, "parergonal" features, in no way integral to the object itself. But on the other they would seem indispensably a part of that object in so far as its aesthetic autonomy and character depend upon its being thus "enframed" or set off. And the same applies to the edifice of theory that Kant erects around the privileged domain of aesthetic understanding. To the extent that it deals in concepts only — theoretical abstractions, so to speak, from the jointly sensuous and cognitive experience of art — aesthetics is itself a kind of "parergon," a framing discourse which cannot partake of the enjoyment it seeks to comprehend. But here, once again, it proves difficult to fix or conceptualize the frame as a solid, impermeable boundary between art and the philosophic discourse on art. For there is simply no deciding to what extent our responses are determined by qualities intrinsic to the artwork, or how far they are influenced, shaped, or "framed" by the assumptions peculiar to that discourse. Such is the curious logic of the "parergon," as Derrida describes it: a logic that suspends the decidable opposition between inside and outside, art and philosophy, aesthetic disinterest and everything that should (on Kantian principles) have no role to play in the experience of art.

Thus it becomes clear that this whole system of unstable oppositions is in fact determined by the need to exclude precisely those interests that threaten its precarious structure. (The point could be made more simply by recalling the praise that Kant lavishes at one point on an undistinguished poem by his "enlightened" patron, Frederick the Great of Prussia.) And it receives massive documentary support in a recent study by Pierre Bourdieu, establishing the precise correlations that exist between differences on the scale of social class and income and differences on the scale of aesthetic taste. The claim of disinterest goes along with the preference for certain kinds of art — the more abstract, formal, or "sophisticated" — as opposed to those other, less prestigious kinds that possess a widespread popular appeal. Indeed, it is the function of Kantian critique to deny such "vulgar" (sociological) determinants of taste by appealing to a faculty of aesthetic judgment divorced from all material interests. Thus:

> the social categories of aesthetic judgment can only function, for Kant himself and for his readers, in the form of highly sublimated categories, such as the oppositions between beauty and charm, pleasure and enjoyment or culture and civilization, euphemisms which, without any conscious intention of dissimulating, enable social oppositions to be expressed and experienced in a form conforming to the norms of expression of a specific field.[35]

It is the same mystifying process that Derrida remarks in his deconstructive reading of Kantian aesthetics. And from here his analysis extends to those antinomies in the nature of liberal reason that result from its attempting to drive a wedge between political motives and the pursuit of pure, disinterested truth.

Kant's doctrine of the faculties assumes its modern institutional guise in the idea that certain university departments (those devoted to "pure" research in the sciences and humanities) are exempt from the kinds of external pressure that affect their "applied" counterparts. If this distinction was untenable at Kant's time of writing, it carries still less conviction now, in an age when (as Derrida comments) "so long as it has the means, a military budget can invest in anything at all, in view of deferred profits: 'basic' scientific theory, the humanities, literary theory and philosophy."[36] Quite simply, there is *no* kind of knowledge that cannot be coopted into the service of a means-end rationality whose more obvious symptoms include the arms race, the military-industrial complex, and the whole machinery of persuasive mass-media techniques required to keep these projects in business. And so it might seem that the case against theory can be argued on political grounds; that the only adequate response to this predicament is one that rejects the whole tradition of enlightened critique as merely a legitimizing ruse adopted to conceal the interests of power. In which case of course the neo-pragmatists would carry the day, since this is the conclusion they have urged all along. It would likewise fit in with the prevalent view of deconstruction — including the Critical Legal Studies movement — as an enterprise that aims to discredit the principles of enlightened reason by showing how these principles always come down to the assertion of sheer political self-interest.

I have argued that this is a mistaken understanding, though one with such widespread currency — among proponents and detractors alike — that it threatens to preëmpt the very terms of debate. Deconstruction is viable (as Derrida insists) only to the extent that it respects the Kantian imperatives, even while acknowledging that no such ideal can ever be achieved in practice. It is situated — like the work of the Frankfurt Critical Theorists — at precisely that point where reason holds out for a power of reflective, disinterested grasp unthinkable under present circumstances. In Adorno's words: "Philosophy demands today, as it did in Kant's time, critique of reason through reason, not the banishment or annihilation of reason." And again: "Self-reflection of Enlightenment is not its revocation: this would be its corruption under the present status quo."[37] Habermas assumes the same standpoint with regard to his "ideal speech-situation" — an admittedly utopian community of discourse among free and equal subjects, redeemed from the kinds of distorted understanding that currently prevail. In each case there is a clear recognition of the factors conspiring to prevent any straightforward appeal to the Kantian tribunal of enlightened reason. But there is also a refusal to abandon such thinking and thus fall back on the pragmatist argument that what's true is simply what's good in the way of belief. For this would make it impossible to criticize those forms of institutional unreason or skewed communication that most urgently call for analysis. It would rule out every kind of critical reflection save those that made sense according to presently accepted values and beliefs.

Such arguments effectively collapse the difference between rational, informed consensus on the one hand and a passive ideological formation on the other. Thus — to take an example from Habermas — it would carry no weight, in pragmatist terms, if anti-nuclear protesters were to justify their campaign of civil disobedience by invoking the distinction between *lawful* and *legitimate* modes of behavior.[38] This distinction follows from the principle — supposedly inscribed in all liberal constitutions — that there may indeed be genuine conscientious grounds for breaking the law, provided the action is 1) backed up with good reasons, and 2) undertaken with a willingness to face the likely legal consequences. If these conditions are met then the protest should justly be construed, *not* as a species of violence or coercion, but rather as a form of communicative action intended to awaken other people to their own responsibility as thinking citizens. Any state that refuses to acknowledge this claim is effectively denying — against all the evidence to date — that such actions can provide the impetus for enlightened legal reform. Defining what is legitimate solely in terms of what is lawful would amount to confirming the state as supreme arbiter in all questions of moral and political conscience. It would thus invite the Kantian riposte that governments behaving in this fashion eventually relinquish their own right to govern in the name of representative democracy. And the same objection could be leveled at those philosophies of law, politics, and interpretation which deny that understanding is possible outside the terms of some existing communal enterprise. Here also, the effect must be to delegitimize any form of reasoning that breaks with the established consensual view.

On the pragmatist account these issues are simply unreal, since theory is incapable of resolving them one way or the other. "Positive" theory — the kind that talks a lot about principles, foundations, and right readings — cannot make good (so the argument runs) because it fails to take account of its own self-interested nature. While "negative" theory — deconstruction and its various cognates — must always end up by revealing the delusive or nonexistent grounds of all theoretical inquiry. But this argument rests on the foregone conclusion that thinking is inherently a circular process, discovering only those meanings and values that are sanctioned by present-day belief. It ignores the extent to which change comes about through a constant dialogue between positive and negative theories, those that advance some particular view of emancipated human interests and those that periodically attack such views as inadequate, confused, or contradictory. This is nowhere more apparent than in the history of debate on issues raised by American constitutional law. One extreme position — espoused by the so-called legal realists — is that judges themselves make law, and that therefore (in effect) the Constitution means what the Supreme Court currently says it means. But this argument reduces to nonsense in so far as lawyers, politicians, and laypersons continue to discuss these matters and assume, furthermore, that other parties to the dialogue will try to make rational sense of their position. As one recent commentator puts it, "the very decision to debate an interpretive judgment presupposes the possibility of, and justifies the quest for, the correct constitutional theory."[39] This argument goes clean against the current neo-pragmatist wisdom that urges us to drop such talk of "correct theories" and simply accept that interpretation goes all the way down.

For theories, whether positive or negative, do have consequences beyond the mere fact of allowing certain people to believe what they would anyway believe without benefit of theory. The pragmatist turns this argument around to assert that such harmony between formal and substantive truth-claims is merely further evidence — if any were needed — that knowledge and true belief are synonymous terms. But in so doing the pragmatist argues away the very grounds for seeking an informed, rational consensus on this or any other topic of debate. He or she would then be placed in the same untenable position as those legal realists who equate justice with the currently prevailing idea of what justice ought to be. In this case there could be no serious argument on matters of constitutional law, since such argument presupposes (in the words of Sotirios A. Barber) "the assumption that we can in some respects distinguish what the Constitution means from what the Supreme Court says it means" (*WCM*, p. 16). To reject this reasoning is also to deny "the unavoidable distinction between what is constitutional or just and what is represented as constitutional or just." It would amount to something like a vote of no confidence in moral and legal reason.

Such distinctions are all the more vital at a time when consensus values can be swung to give a semblance of majority support for judgments that scarcely acknowledge the claims of enlightened social interest. It is clearly not enough to denounce any resulting legislative acts on grounds of straightforward moral revulsion, or by simply declaring beliefs opposed to the beliefs of those who framed them. Rather one will need to offer good reason for thinking such judgments wrong and unconstitutional. And at this stage the argument will involve standards of interpretative reason and fitness beyond anything conceivable on pragmatist terms. "This need," as Barber writes, "to perceive enactments as good-faith and reasonably competent versions of the ends of government results in a substantive notion of rationality or reasonableness as part of the meaning of constitutional law." (*WCM*, p. 127) Interpretation would then have to involve something more than an appeal to the hermeneutic circle, to established ideas of what the Constitution means as arrived at on the basis of tacit values and assumptions. On the "positive" side, it would ask what kinds of *theoretical* commitment — what views on the nature of ethical reason, argumentative validity, and truth — were basic to the framing intentions of the document. This would have a clear bearing on those controversial issues (like abortion and religious education) where the claims of conscience are sometimes thought to override the dictates of enlightened secular reason. In such cases an appeal is surely open to the fact that the Constitution embodies a distinctly secular understanding of social rights and obligations; that it represents a principled attempt on the framers' part to ensure that religious views are not imposed to the detriment of reasoned debate. And this gives grounds for arguing that "the Court has an affirmative obligation under the First Amendment to do all that it can to prevent pretextual impositions of religious dogma" (*WCM*, p. 138). Such abuses would indeed be "pretextual" in the sense that they took some unarguable item of faith as a pretext for ignoring the express provisions of the constitutional text.

Positive theorists from Kant to John Rawls have always held the view that justice required an argued, principled account of the nature of justice, one that would not serve merely to articulate the interests of this or that dominant pressure group. Negative theorists like de Man have subjected such claims to various kinds of ideological critique, intended to show how they don't (indeed cannot) live up to this fine ideal. It is through the dialectic of positive and negative theories that there exists the possibility of reasoned debate on our motivating interests and beliefs. This is why it is essential to distinguish negative theory from the pragmatist position which, if acted on consistently, would call an end to such debate. It is also one reason for not going along with versions of the hermeneutic circle which make interpretation wholly dependent on a background of ineliminable presuppositions. For here again the effect is to argue away the grounds for that enlightened community of interests that would constitute a genuine participant democracy. Otherwise the appeal to consensus values can never be more than a disguised apologetics for the current institutional status quo.

6

"The Temptation of Permanence": Reading and History

I

In Chapter 5, my argument turned somewhat aside from the detailed exposition of de Man's writing. My aim was to suggest ways in which his work might relate not only to Derrida's but to other modern forms of critical or negative hermeneutics. Adorno provides perhaps the most useful analogy, with his relentless insistence (as against Hegel) that "the whole is the false," that thinking must reject all premature absolutes, and that truth resides only in those discrepant details — those stubbornly *material* signs and tokens — that cannot be reduced to any grand synthesizing scheme. There is also, in Adorno, a distinction between the false and the presently, contingently untrue which corresponds closely to that in de Man between mere "mistakes" and significant "errors." Such is the function of immanent critique, as Adorno conceives it: to redeem those moments of *authentic* untruth in art and philosophy which correspond to nothing real in our present, distorted, and indigent condition, but which nonetheless possess a power of revealing what truth might be if things were otherwise. Such thinking, he writes,

> takes seriously the principle that it is not ideology in itself which is untrue but rather its pretension to correspond to reality. Immanent criticism of intellectual and artistic phenomena seeks to grasp, through analysis of their form and meaning, the contradiction between their objective idea and their pretension.[1]

This is what leads Adorno — as it leads de Man — to reject all forms of that potent aesthetic ideology which promises to reconcile subject and object, mind and nature, concepts and sensuous intuitions. For Adorno, "the picture of a temporal or extra-temporal original state of happy identity between subject and object is romantic — a wishful project at times, but today no more than a lie."[2] Such claims can only be false in so far as they locate this ideal condition either in a purely mythological past (like the commonplace misreadings of Rousseau), or in an equally mythic present that transcends all the obstacles created by a far from ideal reality. For Adorno, the measure of authentic thinking is its willingness to face up to this knowledge of its own inescapable predicament. "Every thought which is not idle . . . bears branded on it the impossibility of its full legitimation."[3]

But this negative knowledge is not to be confused — as it is so often by opponents of de Man and Adorno alike — with a mood of mere intellectual "nihilism," a perverse will to undermine every source of meaning, value, or cognitive assurance. For it is only by acknowledging the limits placed upon thought by its material and temporal condition that philosophy can hope to preserve some sense of an alternative, better world. "The mind is not this power as a positive which turns away from the negative, as when we say of something that it is null, or false . . . ; it is this power only when looking the negative in the face, dwelling upon it."[4] These words are not Adorno's but Hegel's, in a passage cited by Adorno in his Preface to *Minima Moralia*. They bring out very clearly the ambivalent nature of Adorno's response to Hegel — on the one hand preserving the restless negativity, the impulse to question all received ideas and commonsense intuitions, while on the other rejecting the Hegelian assurance that such questioning might at last have an end with the advent of Absolute Reason, Christianity, and the Prussian nation-state. For history had so far falsified the content of Hegel's sanguine predictions as to leave them as merely a stark reminder of philosophy's impotence in the face of practical events. The only way forward for critical thought was to hold fast to the negative power of Hegelian dialectic — its refusal to acknowledge things as they are — and thereby resist the self-deluding claims of a reason that identified absolute truth with its own, inevitably partial and distorted viewpoint. That dialectical thinking should fall short of the promise implicit in its nature — that it should everywhere manifest the scars of this mutilated state — was for Adorno the characterizing mark of all authentic philosophy and art.

Hence the analogy that Adorno perceives between those "reflections from a damaged life" that make up the disjunct, aphoristic style of *Minima Moralia*, and other modern art forms (like the music of Arnold Schoenberg) that relentless expose the alien conditions of modern social existence. In Schoenberg, he writes,

> The total rationality of music is its total organization. By means of organization, liberated music seeks to reconstitute the lost totality — the

lost power and the responsibly binding force of Beethoven. Music succeeds in doing so only at the price of its freedom, and thereby it fails. Beethoven reproduced the meaning of tonality out of subjective freedom. The new ordering of twelve-tone technique virtually exting-uishes the subject.[5]

Adorno's project in *Minima Moralia* is to give voice to this predicament by writing in a fragmentary mode which preserves the force of negative dialectics — the power vested in the aphorism, last refuge of authentic thought — against all the blandishments of method, system, and large-scale synthesizing creeds. It is an effort, as he knows, that courts self-defeat in every paragraph, every sentence, and detail of formulated theory. But only by accepting this risk — by renouncing the false totality of a reason that has abandoned the realm of individual experience — can thinking hold out against the homogenizing pressures of a socially administered "objective" rationality. Not that this maneuver can be carried through without a sense of culpable failure, a knowledge of its own deep complicity with the forces that have brought thinking to such a sorry pass. But it is still the one authentic option in an age given over to false totalities and versions of premature absolute truth.

> In face of the totalitarian unison with which the eradication of difference is proclaimed as a purpose in itself, even part of the social force of liberation may have temporarily withdrawn to the individual sphere. If critical theory lingers there, it is not only with a bad conscience.[6]

Thus Adorno, like de Man, rejects every form of philosophical or aesthetic ideology that claims in itself to transcend the bad antinomy of subject and object, individual experience *versus* the power of objective dialectical thought. And he does so not in the gloomy Schopenhauerian belief that such conflicts are intrinsic to the human condition, but in order to preserve a margin for imagining how things might stand in some alternative dispensation of knowledge and social life. The only way that thought can occupy this margin of hope is by working with a constantly exacerbated sense of its own inadequate nature — its failure to achieve anything like the utopian condition held out by more positive (and to this extent, more chronically self-deluding) philosophies. But again, such failure is not to be accounted a sign of abject self-defeat or intellectual nihilism. "If a life fulfilled its vocation directly, it would miss it." And again:

> this inadequacy resembles that of life, which describes a wavering, deviating line, disappointing by comparison with its premises, and yet which only in this actual course, always less than it should be, is able, under given conditions of existence, to represent an unregimented one.[7]

So thinking keeps faith with its own best insights by acknowledging the extent to which reality confounds any hopeful prognosis; by maintaining a stance of intransigently negative critique which yet contains the promise, albeit barely glimpsed, of better things to come.

The same can be said of de Man's writings, in so far as they work to demystify those forms of false, premature, or totalizing thought which would seek to obliterate all traces of time, history, and difference. Derrida addresses this question in *Mémoires*, the text of a lecture series delivered by way of tribute to de Man shortly after his death in 1983.[8] One of Derrida's main concerns in these lectures was to turn back the charge often brought against de Man, that deconstruction amounted to a form of "textualist" mystification, a last-ditch retreat from politics and history into the realm of evasive rhetorical strategies. Now this charge has some force — as I argued in Chapter 1 — when applied to those early and middle-period essays (like "Wordsworth and Hölderlin") where poetry and politics are treated as in some sense antithetical terms. That is to say, there is in these essays a marked tendency to write off the claims of political commitment from a retrospective standpoint of undeceived superior wisdom, treating them as products of a blind will-to-power that cannot survive the salutary rigors of a deconstructive reading. Thus Wordsworth's narrative of his youthful involvement with revolutionary events in France is read by de Man not only as a chapter in the poet's subsequent, revisionist account of his own experience, but as a veritable "allegory" of how poetry works to chasten and subdue such misguided hopes. And this pattern is repeated elsewhere in his work, often with the same series of implications: 1) that all authentic poetry is the outcome of prolonged reflective self-knowledge; 2) that all political involvements are the upshot of impulsive, unreflecting action; 3) that criticism is therefore best occupied in drawing out those "allegories" of frustrated hope or non-fulfillment that constitute poetry's chief lesson in the reading of political events. Such I take to be the coded affirmation, the underlying "point" of those early essays. It is a reading that finds at least a measure of support in what we learn of Hendrik de Man and the fortunes of Belgian socialist politics in the immediate pre-war period. It is hardly surprising, in light of such experience, that Paul de Man's work should at this stage manifest a strong mistrust of activist creeds, an insistence on the virtues of reflective non-involvement, and an ironic stance toward political beliefs that at times leans over into downright cynicism.

But thereafter, as I have argued, his writing became steadily more preoccupied with issues of aesthetic ideology and the politics of representation. The last chapter of Derrida's *Mémoires* assembles some of the evidence that de Man's was indeed an "engaged" discourse, one that "more and more explicitly . . . [said] something about institutional structures and the political stakes of hermeneutic conflicts."[9] In support of this claim, he cites de Man's essays on Rousseau in *Allegories of Reading*, especially his chapter on the *Social Contract*, where issues of textual "undecidability" — of the tension, in this case, between constative and performative aspects of language — are inseparably linked with questions of history, politics, and legislative power. Those who would deny this connection fail to perceive how the specific misreading of passages in Rousseau (as in Kant or Hegel) gives rise to a mystified aesthetic ideology whose effects are none the less real for their "textual" character. In Derrida's words: "'reactionaries' and 'political activists' in truth misunderstand, in order to protect themselves, the political stake and structure of the text, the political allegory of the literary text, no less than the allegorical and literary structure of the political text."[10] Thus Rousseau, Kant, and Hegel have each been subjected to political readings which turn crucially on the sense attributed to certain problematic passages. And it is the hallmark of conservative ideologies that they tend to elide these problems by adopting an organicist or naturalizing view of language, thought, and perception whose motivating interests de Man was much concerned to reveal.

Of course Derrida himself has a stake in turning back the charge of political quietism so often brought against himself and de Man. What he writes here would equally apply to his reading of Rousseau in *Of Grammatology*, a reading that is likewise intended to demystify those "logocentric" topoi (of speech, self-presence, nature, origins) which play such a prominent role in Rousseau and dominate the thinking of his mainstream interpreters.[11] Again, there is a clearly marked political dimension to Derrida's text, though one that is routinely ignored by those commentators who see only the promotion of a massively generalized "writing" and hence — as they think — an indifference to everything "outside" the text. What this reading passes over is Derrida's argument that the repression of writing has always gone along with a certain mystique of origins that works to efface real history — the history of civil and political institutions — by evoking a long-lost "organic" community of souls where speech would suffice for all authentic social needs. And this mythology is still very much at work in those linguists, anthropologists, and exponents of the present-day structuralist "sciences of man" who preserve something of Rousseau's attitude to the innocence of origins and the corrupting effect of history, culture, and civilization. Derrida makes the point with maximum force in his reading of Lévi-Strauss's *Tristes Tropiques*. "Self-presence, transparent proximity in the face-to-face of countenances and the immediate range of the voice, this determination of social authenticity is therefore classic: Rousseauistic but already the inheritor of Platonism. . . . "[12] On the one hand speech,

presence, origins, and nature, all of them strongly marked positive terms;
on the other writing, absence, hierarchy, delegated power, and all the
manifold forms of decadent modernity that Rousseau never ceases to
denounce. For it is writing that breaks in upon the idyllic scene of Lévi-
Strauss's wishful imagining, whose advent creates the possibility of
exercising power *at a distance*, and thus destroys the authentic face-to-
face communion of primitive life.

So there are clearly political interests in play when Derrida shows
how this binary logic is constantly subverted in the course of Rousseau's
arguments; how writing refuses to play its properly subordinate role (as a
mere "supplement" to speech), and becomes in effect the structurally
dominant feature of everything that Rousseau has to say about language,
culture, politics, ethics, and social evolution. This is *not* to claim — as
that simplified polemical reading would have it — that there is no possible
access to a world of reality "outside" the text, since nothing could serve
as an anchor or endpoint to the infinitized play of linguistic *differance*.
Rather it is to urge, like de Man, that we should read with a sense of the
material resistances that writing puts up to any kind of aesthetic
idealization that would seek to transcend history and politics in the name
of some mystified organicist creed. Quite simply, writing is the
precondition of all historical knowledge, all thinking that would pass
beyond the timeless complacencies of myth to a grasp of what exceeds
and baffles this craving for long-lost authentic origins. And so one can
fairly say of Derrida, as he says of de Man, that "'politics' cannot be
separated, neither in its acts nor in what it leaves to be deciphered, from
that thinking of the political and of law which traverses all of his
writings."[13]

We have seen already how de Man takes issue with Derrida on the
question of how far Rousseau's texts effectively prefigure or rehearse in
advance the kind of reading that Derrida brings to bear. For de Man,
those texts have no "blind spots" in themselves, but on the contrary
"account at all moments for [their] own rhetorical mode" (*BI*, p. 139). It
is Rousseau's interpreters who stand in need of deconstruction, since
even the best of them — Derrida included — seem destined to repeat the
same alternating rhythm of coimplicated "blindness" and "insight." What
is odd about this argument (as I suggested) is the fact that it ignores those
frequent passages in *Of Grammatology* where Derrida *does* quite
explicitly acknowledge that Rousseau's text provides all the materials for
its own deconstructive reading. Thus it is Rousseau (not Derrida) who
most strikingly reveals the aporias engendered by a logocentric discourse
on the origins of language; whose *Confessions* are everywhere haunted by
the "dangerous supplement" of writing; and whose mythical account of
social evolution — of the evils attendant on civilized existence — is

thrown into doubt by a close reading of his own ambivalent texts. All this
Derrida himself points out with scrupulous reference to the details of
Rousseau's often tortuous argumentation. So there remains, to say the
least, some doubt as to who is misreading whom in this curious sequence
of claims and counterclaims.

But if one point does emerge clearly, it is de Man's insistence on the
power of Rousseau's texts to demystify those subsequent readings which
annex him to a vaguely "Rousseauist" mythology of nature, presence,
and origins. Thus Derrida reflects on Rousseau's importance for de Man
as a strong precursor, an author whose texts exhibit a degree of rhetorical
self-awareness not to be found in the later Romantics. Hence the desire
— as he subsequently remarked in correspondence with Derrida — to
"exempt Rousseau *at all costs* from blindness," a desire in which de Man
yet perceives "a gesture of fidelity to my own intinerary."[14] We can best
understand this remark, it seems to me, in relation to de Man's deepening
concern with issues of aesthetic ideology. For it is in Rousseau, more than
any other writer, that he locates a resistance to those potent forms of self-
mystifying rhetoric that results from a failure to acknowledge the
distinction between language and the realm of phenomenal or sensuous
experience. This is why there develops, according to de Man, a
"particularly rich aberrant tradition" in the case of those writers who, like
Rousseau, "can legitimately be called the most enlightened" (*BI*, p. 141).
That it is to say, there is something like an inverse relationship between
the rigor, the un-self-deceiving clarity of Rousseau's discourse, and the
tendency in his orthodox interpreters to ignore this whole dimension of
his writing and fasten on to themes which merely give back the reflected
image of their own preoccupations. And so it came about, in de Man's
words, that

> Derrida found himself in the most favorable of all critical positions: he
> was dealing with an author as clear-sighted as language lets him be who,
> for that very reason, is being systematically misread; the author's own
> works, newly interpreted, can then be played off against the most
> talented of his deluded interpreters or followers. (*BI*, p. 139)

One may question the justice of de Man's observations in so far as they
ignore what is patently there in Derrida's reading of Rousseau. But still it
must be asked just why de Man should have laid himself open to this line
of *tu quoque* response. I would suggest that his motives are primarily
political, and have to do with that version of *Ideologiekritik* that de Man
increasingly came to identify with the strategies of deconstruction. When
he calls Rousseau the most "enlightened" or "clear-sighted" of authors,
and when he talks of "playing off" these qualities against the errors and

delusions of mainstream Rousseau criticism, what de Man seeks to stress is the power of these texts to demystify the kinds of false understanding that result from aesthetic ideology. Hence his desire to defend Rousseau against any imputations of "blindness," even where these come — as in Derrida's case — from a critic whose extreme acuity and strength of demythologizing insight de Man is more than willing to acknowledge.

II

One can only conjecture as to the reasons — circumstantial or otherwise — for the clearly marked shift in de Man's ideological stance over three decades of intensive critical thought. In Chapter 1, I suggested that his early and middle-period essays, to the extent that they touched at all on such themes, did so from a viewpoint of profoundly disenchanted irony, with the clear implication that politics — or political activism — was a species of endlessly recurrent delusion for which poetry (or the depth of reflective self-knowledge that poetry required) was a kind of salutary antidote. And I argued further that this attitude may have been induced, at least in part, by his experience of events in pre-war Belgium and, nearer home, by the ill-starred socialist involvements of his uncle, Hendrik de Man. Thus the typical movement of thought in these essays is one that discovers in poetry — especially in Wordsworth and Hölderlin — an image of its own preoccupation with time, memory, reflective hindsight, and the self-deluding character of actions undertaken on the spur of the moment, or in hope of achieving some radical change in the order of secular affairs. This can easily be taken to imply a stance of political quietism, a will to discredit all forms of activist commitment by showing them to rest on the dangerous illusion that our present imaginings can be somehow translated into long-term practical effects. Such — as we have seen — is Frank Lentricchia's main charge against de Man: that his writings systematically exploit the kind of Nietzschean aporia that drives a wedge between "history" and "modernity," or knowledge and reflective wisdom on the one hand and blind, impulsive action on the other.[15] And indeed it is possible to read these texts as conducting a sustained ironic meditation on the ways in which history — especially the history of revolutions — turns out to be no more than a melancholy lesson in the vanity of human wishes.

But there is another aspect to those early essays which this reading leaves out of account. It has to do with de Man's principled mistrust of any thinking that claims to go straight to the truth or the heart of the matter, without leaving room for such critical reflection as might serve to indicate the dangers involved. We should recall, in this connection, his diagnostic reading of Heidegger's commentaries on Hölderlin, especially his point that Heidegger misinterprets — indeed "violates" — his texts exactly in so far as he wants them to *state* what can only be shadowed forth obliquely in a mode of self-denying or negative assertion. To cite the crucial passage once again:

> The ineffable demands the direct adherence and the blind and violent passion with which Heidegger treats his texts. Mediation, on the other hand, implies a reflection that tends toward a critical language as systematic and rigorous as possible, but not overly eager to make claims of certainty that it can substantiate only in the long run. (*BI*, p. 263)

Again, one can read these words as recommending that thought renounce the temptations of real-world commitment, that it withdraw into a realm of inward, ironic detachment where those temptations would no longer be able to exert their seductive appeal. The passage would then go to confirm all the charges that Lentricchia brings against de Man. But this is to ignore both the evidence of de Man's later writings on the topic of aesthetic ideology, and the pressured situation to which he was responding at the time of these early texts. For it was Heidegger whose meditations had led to the point of equating "authentic" thought with the interests of a single, self-privileged national culture; who had identified truth with the unveiling of a temporal destiny whose origin lay in the sources of Greek (pre-Socratic) speculative thought, and whose signs were now there to be read in the texts of German poetry and philosophy. And it was also the question of Heidegger's conduct in the years of the Nazi ascent to power that had posed most starkly the whole vexed issue of how far philosophers, from Nietzsche down, had paved the way for National Socialist ideology. At least one can say that Heidegger, and especially Heidegger's readings of Rilke and Hölderlin, presented de Man with a challenge whose terms were inescapably marked by the shadow of recent historical and political events.

Of course there has been much scholarly debate as to just how far Heidegger's thinking was complicit with the purposes of Nazi cultural propaganda.[16] Then again, it is agreed among his commentators that there occurred a decisive "turn" (*Kehre*) in Heidegger's thought, a movement away from the kind of appropriative reading that strikes de Man as a form of hermeneutic "violence."[17] This change led Heidegger to stress the need for a self-denying openness (*Gelassenheit*) to meanings and values that lay beyond the grasp of our modern, rationalistic, "enlightened" understanding. The texts on Hölderlin to which de Man makes reference were written over the period from 1939 to 1954, a period which spans not only the war years but also — significantly —

Heidegger's "turn" toward this new, less assertive or culture-specific way of reading. So it is simplifying matters to treat de Man's essay as a direct response to those elements in Heidegger's thought that lent themselves directly to the purposes of nationalist propaganda. But we shall also do less than justice to de Man's early essays if we ignore — like Lentricchia — that aspect of his thinking which does hold out against the mystifying power of organicist creeds and ideologies. For this is precisely what de Man resists in Heidegger's readings of Hölderlin: the impulse to identify revealed poetic truth with the power of language — preëminently the German language — to articulate the nature of Being itself. For Heidegger, "the essence (*Wesen*) of what is named (Being) is revealed in the word. By naming Being's essence, the word separates the essential from the non-essential (or the absolute from the contingent: *das Wesen vom Unwesen*") (*BI*, p. 259). While for de Man, as we have seen, this reading amounts to a reversal, a determinate negation of what Hölderlin actually says. The poet may experience this gulf between desire and fulfillment as the "anguishing question" that impels all authentic thought: "how can one not only speak *of* Being, but say Being itself?" (*BI*, p. 256). But when Heidegger finds an affirmative response in Hölderlin's texts — when he reads them as stating the essence of Being in a mode of self-present, demonstrative truth — he can do so only through an act of hermeneutic "violence" that ignores all the signs of a contrary meaning. Thus, according to de Man, "as soon as the word is uttered, it destroys the immediate and discovers that instead of stating Being, it can only state mediation" (*BI*, p. 259).

It is in de Man's resistance to this appropriative drive in Heidegger's reading that I think we can make out the earliest signs of his own distinct "turn" toward a form of implicit ideological critique. This conjecture finds support — albeit obliquely — in some recent research by the Belgian scholar Ortwin de Graef.[18] For it emerges that de Man in fact produced a quantity of published work during the period 1938–42, during and after his period of study at the Free University in Brussels — having enrolled first for courses in Civil Engineering, then switched to Chemistry, and finally opted for Social Sciences. His articles appeared in two journals of very different character, *Les Cahiers du Libre Examen* and *Het Vlaamsche Land* ("The Flemish Land"). More recently still — after this book went to press — de Graef made known his discovery of a great number of articles (some 170 in all) that de Man had written for the Belgian paper *Le Soir*, and which were published during the early years of Nazi occupation. These writings have occasioned bitter controversy in America as to the extent of de Man's collaborationist involvement and its bearing on the politics of his later work. Clearly this must raise painful questions for anyone who has read that work and been impressed not only by its intellectual force but its claims to articulate a politics and an ethics of reading that run strongly counter to received ideas. In a Postscript (Chapter 7) I offer some account of these writings and the historical circumstances in which they were produced. For the moment, however, I shall concentrate on de Man's articles in *Het Vlaamsche Land*, a journal that likewise exhibited very marked pro-German sympathies, though mainly at a level of generalized reflection on cultural history and comparative literary studies. De Man reviewed a number of books in this area, clearly selected (by himself or the editors) for their relevance to wartime political events. And among the main themes that run through these articles is the question of national identity, of European culture and the place within it of the various literatures — especially the German and the French — whose destiny de Man regards as closely interlinked.

In fact there are two strains of thought at work in these essays, and between them they generate signs of unmistakable conflict and tension. One is the idea of national traditions as existing ideally in a state of complementary or mutually enriching exchange. Thus he writes (in a passage cited by de Graef) that the future of civilized values must rest on a faith in "national personality as a valuable condition and a precious possession," along with a will "to unite the creative forces of all European states."[19] But elsewhere one finds the argument that these various national cultures can best take a lead from German writers, artists, and intellectuals, since it is their particular virtue — in so far as they are "authentically" German — to have given the most articulate expression to this sense of cultural nationhood. And in advancing this case, de Man's rhetoric strays more than once onto the dangerous ground of "blood and soil," of cultural identity as rooted in a sense of predestined (organic) development and growth which can only be asserted over and against all rival nationalist claims. De Graef takes note of these discomforting metaphors, but also points out — very fairly — that they possessed at this time nothing like the charge of ideological meaning that we may now be tempted to read back into them. Any hint of "ambivalence" in de Man's thinking must at all events be seen in the context of a Belgian nation already subject to deep linguistic and cultural divisions, and whose very existence was now threatened by German imperialist designs. As with his uncle's tortuous attempts to save at least some remnant of the socialist ideal by drastically reinterpreting history and politics, so one can read Paul de Man's earliest essays as a search for some conceivable way forward from this stark and oppressive reality.

Nevertheless, the main impression left by these texts is of just how remarkably little they have in common with the writings that began to appear some ten years later in *Critique* and other French-language journals. Thus de Graef comments on the "enormous distance" that de Man had traveled in the interim, a distance marked chiefly by his total rejection of organicist models and metaphors. "In 1942, de Man sees literature as an expression of a specific national disposition which can profitably be used as one kind of reliable historical material for the deduction of 'a general idea about the destiny of mankind.'" Nothing could be further from his subsequent attitude of extreme scepticism with regard to all totalizing notions of history, all attempts to bypass the problems of attentive close reading through an appeal to some overt or tacit analogy between historical knowledge and the "hermeneutic circle" of achieved understanding. Such was indeed, as de Man came to think, the principal source of that potent aesthetic ideology that worked to naturalize — and hence to legitimate — the errors and delusions of organicist thinking. In fact one could read the entire course of his subsequent work as a single-minded effort to redeem or to exorcise the memory of those early reviews.

Such a reading would of course have to ignore those strategically placed passages where de Man fairly warns us not to expect any satisfying sense of shape, coherence, or developmental logic in his work. We have already noted one such passage in his Foreword to *The Rhetoric of Romanticism*, a passage that registers the "melancholy spectacle" these essays present in their failure to achieve any unified historical perspective.[20] And there is a similar moment of self-denegating irony in the opening sentence of *Allegories of Reading*, where de Man recalls that this book "started out as a historical study and ended up as a theory of reading." More specifically: "I began to read Rousseau . . . in preparation for a historical reflection on Romanticism and found myself unable to progress beyond local difficulties of interpretation."[21] But of course we would be wrong — naive in the extreme — if we took these admissions at anything like face value. If there is one thing clear about *Allegories of Reading*, it is de Man's determination from the outset to discredit that form of illicit metaphorical transfer that assimilates history to organicist models of development, growth, and change. His treatment of Nietzsche — especially in the chapter "Genesis and Genealogy" — brings out the degree of de Man's resistance to all such seductive schemes (*AR*, pp. 79–102). I shall need to quote at length since his formulations here are among the most remarkable, condensed, and far-reaching in all de Man's published work.

The passage in question occurs toward the end of his chapter on *The Birth of Tragedy*, at a point where the emphasis has already shifted "from a thematic to a more rhetorical reading," and where the play of figural tropes and substitutions has blocked any straightforward appeal to principles of organic continuity or historical development.[22] What de Man brings out is the constant pressure exerted on these arch-Romantic metaphors and themes by a language whose workings Nietzsche can scarcely control, and whose effects are such as to disrupt every form of self-assured hermeneutic grasp.

The dependence of narrative, continuous texts, such as *The Birth of Tragedy*, on discontinuous, aphoristic formulations . . . turns out to be a recurrent structural principle of Nietzsche's work from the start. From a historiographical point of view, it is instructive to see a genetic narrative

function as a step leading to insights that destroy the claims on which the genetic continuity was founded, but that could not have been formulated if the fallacy had not been allowed to unfold. This may well turn out to be an exemplary model in trying to understand the aberrant interpretation of Romanticism that shapes the genealogy of our present-day historical consciousness. (*AR*, pp. 101–2)

This is one of many passages in *Allegories of Reading* that mark the extent of de Man's disenchantment with all versions of historicist thinking grounded in organic, genetic, or totalizing metaphors. And indeed, one finds much evidence in his previous writings — especially the essays collected in *Blindness and Insight* — that he had long been working toward a stance of extreme and principled scepticism with regard to such delusive ideas. So there is, to say the least, something disingenuous about de Man's wry concession in the Preface to *Allegories of Reading* that this book "started out as a historical study" and "ended up as a theory of reading." What he writes about Nietzsche in the above-quoted passage would clearly apply with equal force to his own example, here and elsewhere. That is to say, the pretence of his having set out to produce some continuous, developing form of argument is everywhere belied by the way his readings undermine all belief in their power to achieve such an end. As with Nietzsche, so with de Man: the "recurrent structural principle" at work in his texts is one that will always have been in force "from the start," though to some extent concealed by the need to produce at least a semblance of unified, continuous argument. For the alternative is a mystified view of language and history which de Man had once espoused — in those early reviews — but which he subsequently set about to deconstruct with the aim of exposing its dangerous ideological consequences.

Now this is just the kind of reading that de Man ultimately rejects in Nietzsche's case. One might suppose that there was, after all, a certain narrative shape to be discerned in the stages of Nietzsche's intellectual progress, a development that would run — broadly speaking — from the organicist myths and metaphors of *The Birth of Tragedy* to those later, more rigorous and undeceived writings where an aphoristic style goes along with an outlook of extreme epistemological scepticism. Thus "a great number of passages from *The Birth of Tragedy* seem to place [this] text forcefully within the logocentric tradition. The later evolution of Nietzsche's work could then be understood as the gradual 'deconstruction' of a logocentrism that receives its fullest expression in *The Birth*"

(AR, p. 88). And this reading could moreover be applied to de Man's own texts, since here also — as we have seen — there is evidence of a strongly marked shift from organicist models of history, language, and representation to a stance that firmly repudiates such thinking in favor of a radical discontinuity between these levels or modes of explanatory grasp. But for de Man, this move can only amount to another form of redemptive ploy, a reading that makes coherent sense of Nietzsche by imposing its own teleological scheme of values. The only difference is that now those values are derived from a foregone set of *deconstructionist* assumptions that equates progress with the steady onward march toward a fully demystified state of understanding.

The assured route from "logocentrism" to "deconstruction" would then be exactly what is thrown into doubt by a rigorous accounting for the problems and resistances of Nietzsche's text. For it is simply not the case, as de Man is at pains to point out, that *The Birth of Tragedy* develops its "themes" in a manner of straightforwardly coherent exposition which would make it a kind of innocent foil-text to the later, more rigorous or "deconstructive" writings. On the contrary: *The Birth of Tragedy* is marked through and through by thematic and rhetorical tensions which everywhere turn out to subvert its mythic or pseudo-historical claims. Thus

> the outward narrative transitions . . . often consist of mere formal symmetries devoid of thematic weight. Thus the rebirth of Dionysos in the person of Wagner, crucial as the event may be, is described as a mere reversal of the regressive movement that destroyed the Hellenic world into a symmetrical movement of regeneration by which the modern, Germanic world is to be reborn. Passages of this kind are valueless as arguments, since they assume that the actual events of history are founded in formal symmetries easy enough to achieve in pictorial, musical, or poetic fictions, but that can never predict the occurrence of a historical event. *(AR*, p. 84)

So we are wrong to see *The Birth of Tragedy* as a text still captive to those themes and motifs that Nietzsche would subsequently expose to the rigors of a full-scale deconstructive reading. Already there are signs of his argument generating conflicts and tensions of rhetorical strategy that cannot be contained within the governing terms of a straightforward thematic reading.

And the same applies to that other main component of the Nietzschean myth, his idea of Western culture as having evolved from the clash of opposing ("Dionysian" and "Apollonian") principles — with Greek tragic drama providing the originary ideal case of how those principles once came together in a moment of short-lived creative synthesis. What destroyed this condition was of course, in Nietzsche's view, the intrusion of a rationalist philosophy whose first and chief spokesman was Socrates, and whose effect was so far to unbalance the equation that Dionysian instinct and energy gave way to the calculating spirit of abstract thought. But de Man finds this narrative no more coherent than the story of Wagnerian music-drama arriving on the scene just in time to restore German culture to its authentic, predestined ancient Greek heritage. For it can be shown, he writes,

> that whenever an art form is being discussed, the three modes represented by Dionysos, Apollo, and Socrates are always simultaneously present . . . The Dionysian moments always occur in revolt against the tyranny or as a result of the failure of the Socratic claim to knowledge; the Dionysian insight must always be doubled at once by the Apollonian shelter of appearances; and the Apollonian vision is always the vision of "the eternal contradiction, of the father of all things." [i.e. Dionysos] (*AR*, p. 85)

So there is no question of translating Nietzsche's mythology into anything like an intelligible order of concepts, themes, or historical developments. One the one hand his text is undeniably cast in the form of a providential narrative or secularized salvation-history — one that moves from stage to stage through a sequence of gains and losses whose last, redemptive twist is the advent of a new culture hero in the person of Richard Wagner. But on the other this message is shrewdly undercut by the evidence that Nietzsche "might be in the grip of a powerful assumption about the nature of language, bound to control his conceptual and rhetorical discourse regardless of whether the author is aware of it" (*AR*, p. 87). One result is Nietzsche's apparent acceptance, in this early text, of organicist models and metaphors that his subsequent writing would strenuously seek to deconstruct. But the other — more important for de Man at this stage — is that Nietzsche's narrative and rhetorical strategies *already* show every sign of subverting the manifest drift of his text. So we should merely be falling into another version of the same geneticist trap if we took it that Nietzsche's productions exhibited a straightforward progress from mystified thinking to a stage of enlightened, self-conscious rhetorical critique.

I have suggested that one of de Man's motives here is to head off any possible reading of his work that would seek out evidence of a radical "turn," a complete repudiation of early ideas that had since come to strike him as naive, deluded, or ideologically dangerous. And I think that we should not be too readily inclined to go along with these injunctions and abandon the attempt to make sense of de Man's work in "genetic" or developmental terms. Just as his account of *The Birth of Tragedy* does — whatever his assertions to the contrary — read it very much in the light of

Nietzsche's subsequent texts, so again with de Man there is much to be gained if one traces the sequence of visions and revisions that make up his intellectual history. And by far the most significant factor here is his turning away from that seductive organicist creed that identifies authentic language with the power to redeem man's fallen, self-alienated existence by somehow restoring a naturalized relation between words, thought, and experience. Such had indeed been de Man's way of thinking in those early reviews — published in *Het Vlaamsche Land* — that fastened their hopes for the survival of European civilization to a sense of the distinctive destiny at work in various languages and national cultures. With the collapse of those hopes — and no doubt the recognition that similar beliefs had played a more sinister role — one can see why de Man should have gone to such lengths to dissociate his subsequent writings from every last form of organicist ideology.

III

Perhaps the most revealing text in this connection is his essay "The Temptation of Permanence," the French original of which first appeared in 1955, and an English translation (by Dan Latimer) as recently as 1983.[23] This text marks a definite transitional stage in de Man's work, not only in so far as it reflects obliquely on his move from Europe to America, but also in the sense of profoundly revaluing those ideas and influences that had shaped his early thought. The essay can be read as a companion piece to "Heidegger's Exegeses of Hölderlin," since it finds de Man once again measuring his distance from any criticism that claims to interpret poetry in a language of unmediated truth or proximity to Being. Such is indeed the "temptation of permanence" that manifests itself as the desire to have done with all mediating secular interests — like those of politics and history — and so pass directly to the kind of authentic, primordial concern that finds an answering voice in poetry.

For Heidegger, the antithesis of these values is to be seen in modern technological civilization, in a process of accelerating secular change that alienates man from nature and destroys the very grounds of remembrance. De Man cites some passages from Heidegger's later writings where poetry figures as the one potential source of a wisdom that can yet hold out against this drift toward oblivion, and thus offers hope of restoring mankind to a proper relationship with nature and Being. "Poetically, man dwells," as Heidegger writes in a sentence drawn from Hölderlin that provides the starting point for one of his best-known meditations on the name and nature of poetry. Through poetry, one glimpses the possibility of an unforced, authentic being-in-the-world that enables man to experience once again that sense of rootedness in time and place that is lost through the will to subjugate nature to the purposes of human technological control. It is this capacity for "dwelling" within language, for inhabiting a world that reveals itself gradually to contemplative thought, and which cannot be grasped through any kind of restless, self-interested striving after knowledge — it is this mode of wise receptiveness that Heidegger identifies with the saving power of poetry. Only by listening patiently to such language can we hope to regain the sense of that primordial destiny whose signs have been persistently ignored or misread by thinkers from Socrates to the present.

"The Temptation of Permanence" is a diagnostic reading of Heidegger's texts that questions this idea of poetry as somehow giving access to a timeless, aboriginal truth prior to all mere determinations of historical or conscious, reflective grasp. For it now appears to de Man that such thinking has a dangerous aspect, a tendency to promote forms of mystified understanding whose effects are not confined to the realm of aesthetic speculation. For Heidegger, as he remarks, language takes on a power of etymological suggestion that can easily translate into a nationalist mystique with potentially far-reaching implications. "Relying on the relation, in the German language, between the word 'destiny' (*Geschick*) and the word 'history' (*Geschichte*), he [Heidegger] affirmed in various ways that history is the concrete manifestation of the very movement of Being, a movement whose fundamental ambiguity is the origin of the historicity of our destiny" (TP, pp. 214–15). And this strain of highly charged etymopoeic thinking goes along with Heidegger's constant desire to assimilate language to organicist metaphors of origin, growth, and natural evolution. Hence the frequent occurrence in his late essays of "examples and metaphors borrowed from the life of the earth: the forest, labor, the land, etc. The fixed idea seems to be the necessity of protecting the earth, of watching over it as a peasant watches over his fields; technology takes on diabolical proportions in so far as it is the enemy of the earth" (TP, p. 220). It is in this sense precisely that Heidegger's thought manifests the "temptation of permanence," the will to distinguish an *authentic* temporality — one that respects the predestined vocation of Being and truth — from a secular or fallen historicity that bears witness to man's fateful swerve from that original destiny. What is always in question for Heidegger is the power of thinking in its genuine, creative or poetic mode to repair the divisions thus inflicted upon human experience. And the metaphors that serve to advance this case — as in the title of Heidegger's essay "Building Dwelling Thinking," to which de Man makes particular reference[24] — are figures that invite an identification between the process of thought and processes or activities in the physical world that have to do with man's relationship to nature. They are tropes intended to reinforce the point that man's true vocation as a thinking, speaking, listening subject is so closely tied up with his being in the world that only such organicist metaphors can express the truth of his condition.

Now it is a part of the burden of de Man's argument that these metaphors don't go together as naturally as Heidegger would have us believe. "Building" and "dwelling" may appear to be aspects of a common enterprise, one that is directed toward furnishing man with a "shelter" whose construction is yet a part of nature, since it enables him (in Heidegger's words) to "dwell on the earth and in his dwelling let the earth be earth." That is to say: the essential activity of building is one undertaken in *natural* accord with the conditions — those of our being-in-the-world — that require such constructive enterprise as an aspect of man's authentic destiny. And the same would apply to creative thinking, in so far as it requires that we harken to a truth that only language can impart, no matter how far we think to elaborate ("build") that truth in verbal constructions of our own apparent creating. It is by means of this complex metaphorical transfer between "building" and "dwelling" — between the constructive and the passive or contemplative aspects of thought — that Heidegger can claim for poetry a power to reconcile all those conflicts and antinomies that plague the discourse of philosophic reason. In de Man's words:

> Heidegger promises explicitly the transcendence of division and speaks more overtly than in his earlier work of the necessity to learn to think the simplicity of the earth: the earth, the sky, mortal man, and God thought in their unity. This unity is *thought as an act*; to take care of things and in raising them up, to approximate building (*bauen*) which approximates in its turn dwelling (*wohnen*). Heidegger uses the same term "dwelling" to indicate this action and to indicate poetic action; he thus invites the mind to make with him this leap which identifies the two kinds of act. (TP, pp. 218–19)

But it is de Man's point that this presumed identification is in fact the product of a certain linguistic subterfuge; that Heidegger's claims for the profound unity of "building" and "dwelling" can only seem deluded if one reads his text with an eye to its covert rhetorical strategies. For there is all the difference in the world between an act, whether physical or verbal, that issues in the construction of a hitherto nonexistent edifice, and a mode of habitation — or poetic "dwelling" — that occupies a place already thus built. Heidegger's metaphors work to efface this distinction, and along with it the difference between lived history, as a realm of practical choices and decisions, and "authentic" destiny as that which unfolds through a process of quasi-organic evolution quite apart from such issues.

De Man never goes as far as Adorno in condemning the Heideggerian "jargon of authenticity" as a vehicle for the kind of irrationalist mystique whose political expression was the rise of Nazi ideology.[25] His writings continued to engage critically with Heidegger's thought, but always on the basis of a shared concern with questions that de Man finds Heidegger to have raised to a high point of philosophic subtlety and grasp. This is clearly why he thinks it so important to distinguish the moments of genuine insight in Heidegger's readings of Hölderlin or Rilke from the passages where a certain self-motivated "blindness" to the workings of his own rhetoric leads Heidegger to mystify the nature of poetic understanding.

> If therefore one agreed to make the identification that Heidegger suggests . . . one would have in fact succumbed to the temptation of permanence. Insofar as the *building* of the essay "Building Dwelling Thinking" is the building of the earth, it is certain that it is eternal and that it abides. But it passes to the side of history, for it does not establish a transcendence of the division of being. (TP, p. 219)

The somewhat abrupt change of tack midway through this passage is crucial not only as the turning point in this particular essay but as a clear indication of the course de Man's thinking would pursue over the next two decades and more. It signals the point at which a Heideggerian meditation on origins, destiny, and authenticity gives way to a form of *Ideologiekritik* alert to precisely the dangers and "temptations" that attend such a project. And this emphasis emerges in de Man's writing alongside a shift of geopolitical priorities that begins to discover more hopeful portents in American than in European culture. Thus Heidegger is cast as the "authentic" but none the less deluded voice of a self-proclaimed national destiny — a destiny that is identified all too closely with the German language, its expressive resources and its power of conserving a threatened truth against the ravages of modern technocratic reason. To de Man, on the contrary, such thinking now appears a species of seductive illusion. "It is more dangerous than technical thinking since, instead of attacking an earth which is quite capable of defending itself, it betrays the movement of being" (TP, p. 220).

One might gather from this last formulation that de Man's language is still in thrall to a strongly Heideggerian thematics of origins, Being, and truth. But his point is again that Heidegger falls into error in so far as he thinks that language can articulate such truths in a mode of immediate, self-present apprehension that would finally transcend history, reason, and the antinomies of conscious thought. Such, we may recall, is de Man's chief objection to Heidegger's readings of Hölderlin: that they presume to *state* directly and explicitly what the poet can only suggest through a language that everywhere acknowledges its own inevitable failure to reconcile these disparate realms. This strikes de Man as a form of hermeneutic violence, a will to penetrate to the truth of a text whose truthfulness lies in its way of avoiding such premature and dangerous absolutes. And in "The Temptation of Permanence" we can see just why — and on what ideological grounds — de Man arrived at this position. Heidegger's desire to have poetry achieve an authentic overcoming or transcendence of man's divided condition is complicit with his will to identify language — and the German language preëminently — with the voice of revealed truth. In both aspects his thinking courts the danger of confusing history with processes of natural evolution and growth, a confusion which — as we have seen already — de Man was to track through its numerous showings in the discourse of post-Romantic critical thought. His commentary on Yeats's "Among School Children" in *Allegories of Reading* is probably the best-known example of this resolute demythologizing drive (pp. 11–12). But we can best understand its political implications in the context of an essay like "The Temptation of Permanence," where de Man is clearly striving to articulate themes that bear directly on the course of world-historical events.

In fact the essay begins, not with Heidegger's reading of Hölderlin, but with a commentary on some texts of André Malraux, in particular his novel *The Walnut Trees of Altenburg* (1943).[26] The scene that first engages de Man's interest is one in which "the principal character receives a revelation of the permanence of man by seeing the ancient trees of the ancestral manor" (TP, p. 212). And this epiphany takes place shortly after his discussion with a philosopher of history whose arguments have to do with the choice between an organicist, naturalizing concept of human destiny and one that accepts the discontinuous, unpredictable, contingent character of actions and events. De Man's commentary on this episode prefigures what he will have to say in *Allegories of Reading* about the seductive appeal of organicist metaphors and the need to guard against them by an effort of vigilant critique. The opposition, he writes,

> resides in the nature of the two movements confronting each other. The historical movement is that of becoming: *being* consciously created, whether as the work of art or historical deed in general, is unstable in its essence, and it denies itself to be reborn in another *being*. The two are separated by the abyss of a negation (in organic language: a death), and the passage from the one to the other is essentially discontinuous. The movement of the ancient tree, on the other hand, is a growth: its being

remains immediately identical with itself, and its movement is only the extension of what already is and always will be. (TP, p. 212)

In this particular text, de Man finds Malraux to have posed the crucial question in a language that indicates his own vivid awareness of the tempting, delusive nature of organicist models and metaphors. But in a subsequent work (*The Voices of Silence*) this attitude gives way to a quite different set of values and priorities, one where historical destiny appears always under the aspect of organic form, and where discontinuity is directly equated with the death of individuals and civilizations.[27] And it is at this point — with the shift in Malraux's thought toward a certain "temptation of permanence" — that de Man draws out the essential kinship with Heidegger's readings of Hölderlin.

> [H]istorical consciousness becomes the acceptance of destiny, acceptance which is passivity . . . In becoming trees, we have lost the precarious situation of being *on* the earth to become creatures *of* the earth . . . For art so considered is in reality only a sediment without life, which integrates itself with the soil without opposing it. Pretending to think being, Malraux thinks in reality earth which he desires. (TP, p. 213)

This passage makes it clear that de Man has already traveled a long way from any straightforward allegiance to the Heideggerian ethos of origins, presence, and truth. If his language still acknowledges the claims of a "being" that in some sense stands as the measure of authentic existence, it is a being whose condition is always to be presently unfulfilled, to take shape through man's struggle for a better way of life, and not — as in Heidegger — to point thinking back to its ground in some remote predestination of language or culture. So it is that de Man can write, in the single most striking sentence of this essay: "Far from being anti-historical, the poetic act . . . is the quintessential historical act: that through which we become conscious of the divided character of our being, and consequently, of the necessity of fulfilling it, of accomplishing it in time, rather than undergoing it in eternity." (TP, p. 214)

From a certain point of view — undoubtedly that which de Man espoused in his subsequent writings — one has "explained" nothing by pointing to these likely influences and pressures on his early development. The texts, after all, are there to be read, and indeed no critic has done more than de Man to discourage the kind of lazy or short-cut "reading" that passes clean through the complexities of textual understanding to arrive at some putative psycho-biographical content. To this extent we read in defiance of his own repeated counsel if we respond to the extreme critical rigor of his later texts by asking what might have been the motives, political or otherwise, that led to his adopting this stance. Nevertheless I would argue that the two approaches are not incompatible; that we can read those texts with a due regard to their rhetorical and argumentative structures yet without in the process renouncing all interest in de Man's intellectual life history.

In his essay "Criticism and Crisis," de Man himself makes a comparable claim in relation to Husserl and the project of transcendental phenomenology (*BI*, pp. 3–19). This project was epitomized in the lectures that Husserl delivered in Vienna during 1935, subsequently published under the title *The Crisis of the European Sciences*.[28] In them, Husserl laid out the program of a new philosophy that would finally secure the bases of knowledge, reason, and truth; that would combat the threat of an encroaching relativist or nihilist outlook by grounding thought in an apodictic "science" of primordial intuitions immune to further questioning or doubt. He would thus carry through the foundationalist project that others before him (like Descartes and Kant) had attempted but ultimately failed to achieve. And he would do so by suspending all commonsense or merely "psychological" sources of knowledge, by systematically doubting whatever could be called into doubt, and thus working down to the bedrock of epistemological certitude that philosophy and science required. Only by such a radical rethinking of knowledge, its constitutive powers and limits, could European culture be restored to a sense of its authentic historical destiny.

For de Man, this program offers a striking case in point of the link between "criticism" and "crisis," a link that is of more than merely etymological interest. For it is always through a certain "rhetoric of crisis" that criticism seeks, like Husserl, to escape the relativity or the partial insights of a previous, deluded way of thinking, and to ground its own truth-claims in a discourse of enlightened knowledge and truth. But such claims can be advanced only by virtue of a certain correlative "blindness" to the limiting conditions that govern their utterance. This Husserl speaks on the one hand for a concept of *universal* human reason, for a supranational community of mind which philosophy can best work to achieve by discounting those merely local or culture-specific differences that would stand in the way of such an ideal consensus. Indeed, his entire project is premised on the faith that this "transcendental" viewpoint can at last be attained, thus refuting the kind of relativist argument that follows from acknowledging the ultimately incommensurable character of different languages and cultures. But this set of claims must be seen to conflict with Husserl's stress on the fate of *European* philosophy and science, on the need for a certain, highly developed form of theoretical reason to assert its authority over and against those other, less enlightened or self-critical traditions. Thus "Husserl speaks repeatedly of non-European cultures as primitive, pre-scientific and pre-philosophical, myth-dominated and congenitally incapable of the disinterested distance without which there can be no philosophical meditation" (*BI*, p. 15). Such an outlook is implicit in the very structure of Husserlian reflection, in its will to suspend all ideas deriving from the "natural" or commonsense attitude, and to put in their place a more adequate knowledge acquired through rigorous, self-disciplined thought. Clearly there is a sense in which these categories work to endorse the superior vantage point and privileged destiny of European man. And this despite the fact that, by his own definition, philosophy transcends such limiting cultural perspectives in the quest for "eidetic" or self-evident truths accessible to all humankind.

Husserl is thus caught up in precisely that alternating rhythm of "blindness" and "insight" that de Man will go on to analyze at length in his subsequent essays. But in Husserl's case we can see most clearly what might be the ultimate *political* stakes of this seeming obsession with textual aporias or moments of rhetorical stress and strain. For it is Husserl's situation as self-elected spokesman for Europe in its moment of greatest crisis and danger that sets the main terms for de Man's discussion in these pages. His text reveals "with striking clarity the structure of all crisis-determined statements" (*BI*, p. 16). It programmatically asserts what *cannot be the case* according to its own more consequent logic, or what has to be exempted from critical inspection in order to provide a starting point for criticism itself. The privilege attaching to "European" values (reason, self-criticism, disinterested inquiry) is the one thing that cannot be called into question without undermining the very rationale of Husserlian phenomenology. Thus "the crucial, determining examination on which depends Husserl's right to call himself, on his own terms, a philosopher, is in fact never undertaken. As a European, it seems that Husserl escapes from the necessary self-criticism that is prior to all philosophical truth about the self" (*BI*, p. 16). Yet de Man is not suggesting that this blindness was in any sense avoidable, or that Husserl should stand accused of bad faith on account of his failure to perceive these contradictions. Their significance lies in the fact that Husserl gave voice to a *genuine* crisis in the European sciences of man — a crisis whose outcome he could scarcely foretell (writing in 1935), but whose conflicts are already deeply inscribed in the character of his project. "Since we are speaking of a man of superior good will, it suffices to point to the pathos of such a claim [i.e., philosophy's task of preserving the high destiny of European culture] at a moment when Europe was about to destroy itself as center in the name of its unwarranted claim to be the center" (*BI*, p. 16).

IV

It is not, I think, too much to claim that de Man experienced his own predicament as in some ways closely resembling that of Husserl. In his case also, the very future of European civilization had presented itself under the aspect of crisis — a crisis that de Man (in his earliest writings) had hoped to see averted through the reconciling power of an authentic meditation on the destiny of national cultures. But this hope had collapsed, and with it his belief that such thinking could offer any prospect of enlightened change. No doubt this sense of failure was intensified by the spectacle of Heidegger's apparent willingness, at one stage, to identify National Socialism with the resurgence of authentic Being and truth. And one could speculate further that Heidegger's radical reinterpretation of Husserl — his turn away from the rigors of transcendental critique toward an existentialist brooding on mortality, finitude, Being, and time — came to strike de Man as a dangerous betrayal of Husserl's original project. At all events de Man's own writing would henceforth take on a demystifying rigor more akin to Husserl's than to anything in Heidegger's work. And this despite his clear perception (in "Criticism and Crisis") that enlightenment as Husserl understood it — "a process by means of which naive assumptions are made available to consciousness by an act of critical self-understanding" — must always go along with a certain blindness to its own constitutive motives and interests.

For the only way forward, as it now appeared, was to acknowledge this predicament and yet keep faith with the project of enlightened critique.

> Speaking in what was in fact a state of urgent personal and political crisis about a more general form of crisis, Husserl's text . . . establishes an important truth; the fact that philosophical knowledge can only come into being when it is turned back upon itself . . . The rhetoric of crisis states its own truth in the mode of error. It is itself radically blind to the light it emits. (*BI*, p. 16)

In this passage, de Man sets out what amounts to a program for his own critical work over the next two decades. That work will undertake to demystify the sources of aesthetic ideology in its various forms, especially where these lend credence to the illusion of history as a process of predestined organic evolution. It will do so, very much in the manner of Husserl, by as far as possible suspending such naturalized habits of thought, exposing them to the kind of lucid critique that draws out their unacknowledged blind spots of prejudice. But de Man also preserves a keen sense of the structural irony that emerges in his reading of Husserl: namely, the tendency of all such "enlightened" or demystifying projects to posit another, naive or deluded state of consciousness against which to play off their own superior insights. Hence, on the one hand, de Man's insistence that *all* critical thinking — his own included — partakes of a certain constitutive "blindness" in relation to the text it seeks to comprehend. Hence also his refusal of the constant temptation to evade this negative knowledge by ignoring textual or rhetorical complications and thus claiming access to truths of experience untouched by critical self-doubt. This is the temptation that Husserl falls into when, writing "as a European," he assumes a standpoint of superior cognitive grasp and so exempts his own discourse from the kind of sceptical scrutiny which alone might justify its philosophic claims. Husserl is committing "precisely the mistake that Rousseau did not commit when he carefully avoided giving his concept of natural man, the basis of his anthropology, any empirical status whatever" (*BI*, p. 16). That is to say, Husserl is moving prematurely from the realm of transcendental critique — of reflection on the powers and limits of *all* cognitive inquiry — to a form of anthropological thinking that equates naive or commonsense awareness with something strictly outside its own domain.

It is characteristic that de Man should here cite Rousseau as a counter-instance to this mystifying tendency in Husserl's thought. For Rousseau, as we have seen, figures always in the role of an author whose texts put up the greatest possible resistance to mystified readings; whose degree of rhetorical self-awareness is such that interpreters, even sharp-eyed interpreters like Derrida, are consistently played off the field. And this goes along with de Man's larger claim: that it is only through the rigors of *rhetorical* exegesis that thinking can avoid such delusory claims. I have already discussed in some detail the way that de Man reconceives the relationship between logic, grammar, and rhetoric, arguing that rhetoric has long been demoted to a merely ancillary position on account of its power to disrupt or unsettle the certitudes of commonsense reason. And we have also seen how this increasing stress on the virtues of rhetorical close reading coincided with de Man's passage from Europe to America and his encounter with the New Criticism in its most productive and stimulating moment. That these facts are not unconnected is clear enough from his retrospective comments on the New Criticism in "The Return to Philology" (1982). I have cited this passage once before but do so now more specifically in the context of de Man's response at this crucial point in his scholarly career. What most impressed him about the New Criticism was its inbuilt resistance to premature absolutes:

Mere reading, it turns out, prior to any theory, is able to transform critical discourse in a manner that would appear deeply subversive to those who think of the teaching of literature as a substitute for the teaching of theology, ethics, pyschology, or intellectual history. Close reading accomplishes this often in spite of itself because it cannot fail to respond to structures of language which it is the more or less secret aim of literary teaching to keep hidden:[29]

At this time de Man was clearly, so to speak, on a state of maximum alert against any temptation to bypass those rhetorical checks and resistances that offered a guard against the seductions of aesthetic ideology. And his subsequent writings give evidence enough of his determination to maintain this stance through a sequence of increasingly complex theoretical positions.

His passage to America can therefore be seen as a turning point in de Man's intellectual history. It marked his transition from a strongly Eurocentric standpoint — one still characterized by a deep, if ambivalent regard for the writings of Husserl, Heidegger, and phenomenological criticism — to a stress on the virtues of textual close reading and on rhetoric as the chief and most reliable means of exposing the blind spots engendered by that same tradition. In "Crisis and Criticism" de Man asks pointedly just why Husserl should have drawn such sharp geopolitical limits to the otherwise (and in principle) universal spread of enlightened critical thought. "Why this geographical expansion should have chosen to stop, once and forever, at the Atlantic Ocean and at the Caucasus, Husserl does not say" (*BI*, p. 15). And the same question is raised in "The Temptation of Permanence," where there develops a kind of dialectical agon between Europe and America, the latter conceived as a land of open possibilities unburdened by the sense of cultural destiny that bears down so heavily on European thinkers. Thus de Man cites a passage from Rilke, also taken up by Heidegger, in which the poet complains that "from America have come to us now empty, indifferent things, artificial things which deceive us by simulating life . . . A house, or an apple tree, or a grapevine has nothing in common with the house, the fruit or the grape in which our ancestors have invested their hopes and cares."[30] These sentiments of course chime exactly with Heidegger's contempt for American civilization, in particular those two aspects of it — technology and pragmatism as a home-grown philosophic creed — which he saw as symptoms of well-nigh terminal decline. But de Man responds to these charges by suggesting that "perhaps in the degree to which technology is impoverishment and burns history without leaving material residue, technology forces us to rid ourselves of what is after all only a false serenity" (TP, p. 211). Rilke's and Heidegger's ancestral dreams would then appeal not only as wishful illusions but as symptoms of a deep-laid conservative mystique inimical to history and change.

It would plainly be absurd to present de Man as a starry-eyed convert to all things American. In Chapter 5, I pointed to some of the ways in which his work, like Derrida's, holds out against the current neo-pragmatist drift in American philosophy and criticism. When de Man speaks of the "resistance to theory" — the fact that close reading can "transform critical discourse" in a manner that inevitably tends to disrupt any method, system, or preconceived approach — he is far from adopting the anti-theoretical line espoused by a philosopher like Richard Rorty or a literary critic like Stanley Fish. For de Man, the resistance must come from within theory itself, in a movement of thought that both acknowledges the claims of theoretical reflection — the call for enlightened critique — and perceives the obstacles that rise up against it in the course of a rhetorical close reading. This is why he insists that any responsible practice of criticism — any "ethics of reading" that merits the name — will need to forego the kind of self-assured hermeneutic grasp that comes of pretty much knowing in advance what a text or a passage is likely to mean. Thus "reading is an argument . . . because it has to go against the grain of what one would expect to happen in the name of what has to happen."[31] Nothing could be further from the current neo-pragmatist position, according to which it is strictly impossible to read, criticize, interpret, or argue a case that doesn't in the end fall in with those tacit values and assumptions which make up the enabling precondition of all understanding. In the words of Walter Benn Michaels: "Our beliefs are not obstacles between us and meaning; they are what makes meaning possible in the first place."[32] Such arguments, if accepted, would totally disqualify not only de Man's project of deconstructive reading but also any form of *Ideologiekritik* that sought to go beyond received, commonsense beliefs to an account of their unrecognized motives and interests. It would amount, as I have argued, to a vote of no confidence in reason itself. This is why de Man insists that close reading — or the practice of rhetorical exegesis — must indeed go against any version of the so-called "hermeneutic circle," that principle which equates true understanding with a tacit foreknowledge of what the text says, and which would thus block the way to any genuinely critical or contestatory reading.

It may be that what first appealed to de Man in the American New Criticism was precisely its "pragmatic" character, its resistance to theories of the generalizing kind that promoted an indifference to the disciplined activity of reading. In fact he suggests as much in a passage from "The Return to Philology" which commemorates his teacher Reuben Brower, one who "had a rare talent . . . for keeping things as tidy as a philosophical investigation ought to be yet, at the same time, entirely pragmatic" (p. 24). But it is clear from what de Man has to say more specifically about Brower's teaching that the term "pragmatic" must here have very different connotations from those it possesses for the apostles of neo-pragmatist fashion.

> [Students] were asked . . . to begin by reading texts closely as texts and not to move at once into the general context of human experience or history. Much more humbly or modestly, they were to start out from the bafflement that such singular turns of tone, phrase, and figure were bound to produce in readers attentive enough to notice them and honest enough not to hide their non-understanding behind the screen of received ideas that often passes, in literary instruction, for humanistic knowledge. (*RP*, p. 23)

Such "pragmatism" is far from confining itself to the closed circle of interpretive foreknowledge or (in Gadamer's phrase) hermeneutic "pre-understanding." It encourages a willingness to read texts with an eye to those disruptive elements of sense that cannot be accounted for by any kind of "theory," but which equally confound the neo-pragmatist idea that we must always, in some way, know *in advance* how our interpretations are going to turn out — so that no kind of theory can affect the issue one way or another.

I have argued that de Man's most persistent endeavor, from the mid-1950s on, was to articulate a form of ideological criticism that would not repeat those errors to be found in Husserl's — and more ominously, in Heidegger's — writings on the destiny of European culture. This led him to adopt the stance of conceptual rhetorician, one for whom all truth-claims must be called into question through a close examination of language in its suasive and tropological modes, but for whom nevertheless such questioning conduces to better, more enlightened thought. In his last few years of concentrated activity, de Man laid plans for a detailed study of Marx, Adorno, Althusser, and other such thinkers in the tradition of radical *Ideologiekritik*.[33] It is possible that some of these texts may yet be published, or at least that sufficient material exists to reconstruct the main outlines of de Man's argument. But on the basis of those writings we do possess — especially his essays on Rousseau, Kant, Hegel, Nietzsche, Husserl, and Heidegger — it is clear that his work had long been directed toward problems in exactly this area. If the foregoing chapters manage to dispel some of the errors and persistent misreadings that have so far obscured the nature of that work, this book will have served its purpose well enough.

7

Postscript: On de Man's Early Writings for "Le Soir"

I

On December 1st, 1987 the *New York Times* ran a piece under the title "Yale Scholar's Articles Found in Nazi Paper." The scholar in question was Paul de Man, who had written these pieces during the early 1940s, before leaving Belgium for America. They were published in *Le Soir*, a newspaper of decidedly pro-Nazi sympathies, and contain many passages that can be read as endorsing what amounts to a collaborationist line. There is talk of the need to preserve national cultures against harmful cosmopolitan influences, and of German literature as a model for those other, less fortunate traditions that lack such an authentic national base. Their language often resorts to organicist metaphors, notions of cultural identity as rooted in the soil of a flourishing native literature. One could draw comparisons with a work like T.S. Eliot's *Notes Towards the Definition of Culture*, where it is likewise argued that the vitality of "satellite" traditions (for de Man most crucially the French, Dutch, and Belgian) must depend on the continuing existence of a strong hegemonic center. But of course de Man was writing at a time and in a political situation where thoughts of this kind carried a far more ominous charge. It is hard, if not impossible to redeem these texts by looking for some occasional sign that they are not to be taken at face value. They are utterly remote from de Man's more familiar writings, not only in their frequent naivety of utterance and sentiment, but also in the way that they uncritically endorse such mystified ideas as the organic relation between language, culture, and national destiny — ideas which he would later set out to deconstruct with such extreme sceptical rigor.

This is not to say that they can now be written off as mere youthful aberrations, texts for which he cannot fairly be held to account since they go so much against his subsequent thinking. Though their existence remained a secret all those years de Man would, I think, have acknowledged their discovery with the attitude "scripta manent"; that what is written is written and cannot be tactfully ignored, no matter how far his convictions had changed in the interim. But there are several points that need to be made before we can assess their real significance. One is the fact that he wrote these pieces as a very young man under pressures of political and personal circumstances that may help to explain, if not to justify, their writing. As we have seen, his uncle, Hendrik de Man, was a prominent Belgian socialist thinker during the 1920s and 1930s, a government minister whose two terms of office had been marked by numerous disappointments and policy setbacks. His response to the catastrophe of German occupation was to draw up a last-ditch tactical plan arguing that Nazism might, after all, evolve into something like a genuine National Socialism, and that therefore the only course open was to pin one's hope to that saving possibility and not hold out against the occupying forces. His biographer, Peter Dodge, traces all the tortuous visions and revisions that led up to this ultimate misjudgment.[1] Dodge sees Hendrik de Man as a genuinely tragic figure, forced into exile (and convicted of treason in his absence) not so much through opportunism, compromise, or worse, but through a desperate attempt to reinterpret history in light of his residual socialist faith. Paul de Man was clearly not in a position where any pronouncements of his would take on such a burden of fateful consequence. But it is fair to conjecture — on the basis of numerous passages in these articles — that he thought the only prospect of survival for the Belgian people, languages, and culture lay in making terms (at least temporarily) with the fact of German occupation, and hoping that Nazism might indeed be "reinterpreted" in a more favorable light. Again, this is not to excuse those early writings, but to see how they might have been produced by a thinker whose subsequent reflections took such an utterly different path.

For this is what will strike any reader acquainted with the texts that de Man published after his passage to America. One could read this entire production as an attempt to exorcise the bad memory, to adopt a critical standpoint squarely opposed to that mystified philosophy of language, tradition, and organic national culture. Of course it is possible to argue the opposite case, to declare with the wisdom of hindsight that deconstruction was always a "nihilist" activity, that its politics were clearly reactionary, if not proto-fascist, and that therefore these latest revelations merely confirm what should have been evident from the start. Already the professors are lining up to make statements to this or similar effect. (Thus R.W.B. Lewis, quoted in the *New York Times* article: "deconstruction is anti-historical . . . it encourages scepticism about almost anything in the realm of human experience. That's one of the things I hold against it.") Jeffrey Mehlman went so far as to surmise that deconstruction in America was really nothing more than an elaborate cover-up campaign, an "amnesty" organized by literary intellectuals who could find no other means to evade or excuse their burden of collective guilt. Such arguments, for all their patent absurdity, have found a ready platform in the American press and convinced many people that there must after all be something deeply suspect about the whole deconstructionist enterprise. Others — Frank Lentricchia among them — have fastened on passages from de Man's later work where he addresses the matter of guilt, responsibility, and self-exculpation in terms that can easily appear to invite a crypto-autobiographical reading.[2] One such passage is the sentence on Rousseau from *Allegories* where he explains how any fault may be excused in confessional narrative since "the experience always exists simultaneously as fictional discourse and as empirical event and it is never possible to decide which one of the two possibilities is the right one. The indecision makes it possible to excuse the bleakest of crimes" (*AR*, p. 293). As Lentricchia says, it is difficult to read such passages now without being put in mind of de Man's early writings and his burden of guilty memory.

The same applies to those middle-period essays (like "Literary History and Literary Modernity") where de Man takes a lead from Nietzsche's meditations on the dead weight of historical memory, its paralyzing effect on present thought and action, and the modernist desire to achieve a radical break with all such disabling legacies. Lentricchia once again has the relevant passages ready to hand, passages where de Man writes of "a past that . . . is so threatening that it has to be forgotten," and of the way in which "we try to give ourselves a new past from which we should have liked to descend."[3] There does seem reason to suppose de Man is here engaged in something more than a piece of purely diagnostic commentary; that his relentless pursuit of these Nietzschean aporias shows him in the grip of a compulsion to rehearse and yet somehow repress or sublimate the facts of his own past history. Such is at any rate a part of the significance these texts must bear for us now, whatever may have been de Man's conscious or unconscious intentions in the matter. But we should also bear in mind one further passage cited by Lentricchia, a sentence from the same essay where de Man remarks of Nietzsche that "the rejection of the past is not so much an act of forgetting as an act of critical judgment directed against himself" (*BI*, p. 159). The hostile commentators are united in supposing that de Man wished only to conceal the truth from himself and others; that his subsequent work was indeed nothing but a series of oblique strategies for pretending that it never happened, or at least that there existed no present responsibility for past thoughts and actions. I have argued, on the contrary, that de Man's later writings bear witness to a constant, often agonized attempt to explain the sources of that powerful "aesthetic ideology" which had played a prominent seductive role in his own youthful thinking. Of course there is still the question why he chose to pursue such a tortuously roundabout path of self-reckoning and didn't, so to speak, come clean by acknowledging what he had written in those early years. There is no way of answering this charge, save by pointing out that a public admission would almost certainly have meant a break with some of his closest, most valued colleagues, the loss of his academic livelihood (after ten years of wandering from one part-time job to another), and also of the one chance he now had for making some kind of intellectual reparation. In this respect at least I think there is room for a measure of charitable judgment.

The historian Jon Wiener, writing in *The Nation*, does at least make some effort to weigh up the evidence and establish just how much de Man could have known about the fate of Belgian Jews and the ultimate direction of Nazi policy.[4] He points out that de Man's articles ceased to appear in *Le Soir* toward the end of November, 1942, at a time when such knowledge was becoming more widely available. Wiener declines to offer any definite conclusion but cites the views of two experts on the period, one of whom declares that all "educated Belgians" must have gathered something of the terrible truth by "at the latest, 1942,"[5] while the other thinks that few were as yet in a position to know that Nazi sources were lying when they spoke of deporting large numbers of people for emergency work in the "labor camps." At least it seems clear that, for whatever reason, de Man had severed his links with *Le Soir* before the time when any further involvement would have pointed to a knowing complicity with Nazi war crimes. This gesture might indeed have entailed some considerable risk, not only to his standing in Belgian cultural life but also to his safety under the new regime. All the same, as Wiener points out, he was still contributing articles during a period when various anti-Semitic laws were promulgated, when feeling against the Jews was being whipped up by successive propaganda campaigns, and when no Belgian citizen could possibly have failed to recognize the ominous turn of events.

Besides, there is an article by de Man — "Jews in Contemporary Literature," published on March 1st, 1941 — which shows all too clearly how willing he was to go along with at least certain currents of anti-Semitic prejudice. In it he rejects the idea that modern European culture has been "polluted" by Jewish influence, and asserts on the contrary that no Jewish artist or thinker has achieved such eminence as seriously to threaten the purity of the great national traditions. It could just conceivably be argued — putting the best case for de Man — that one effect of such statements might have been to head off "vulgar" anti-Jewish sentiment by persuading people that no real "threat" existed, since the current campaign (as waged so zealously by other contributors to *Le Soir*) was based on a paranoid misperception of social and cultural realities. But in the end this defense won't do, any more than the idea that when de Man speaks of resettling large numbers of Jews in a separate "island colony," his suggestion might be read as prefiguring the establishment of Israel as an autonomous Jewish nation-state. On the evidence of this piece at least one is obliged to accept Wiener's conclusion that de Man was at one stage willing to collaborate in anti-Semitic cultural propaganda.

But on other points Wiener's article goes seriously wrong and shouldn't be allowed to pass without challenge. For instance, he remarks that de Man wrote some appreciative comments for the jacket of Julia Kristeva's book *Powers of Horror*, published in translation in 1982.[6] That book has a chapter on Ferdinand Céline, the French writer whose virulently racist, anti-Semitic, and misogynist views placed him in the front rank of pro-Nazi ideologues. Wiener takes it on trust — without the least effort to substantiate his claim — that Kristeva's interest in Céline must be proof of her own anti-Semitism, and therefore that de Man, by "singling out these sections of the book for praise" and calling them "indispensable readings," was more or less openly professing similar sentiments. In fact *Powers Of Horror* is a diagnostic study of the political unconscious as revealed by writers whose work responds to extreme conditions of repressed hatred or desire. Kristeva's chosen authors — Lautréamont, Artaud, and Céline among others — are brought together *not* because she endorses their politics (how could she, given such a motley collection?) but because they all exemplify something in the character of language forced up against the limits of logic and representation. What she finds everywhere at work in these writings is a deep *déréglément* of sense, syntax, and prose rhythm that breaks through the structures of meaning imposed by a socialized symbolic order. This manifests itself most strikingly in the work of Céline, a writer who wrenches language apart by exposing its civilized, self-regulated discourse to extremes of dislocating violence. The breaking of taboos and invasion of language by the dark repressed forces of instinctual desire are the signs, for Kristeva, of a textual unconscious that overturns all conventional judgments of morality and value. Now one can certainly argue that there is something very wrong with this *soi-disant* "radical" line of textual semiotics, especially when linked — as in Kristeva's work — to a politics of supposedly left-wing and feminist character. Such objections have been voiced often enough, so there is no need to repeat them in detail here.

But the notion that Kristeva is somehow *endorsing* Céline's politics — and that de Man must be doing the same by calling her book "indispensable" — is so grossly mistaken as to constitute a well-nigh slanderous act of misprision. Whatever the significance that de Man attached to her chapter on Céline, it wasn't on account of his continued allegiance to a strain of hitherto covert anti-Semitic sentiment.

I have no wish either to minimize the disturbing force of de Man's contributions to *Le Soir* or to argue that they are simply unconnected with everything he went on to write. Nor can I speak with any first-hand knowledge of his personal qualities as teacher, colleague, and intellectual mentor, although a recent volume of tributes (*Yale French Studies*, 1985) bears eloquent witness in this regard. I want to suggest rather that opponents like Lentricchia have ignored one important aspect of the case; that deconstruction evolved, in de Man's work at least, as a form of ideological critique directed against precisely that seductive will to treat language and culture as organic, quasi-natural products rooted in the soil of some authentic native tradition. There is no question of excusing those early productions by showing just how far he went to disown and discredit their basic premises. They came to light — as the reader will have gathered by now — when this book was nearing completion, at a time when I had read only the handful of near-contemporaneous articles and reviews that de Man published in the journal *Het Vlaamsche Land*. These pieces (as I argued in Chapter 6) showed signs that his thinking was influenced at this stage by certain elements of National Socialist ideology. But they were mostly concerned with topics in the area of literary history and comparative criticism, topics which indeed had a bearing on current political events, but which none the less allowed de Man to conduct his arguments at a level quite remote from the sordid practicalities of day-to-day life in occupied Belgium. No such defense can be entered in the case of his writings for *Le Soir*, a national paper of wide circulation and known pro-German sympathies whose editorial policy was closely monitored.

That he agreed to write for such a paper, and under such circumstances, might seem to constitute evidence enough of strong collaborationist leanings on de Man's part. All the same it must be said that the pieces in question — 169 in all, contributed over a two-year period — are many of them wholly innocuous, apart from the fact of their having appeared alongside material of a much worse character. There is a strong suggestion in the *Newsweek* and *New York Times* reports that everything he wrote at this time was either overtly anti-Semitic or designed to lend support to Nazi cultural propaganda. In fact very few of these pieces can honestly be said to serve such a purpose, and only one — his article on the Jewish influence in contemporary culture — to warrant the charge of downright racialist sentiment. Of those remaining, many are reviews of various cultural events — concert performances, chamber recitals, university seminars, poetry readings, and so forth — which occasionally touch on the question of national identity *vis-à-vis* the war and the current upheavals in European politics, but which cannot in all fairness be accused of exploiting those events for propaganda purposes. In what follows I shall look at some of the more substantial and revealing pieces in an attempt to explain what led de Man to identify — in however ambivalent a fashion — with the cultural policies adopted by *Le Soir*.

II

A large number of these articles appeared under the title "Notre Chronique Littéraire," a column devoted mainly to reviews of books that offered some pretext for generalized thoughts about the current state of European politics. One such piece (August 19, 1941) was de Man's fairly lengthy assessment of a work by Frédéric Grimm entitled *Le Testament Politique de Richelieu*. In it de Man reflects on the shifting balance of power within Europe over the past three centuries, from the high point of French cultural hegemony to the period of Bismarck, the growth of a unified German nation-state, and the triumph of National Socialism. De Man presents this history as a matter of accomplished fact, a product of inexorable forces which the French (and of course the Belgians) must accept without further pointless shows of resistance. In short, he adopts what looks very much like a collaborationist line, using the book as an object lesson in the destiny of nations and the need for adjustment to present political realities. It was the weak and disunited condition of Germany in Richelieu's time that enabled the French to maintain their position and overcome any threats from outside. But now (de Man argues) this position has been reversed; Germany has not only survived the defeat of 1918 but in some sense been strengthened by it, while French domestic and foreign policy has stumbled from one disaster to another. From which he derives the moral: that there may come certain periods in a nation's development when "it finds itself in a state of division and weakness such that it should allow itself voluntarily to be guided and dominated by its cousin-nations." Since 1920 France has failed to produce any leader, any truly inspirational figure "equipped with a power of rigorous directive thinking" and "capable of maintaining a firmly held political line." It is all too evident — here and elsewhere in de Man's writings of the period — just who must occupy this role in the context of Germany's latter-day rise to power.

The best that can be said for this piece and others like it is that de Man seems to treat European history on a vaguely cyclic model, such that the predominance of any one nation might always yield to yet another change of political fortunes. After all, this follows from the logic of his argument: that just as French supremacy declined partly through effects of internal "weakness and division," partly through the pressure of external events, so it might come about that the current ascendancy of German national culture would eventually suffer the same predestined fate. This may seem an overly generous reading, but it does find support elsewhere in his writings for *Le Soir*. On more than one occasion de Man plays down the significance of present events by suggesting that his readers shouldn't be misled into treating them as an endpoint or ultimate upheaval in the history of nations; that in fact the war is a passing episode which may turn out to have little effect on the long-term evolution of European history. Thus he writes ("Chronique Littéraire." September 30, 1941) that the Belgian public tends to overestimate the influence of current political events, but that really this has been confined to a "modification of tone, not in the work of [creative] writers themselves, but in the ideas and governing principles of criticism." And there are many other passages where de Man insists on this difference between art and the business of day-to-day intellectual life, the latter having to do with short-term adjustment to pressures of political circumstance, while the former transcends such interests by obeying its own mysterious laws of creative evolution, Thus "literature is an independent domain which has a life, laws, obligations that belong only to itself and don't depend in any way on those philosophical or ethical contingencies that exert their influence from its borders" ("Chronique Littéraire," December 2, 1941).

Now this could well be seen as just another piece of mystifying rhetoric on de Man's part, an attempt to disown any deep complicity by pretending that his kind of day-to-day cultural critique has no real impact in the long term. But I think there is a strong suggestion, in this and other articles, that de Man saw a hope for some future turn of events that would end the period of outright German hegemony and restore French cultural influence to its rightful place within the context of European history. In his column of April 28, 1942 de Man returns to this question by way of discussing "Le Probleme Français" and the question of Franco-German cultural relations. There is, he writes, "a certain French form of reason that seeks above all to fix limits and impose measure . . . ," which possesses "the virtues of clarity, logic, and harmony" that have always characterized "the great artistic and philosophical tradition of that country." But at present this tradition is up against a force of German nationalist sentiment to which it can offer no effective resistance. "We are entering a mystical era, a period of faith and belief, with all that this implies of suffering, exaltation, and rapture." Now there is not much that can be said in defense of this crudely stereotyped piece of collective pseudo-psychology. But it does suggest something of de Man's desire to imagine an alternative future, a Europe where these present conflicts would at length give way to a balanced, integrated form of supra-national coexistence. This is not to deny that, when faced with the choice, de Man comes out over and again in defense of German cultural values, German tradition, and the high destinies of German literature. He even states in one article (April 12, 1941) that the occupying forces have behaved with more generosity of spirit than the French showed toward the Germans at Versailles. And the practical upshot of de Man's arguments is always a counsel of non-resistance: that the ultimate lesson to be drawn from events in France is the pointlessness of presently standing in the way of German political and cultural supremacy. Nobody who reads these articles can remain in any doubt of his defeatist attiude. But I think that if we look more closely at some of them — especially those dealing with the topic of French-German cultural relations — there emerge at least the hints of a different reading, one that would show de Man striving to maintain some hope for better things to come.

One crucial piece here is an article on Belgian cultural politics published in *Le Soir* on April 22, 1941. It is concerned mainly with the question of how far Belgium can claim any kind of national identity, given its division into two distinct cultural and linguistic communities, the Flemish and the Walloon. "Flemish belongs to the low-German group and resembles those dialects spoken in the plains of North Germany. Walloon is a French dialect which descends from Latin." And as might be expected the article goes on to discuss this fact of linguistic division in a broader socio-political context. One can see why this question presented itself with particular urgency to de Man, writing (after all) in a French-language paper whose aim was not only to enlist support for the German cause but to do so by creating a new-found sense of unified national purpose. What made this propaganda line possible was the longstanding tendency of Flemish separatists to identify their interests, as a cultural community, with those of their German-speaking neighbors.[7] Long before World War II there had existed a strong current of feeling among some Flemish natives that Belgium ought to be divided on linguistic-cultural lines, with Flanders becoming an integral part of the German nation and Wallonia resuming its "original," authentically French identity. At the outbreak of hostilities this feeling was intensified in many quarters, and one finds distinct echoes of it in various of de Man's writings. But he also holds out, paradoxically, for the notion of a unified Belgium, a sense of national character transcending these short-term differences of interest. "It is false," he writes, "to believe that the Flemings and the Walloons have always considered each other enemies. . . . In those places where they have lived in close proximity they have endured the same sufferings, undergone the same wars and experienced the same joys. From this there has resulted a great sense of solidarity."

Again there is a crucial ambiguity here, depending on whether one takes it that de Man is advocating a unified Belgium modeled on the German-Flemish alliance, or that he rather envisages a genuine state of reciprocal interdependence where the different communities would exercise a degree of autonomy and self-determination. This doubt persists through many of the articles published in *Le Soir*. But one could also pick out numerous passages where he does quite explicitly state the need for recognition of the French and Walloon contributions to a diverse European culture, and therefore the requirement that these values be preserved in any future plan of postwar reconstruction. That is to say, he maintains a certain distance from the line of straightforwardly pro-German, Flemish nationalist sentiment that prevailed among many of his fellow contributors. And this goes along with de Man's argument — despite all his slighting references to French decadence, lack of "spirit," and disabling political divisions — that France still embodies certain values indispensable to European culture at large.

Those values were, I think, too closely bound up with de Man's own sense of intellectual identity for him to betray them entirely in the service of Nazi propaganda work. In the years immediately preceding the war he had been involved with a journal, *Les Cahiers du Libre Examen*, whose editorial policy was utterly opposed to the line later adopted in *Le Soir*. The proper business of criticism — so de Man and his colleagues affirmed — was *not* to give way to political interests or short-term values and imperatives, but to hold out for the freedom of disinterested judgment in preserving a space for enlightened intellectual debate. And furthermore, they pledged the journal to a continued defense of such values specifically against any violent imposition of dogmatic creeds and ideologies. *Les Cahiers* turned out to be a short-lived venture, since the Nazi occupation (just three years after its inaugural number) made it henceforth impossible for any publication openly to espouse such views. That de Man went on to write his pieces for *Le Soir* may seem all the more an opportunist and cynical act of self-betrayal. But I think those later articles do preserve at least a residual, intermittent sense of what is required in order to salvage any civilized values from the present grim state of Belgian national life. And this feeling is at its strongest when de Man touches — as he very often does — on the topic of "l'espirit français" and its role in the history of European thought and culture.

One item of particular interest in this regard is his article on Goethe's *Elective Affinities* (published in *Le Soir*, May 26, 1942). De Man is here reviewing a new French translation and takes it as a pretext for some generalized thoughts about European romanticism and its mixed national sources. The piece starts out even-handedly: "we will restrict ourselves to examining this work with respect to its French and German artistic qualities: the synthesis of these two national temperaments, an achievement rare and difficult, and amply sufficient to justify its particular attraction." Then — within a couple of paragraphs — he appears to abandon this stance and adopt a more partisan attitude on behalf of German romanticism and its supposedly unique qualities. Where works in the French tradition "seem always to come up against a limit, to attain a level where all has been said and understood," there remains in Goethe a sense of further depths, a "metaphysical feeling for the infinite . . . peculiar to German thought." From which it might seem that this article is just one more piece of cultural propaganda, pretending to discriminate the strains of European romanticism in a scholarly and disinterested fashion, while in fact constructing a bogus mythology in order to promote the German cause. But in his last paragraph de Man once again turns the argument around and leaves a rather different impression. "At certain moments," he writes, "the totality of riches dispersed among the nations that compose occidental civilization are concentrated in one individual, who then becomes a universal genius." It might still be pointed out that these crude formulations derive from an all-too-familiar ideology of language, genius, and organic national culture that belongs squarely within the German sphere of influence. But at least it goes along with some attempt, on de Man's part, to think how the emergence of a postwar "reconstructed" order might yet be compatible with the continued flourishing of French cultural tradition. And this suggests in turn that he hadn't so completely abandoned those values of liberal, enlightened critique espoused by the pre-war *Cahiers* group.

In Thomas Mann's novel *The Magic Mountain*, young Hans Castorp finds himself caught between two great opposing forces, personified in the figures of Naphta and Settembrini. On the one side German nationalism under its aspect of a dark, irrational, atavistic, and ultimately sinister force, yet possessing a power over Castorp's untutored mind that clearly captures something of Mann's ambivalent feelings. On the other Settembrini, apostle of enlightenment, freedom, democracy, and liberal reason, by far the more attractive figure yet always losing out in argument with Naphta and presented very often in a faintly ridiculous light. Of course *The Magic Mountain* was published in 1924 and treats of the situation in Europe during the years leading up to the First World War. But I think it is not unduly fanciful to see in Hans Castorp's situation something of the chronic confusions that assailed Paul de Man some two decades later. There is a piece on Charles Péguy (*Le Soir*, May 6, 1941) that offers perhaps the most pointed example of these tensions in de Man's thinking. Péguy was a young French socialist and Catholic intellectual who began writing in the mid-1890s, became passionately involved with political events (including the Dreyfus affair), and died in action during the Battle of the Marne. He was founder and editor-in-chief of *Les Cahiers de la Quinzaine*, a journal that pursued a fiercely independent line and attracted the hostility of right- and left-wing factions alike. De Man clearly admires this stance and regards Péguy as in some sense a model for the conduct of intellectual life under extreme pressures of political circumstance. In particular he praises Péguy's refusal to adopt any simplified party-line creed, his determination not to compromise in matters of religious or political faith. "Caught between these two hostilities [attacked, that is to say, both by right-wing Catholic and mainstream socialist intellectuals] he continued to hold his head high, defending his own work and bringing together, in the *Cahiers*, the most remarkable French literary talents of the period."

Any mention of the Dreyfus affair must of course raise the question of anti-Semitism and the resistance to it mounted by writers like Péguy and, most famously, Zola. De Man is distinctly evasive here, commenting at one point that the affair played an "almost disproportionate" role in French intellectual life at this time, but then praising Péguy for having "remained a Dreyfusard to the end," one who impressed his comrades as a "passionate thinker, imbued with the ideas of socialism and egalitarian justice." No doubt it would be overgenerous to interpret these remarks as a covert profession of faith on de Man's part, signaling his continued allegiance to the ideals set forth in *Les Cahiers du Libre Examen*. But there is more than a hint that those ideas still exercised an influence on his thinking, especially when de Man makes a point of adverting to the title of Péguy's review and its connection with "ses cahiers d'école, si propres, si bien tenus." What he singles out for praise in Péguy's work is its spirit of liberal inquiry, a spirit that owed allegiance to no single party or faction, that allowed him to range freely over various questions and debates "without any governing interest or constraint." It is hard to believe that de Man could have written these words without reflecting ironically on the course of events in Belgium and his own conspicuous failure to uphold such standards. In his writings for *Le Soir* de Man continues to associate the French cultural tradition with these values of liberalism, rational inquiry, and open public debate.

This is not to deny that he often turns such arguments round against the French by attributing their defeat in war to the lack of any genuine spirit of national unity, a condition brought about by precisely that habit of detached, self-critical scrutiny. But these values are never entirely submerged in the strain of pro-German populist rhetoric that sometimes marks his writings for *Le Soir*. In fact there is evidence that de Man's sympathies were not only divided but complex to the point of downright political confusion. What is one to make of his article published in July 14, 1942 — anniversary of the French Revolution — where de Man nominates the Surrealist movement, and particularly Paul Eluard, as the single most striking manifestation of French cultural vitality? It is all the more remarkable that he ventured this opinion while reviewing a journal (*Messages*) known for its links with the Resistance movement as well as with communist or left-leaning elements in the Surrealist group. One could interpret such passages as indicating either a weak grasp of political realities on de Man's part or perhaps — more generously — a will to keep the channels of communication open and to risk what must have been, by this date, the very real threat of reprisals from the German censor. The same might be said of his occasional admiring references to Kafka and other Jewish authors who had long since been condemned as decadent modernists by the Nazi cultural hacks. No matter how one reads them — as courageous or naive — these passages must at least complicate our sense of de Man's "collaborationist" activity. Furthermore, it now seems that he also wrote articles for the Resistance paper *Exercise du Silence*, a fact communicated to the present author by his son, Marc de Man. So I think there is good reason to reject the charge — taken up with such intemperate zeal in many quarters of the American and British press — that de Man was at any time wholly given over to the purposes of Nazi cultural propaganda.

III

There are three possible lines of response to the discovery of these wartime writings. The first — as argued by commentators like Wiener and Lentricchia — would take the worst possible view of their content, and would hold furthermore that everything de Man went on to write must (so to speak) carry guilt by association, and therefore be deeply suspect on ideological grounds. The second would hold, on the contrary, that de Man's later texts have absolutely nothing in common with his early writings, that in fact they exhibit an extreme resistance to precisely that form of dangerously mystified thinking, and should therefore be treated as belonging to a different order of discourse. The third — and this is basically the argument I have presented here — is that de Man's later work grew out of an agonized reflection on his wartime experience, and can best be read as a protracted attempt to make amends (albeit indirectly) in the form of an ideological auto-critique. Geoffrey Hartman has argued a similar case in his essay on de Man published in *The New Republic*. His conclusion is worth quoting at length, not least because Hartman writes as a Jewish scholar-critic as well as a close friend and colleague of de Man. "In the light of what we now know," Hartman writes,

> his work appears more and more as a deepening reflection on the rhetoric of totalitarianism. His turn from the politics of culture to the language of art was not an escape into, but an escape out of, aestheticism: a disenchantment with that fatal aestheticizing of politics, blatant in his own early writings, that gave fascism its false brilliance. De Man's critique of every tendency to totalize literature or language, to see unity where there is no unity, looks like a belated, but still powerful, act of conscience.[8]

It seems to me that Hartman's assessment is not only very much to the point but written out of a deep and painful knowledge of events that, for many of de Man's more strident critics, are matters of historical record only. At least his words should give pause to anyone who thinks to discredit de Man's later work by reference to those early writings.

In the Introduction to his book *Frege: Philosophy of Language* Michael Dummett recalls having experienced something like the shock of belated discovery that has attended these recent revelations about de Man.[9] Dummett had devoted many years to his study of Frege, thinking him the greatest of modern logicians and philosophers of language. At one point he decided to set aside this project temporarily and devote himself to the work of improving race relations and combating the rising tide of racial prejudice. Subsequently he discovered that Frege had himself held views of an extreme right-wing character, that he had expressed overtly racist sentiments, and indeed gone along with the whole pernicious line of half-baked populist rhetoric that Dummett encountered in latter-day National Front propaganda. But in the end, as Dummett says, this discovery made no real difference to his estimate of Frege's contribution to the fields of logic and linguistic philosophy. That work belongs to such a specialized domain — so remote from Frege's individual psychopathology, or the content of his social and political beliefs — that Dummett was able to continue his project with a good (if sadly disillusioned) conscience. After all, it is among the main axioms of Frege's philosophy that truth-values exist independently of thoughts going on in this or that mind, and that language in its logical or truth-conditional aspect has nothing to do with matters of subjective or individual belief. So clearly there is a case for arguing, like Dummett, that one has to draw a firm, categorical line between Frege's logico-linguistic innovations and his repugnant political views.

Now I don't think that this is a real option in de Man's case, despite the fact that so much of his later work is conducted in a style of austere, impersonal rigor that might seem to approximate "pure" philosophy of language. One could recall, in this connection, the passage from his essay on Benjamin's "The Task of the Translator" where de Man writes that "it is not *a priori* certain at all that the mode of meaning, the way in which I mean, is intentional in any way . . . [it] is dependent on linguistic properties that are not only not made by me, because I depend on the language as it exists for the devices which I will be using, it is as such not made by us as historical beings, it is perhaps not even made by humans at all."[10] We cannot any longer read such passages as they ask to be read, that is to say, as referring purely to those questions in the province of language, translation, rhetoric, and the other topics that preoccupied de Man in his last years. From one point of view — that taken by the hostile commentators — they reveal the quite extraordinary lengths to which he went in order to repress, disguise, or evade the memory of those early journalistic writings. From another, they are the endpoint of a long and painful coming-to-terms with the fact of that guilt and the way that what is written possesses a starkly material force that can always return to haunt the writer. As Hartman points out, there is something more than a circumstantial irony in the fact that de Man is here writing about Walter Benjamin, the German-Jewish critic who was driven to suicide while attempting to escape from the Nazi forces of occupation. I have spent a good part of this book arguing the case for de Man's work as a salutary warning against forms of aesthetic mystification which can have very real historical effects. Now, with the discovery of his articles in *Le Soir*, that lesson must be read as bearing directly on de Man's own burden of memory. But we shouldn't, for that reason, be tempted to conclude that the later work is *nothing more* than a species of obscure private atonement; that its claims to offer a rigorous reflection on the powers and the limits of language are simply a last-ditch strategy of evasion on de Man's part.

Michael Sprinker's recent book *Imaginary Relations* argues a case, in some ways similar to my own, for taking these late texts seriously in their attempt to articulate a deconstructive version of Marxist *Ideologiekritik*.

"The permanence of ideology and the exogenous position of history in relation to the power of human will are admittedly not uncontroversial principles within historical materialism, but it is surely too soon to declare them un- or anti-Marxist *tout court*."[11] Sprinker's aim is to point up the relation between de Man's insistence on the non-subjective, humanly eccentric properties of language and the Althusserian dicta that "History is a process without a subject or goals," and that therefore "Ideology has no history." His arguments are too complex to summarize here, but I think that he would have no cause to retract or drastically revise them in light of what is now known of de Man's early writings. There can be no doubt that de Man had reasons enough — urgently personal reasons — for wanting to convince himself that language and history were utterly beyond the control or understanding of the situated individual subject. In this sense the whole of his later production could be read (as critics like Lentricchia read it) as one long attempt to disown responsibility for what he had once written. But this is to take those later pronouncements very much at face value, as if de Man had *really* succeeded in repressing all trace of such haunting memories. It is worth bearing in mind those remarks of Mizae Mizumura, herself hard put to account for the curious coexistence in de Man's work of an intense desire to renounce the pathos of subjective guilt and loss with an equally compulsive need to return to such themes and endlessly rehearse them in his writing. "The impression of deprivation comes closer, nonetheless, to grasping the quintessence of de Man than a placid acceptance of the extreme ascesis that reigns in his work. . . . The one who has not been tempted would not have spoken so often about the necessity (and the impossibility) of renunciation — and would not have done so with such authority,"[12] Mizumura was writing before the existence of those articles for *Le Soir* became public knowledge. But her comments take on an additional force when read — as one inevitably reads them now — in the context of de Man's wartime writings and his lifelong attempt to atone for past errors. The point is not just that his entire subsequent production must henceforth be seen as a species of cryptic autobiography, a confessional record that merely masquerades as textual exegesis, philosophy of language, or *Ideologie- kritik*. Rather, it is the fact that de Man's own experience had left so deep and lasting an impression on his work that one simply cannot separate (in T.S. Eliot's phrase) the "man who suffers" from "the mind that creates," or the strain of anguished self-reckoning from the desire to put these lessons to work in a rigorously critical way. It is wrong to suppose that the two readings are wholly incompatible, or that somehow the presence of these sombre meditations counts against our accepting the validity and force of his arguments.

So we don't have the choice, like Dummett on Frege, of so to speak bracketing all questions of moral and political accountability, and reading de Man's later texts for what they are worth in terms of purely theoretical yield. But neither is it a case, as with Heidegger, of a thinker whose entire life's work is so deeply involved with a certain mystique of language, origins, and national destiny that it becomes impossible to disengage the one from the other. These discoveries about de Man have come at a time when Heidegger's involvement with Nazism has likewise been subject to renewed investigation and charges that it went much deeper — and lasted much longer — than had previously been thought.[13] I have already (in Chapter 6) offered some account of de Man's changing attitude to Heidegger, suggesting that it marks the "turn" in his work from a mystified conception of language and politics to a criticism highly alert to such dangerous ideas. But I think we may better understand what is at stake in this crossing of intellectual paths by looking briefly at Derrida's recent book on Heidegger (*De l'esprit*, 1987).[14] For here Derrida not only addresses the question of Heidegger's relationship to Nazism, but does so in terms that quite explicitly acknowledge a debt to certain passages in de Man's *Allegories of Reading*. It should be said that this text of Derrida is based on the proceedings of a conference held in March, 1987 at a time when (presumably) he had no direct knowledge of de Man's wartime writings. But if one reads it alongside his earlier volume in tribute to de Man (*Mémoires*, 1986) there emerges a pattern of interlinked thoughts about language, politics, historical destiny, and the ethics of writing and interpretation, thoughts that now carry an added charge of significance.

The crucial passage from *Allegories* is that in which de Man takes the well-known sentence of Heidegger, "Die Sprache spricht" — "language speaks" — and changes it to read "Die Sprache verspricht (sich)," or (approximately rendered) "language necessarily misleads, undoes or betrays itself to the extent that no intention can entirely govern its meaning or effects."[15] It is important to be clear about the context and purpose of Derrida's argument here. He is far from suggesting that Heidegger was ultimately *not responsible* for what he wrote during the 1930s, or that his inaugural speech as Rektor of Freiburg University — the occasion on which he came closest to identifying the destiny of German and European culture with the fortunes of National Socialism — was a mere aberration brought about by effects of linguistic undecidability. But he does ask us to read these texts as the shadow-side of a quest for language in its authentic, truth-telling aspect, a quest whose fateful consequences Heidegger at this time could scarcely have foretold. "The upheaval of history," as Derrida writes in *Mémoires*, is clearly what determines what happens to the *Sprechen* (let us say the Heideggerian *Sprechen*, that of *die Sprache spricht*) when it must, always already, give itself up to and be affected by the *versprechen*. This cannot happen to it; from the origin on, it is destined to it; this is its destination, even though the *versprechen* threatens destination in it. . . . These accidents are essential, they do not happen to the *Sprechen* from the outside.[16]

It is possible to read such passages now as applying not only to Heidegger's ill-fated utterances but also to those early texts of de Man whose discovery was shortly to cast a long shadow over everything he had written thereafter. What Derrida says about the fateful "drift" of Heideggerian reflection, its tendency to become "disturbed, corrupted, perverted, affected" by historical forces beyond its control, is very close to de Man's often cryptic formulations in *Allegories of Reading*. And these passages seem all the more charged and ironic when read in the knowledge that de Man was himself engaged in a painful and prolonged reckoning with his own past errors.

Derrida starts out in *De l'esprit* by asking how this phrase, so typically "French" in its usage and range of connotations, can possibly be taken as in any sense equivalent to the German word *Geist* (soul, spirit, animating principle).The difference between them could be posed in terms of that stereotyped national-mentality thinking that once led de Man, in his writings for *Le Soir*, to distinguish the French and German cultural traditions. Thus "esprit" carries along with it a strong suggestion of the Cartesian-rationalist quest for clear and distinct ideas, as well as a typically "French" attachment to wit, as well as wisdom, in the civilizing discourse of reason. With "Geist," on the other hand, we enter a zone of charged etymology and darkly brooding meditation, a region to which — so Heidegger argues — we can now have access only through the German language, since it is here that Being may yet rediscover its authentic voice despite all the damaging effects and accretions of that other, post-Socratic, rationalist spirit. So to write a book about Heidegger under this title is to pose something more than a localized problem of translation. And again, the very form of that title — *De l'esprit* — is such as to suggest a certain "classical" approach to questions of intellectual history, one that treats of philosophic concepts in a spirit of detached, enlightened critique. And in a sense this is what Derrida proposes. He will pursue the word "geist" in its passage through various of Heidegger's texts, remarking in particular its "trajectories, functions, formations, and regulated transformations, its presuppositions and destinations." He will do so, moreover, with a view to the role it plays within a certain thematics of the German language as a privileged vehicle of Being and truth. But in so far as this inquiry is conducted in French — and in so far as it seeks something other and more than an etymological gloss on Heidegger's words — it will also necessarily approach these texts from a certain distance of self-imposed critical reserve.

Derrida's argument may be summarized very briefly as follows. The word "Geist" occurs often in Heidegger's writings, but not always — in fact very seldom — with that force of a wholesale, willing commitment that marks his use of it in the Rectoral Address of 1933 and the years immediately following. Elsewhere the word is not so much *used* as *mentioned*, in the sense of these terms that Derrida derives from J.L. Austin and the discourse of British linguistic philosophy. That is to say, the word appears *entre guillemets* —between quotation marks — either literally or by virtue of its somehow being placed "under erasure," cited (so to speak) in a context that warns us not to read *Geist* as a privileged term in the company of others like *Dasein, Wesen*, or *Denken*. As Derrida notes, *Was heisst der Geist?* is the title of a work that Heidegger never wrote. "Quand ils portent sur l'esprit, les énoncés heideggeriens ont *rarement* la forme d'une définition d'essence. Rarement, c'est à dire par exception, et nous nous intéresserons à ces exceptions, d'ailleurs très différentes, voire opposées entre elles." (*De l'esprit*, p. 32). It is precisely where *Geist* takes on such a force of essentialist definition — as in texts like the Rectoral Address — that Heidegger's thinking is drawn into the orbit of National Socialist ideology. At this point the quotation marks are lifted, language (specifically the German language) assumes its world-historical destiny, and the word *Geist* becomes vibrant with powers of etymopoeic suggestion that associate all too clearly with present and future events.

These have to do with fire, conflagration, and a language of spiritualized burning or ardor. For what lies behind Heidegger's usage of the word is a sense of its kinship with the old German *Gheis*, whose meaning evokes precisely this range of compacted metaphorical traits. Further on in *De l'esprit* Derrida tracks their emergence in Heidegger's commentaries on the poets, especially Hölderlin and Trakl, where he fastens on passages that bring out precisely the deep-laid associative link between fire, spirit, and the power of language to revive ancient sources of imaginative life. But it is the Rectoral Address that shows most clearly how *Geist* takes on an intensely dangerous resonance, a meaning in tune with National Socialist ideas of a uniquely German spirit about to fulfill itself in the here and now of political action.

Il se présente. L'esprit *lui-même*, l'esprit dans son esprit et dans sa lettre, le *Geist* s'affirme sans guillemets. Il s'affirme à travers l'auto-affirmation de l'université allemande. L'affirmation de l'esprit s'enflamme.

> Je dis bien *s'enflamme*: non seulement pour évoquer le pathos du *Discours de Rectorat* quand il célèbre l'esprit . . . mais parce que vingt ans plus tard, exactement vingt ans, Heidegger dira du *Geist*, sans lequel on ne saurait penser le Mal, qu'il n'est *d'abord* ni *pneuma* ni *spiritus*, nous laissent ainsi conclure que le *Geist* ne s'entend pas plus dans la Grèce des philosophes que dans celle des Évangiles, pour ne rien dire de la surdité romaine: le *Geist* est flamme. Or cela ne se dirait et cela donc ne se penserait qu'en allemand. (*De l'esprit*, p. 54)

I have cited this passage at length because it brings out very clearly what is at stake in that single word *Geist* and its essential relation to a mystified, organicist idea of German language and culture. For the word would appear, as Heidegger deploys it, somehow "irreducibly German," its meaning so closely bound up with its etymological resonance that it cannot be translated into any other language, least of all the French, where *l'esprit* brings about such a marked shift of cultural context.

Now this is not just an instance, as Derrida remarks, of that commonplace cultural-relativist argument that points to the incommensurable character of various so-called "conceptual schemes." For Heidegger, there are only two languages — the Greek and the German — that have ever possessed this privileged relation to the sources of authentic thought. It is not that *Geist* resists translation in so far as it "corresponds" to some idea or structure of thought present only in the German language. Rather, it marks what Derrida calls "the singular event of a language capable of naming, of summoning Being, or rather of hearing itself summoned by Being." It is by virtue of its standing in this punctual, self-present, and unmediated relation to truth that *Geist* takes on its unique burden of world-historical destiny. For the Rectoral Address is the one and only text of Heidegger – so Derrida asserts — where the word is directly *used* with its full assertive force, as opposed to being cited, "mentioned," or deployed "under erasure" as a term that requires the utmost vigilance of a deconstructive critique. And this gives it the kind of fateful resonance that appears to absolve the individual thinker of all responsibility for its future meaning and effects. "L'argument de Heidegger paraît ici terriblement équivoque: *mutatis mutandis*, quoi de sa propre tactique — et cette tactique est aussi politique — quand elle change et passe d'une déconstruction à une célébration de l'esprit?' (p. 105).

In Chapter 6 I suggested that de Man's reading of Heidegger — and especially of Heidegger's commentaries on Hölderlin — underwent a decisive change as he came to reflect on the dangers concealed in this notion of a language with privileged access to the sources of authentic thought. Heidegger mistakes the meaning of Hölderlin's texts in so far as he takes them to *name* Being itself, rather than rehearsing the perpetual impossibility of attaining to any such primordial truth. It seems to me that Derrida is echoing this lesson from de Man when he locates the fateful swerve in Heidegger's thinking, the failure of critical and ethical intelligence that leads him to "spiritualize" the National Socialist cause by equating it with *Geist* and the manifest destiny of German language and culture. It is surely with this in mind that Derrida cites the passage from *Allegories* where de Man reflects on the capacity for self-betrayal that resides in a language too confident of its powers to articulate the truths of Being. And this danger persists in Heidegger's texts, a temptation that continues to haunt his language long after that single, most shameful episode marked by the Rectoral Address. "La métaphysique revient toujours, je l'entends au sens du revenant, et le *Geist* est la figure la plus fatale de cette revenance" (p. 66). Perhaps the most damaging charge laid against Heidegger is the fact that he never found cause to renounce or explain his "flirtation" with Nazi ideology. What emerges from Derrida's account in *De l'esprit* is the reason — or at least one reason — why this should be so; namely, the profound complicity in Heidegger's texts between a brooding on themes of language, Being, and national destiny, and a will to locate the very presence of truth in a "spiritualized" jargon that remains in thrall to a crude mythology of nationalist *Geist*.

That de Man once fell under this same malignant spell cannot be doubted by anyone who has read his articles in *Le Soir* and *Het Vlaamsche Land*. But it is equally wrong to ignore the crucial difference between his and Heidegger's case, the fact (as I have argued, and as Derrida's text makes clear) that de Man went on to devote the major part of his life's work to a critique of that same seductive mythology that had once so grievously misled his thinking. And we should also not forget that this episode belongs to de Man's early twenties, an age when very few people have yet had sufficient experience — or time for thought — to render them proof against dominant forms of political indoctrination. It seems to me quite appalling — in straightforward moral and human terms — that these texts should now be used as the basis of a wholesale media campaign to discredit the man and his work. In a passage from *Mémoires*, Derrida reflects on "what could be considered Paul de Man's relation to the 'political,' to what we tranquilly and commonly call politics, to his 'experience' of the thing" (p. 143). That experience, as we now know, was of a kind that Derrida could scarcely have guessed at when he wrote these words. But there is much in *Mémoires* — as indeed in *De l'esprit* — that does seem to bear a pointed, almost uncanny relevance to the issue of de Man's wartime journalism. These texts, along with Hartman's, do more for our understanding of the case than any of the hasty, ill-informed, and often vindicative polemics that have characterized the current media response.

Notes

Introduction

1. "The Lesson of Paul de Man," ed. Peter Brooks, Shoshana Felman, and J. Hillis Miller, *Yale French Studies*, no. 69 (New Haven: Yale University Press, 1985). Hereafter cited in the text as *YFS*.

2. Paul de Man, *The Resistance to Theory* (Minneapolis: University of Minnesota Press, 1986), p. 19. Hereafter cited in the text as *RT*.

3. Paul de Man, *Blindness and Insight: Essays in the Rhetoric of Contemporary Criticism*, 2nd ed. (London: Methuen, 1983), p. 28. Hereafter cited in the text as *BI*.

4. Paul de Man, *Allegories of Reading: Figural Language in Rousseau, Nietzsche, Rilke, and Proust* (New Haven: Yale University Press, 1979), p. 115. Hereafter cited in the text as *AR*.

5. Paul de Man, *The Rhetoric of Romanticism* (New York: Columbia University Press, 1984), p. 122. Hereafter cited in the text as *RR*.

6. See Rodolphe Gasché, "Deconstruction as Criticism," *Glyph*, Vol. 6 (1979): 177–215.

1 Allegories of Disenchantment

1. Frank Lentricchia, *Criticism and Social Change* (Chicago: University of Chicago Press, 1983), p. 115.

2. See for instance Edward Said, *Orientalism* (New York: Pantheon, 1978); and *The World, the Text, and the Critic* (London: Faber & Faber, 1984).

3. See Terry Eagleton, *The Function of Criticism* (London: New Left Books, 1984), pp. 100–4; and his comments on de Man in "The Critic as Clown," *Against the Grain: Selected Essays* (London: New Left Books, 1986), pp. 149–65. The "clown" of Eagleton's title is William Empson, not de Man, though Empson comes off much better in the comparison. For a different view of the relationship between this distinctly odd couple, see my essay "Some Versions of Rhetoric: Empson and de Man," in Norris, *The Contest of Faculties: Philosophy and Theory After Deconstruction* (London: Methuen, 1985), pp. 70–96.

4. Paul de Man, "The Dead-End of Formalist Criticism," in *Blindness and Insight: Essays in the Rhetoric of Contemporary Criticism*, 2nd ed. (London: Methuen, 1983), pp. 229–45; p. 240.

5. De Man, *Blindness and Insight*, p. 240.

6. De Man, *Blindness and Insight*, p. 237.

7. See especially the essays collected in de Man's posthumous volume *The Resistance to Theory* (Minneapolis: University of Minnesota Press, 1986).

8. Eagleton, *The Function of Criticism*, p. 100.

9. Paul de Man, "Literary History and Literary Modernity," in *Blindness and Insight*, pp. 142–65.

10. F.W. Nietzsche, *The Use and Abuse of History*, trans. Adrian Collins (Indianapolis: Bobbs-Merrill Co., 1977).

11. Paul de Man, "Literary History and Literary Modernity," in *Blindness and Insight*, p. 150.

12. Lentricchia, *Criticism and Social Change*, p. 44.

13. Paul de Man, "Wordsworth and Hölderlin," in *The Rhetoric of Romanticism* (New York: Columbia University Press, 1984), pp. 47–65. Hereafter cited in the text as *RR*.

14. See especially de Man, "The Rhetoric of Temporality," in *Blindness and Insight*, pp. 187–208; "Sign and Symbol in Hegel's *Aesthetics*," *Critical Inquiry*, Vol. 8, no. 4 (1982): 761–75; "Hegel on the Sublime," in Mark Krupnick, ed. *Displacement: Derrida and After* (Bloomington: Indiana University Press, 1983); and "Phenomenality and Materiality in Kant," in Gary Shapiro and Alan Sica, eds., *Hermeneutics: Questions and Prospects* (Amherst: University of Massachusetts Press, 1984), pp. 121–44.

15. S.T. Coleridge, *Miscellaneous Criticism*, ed. T.M. Raysor (London: Constable, 1936), p. 30. Cited by de Man in "The Rhetoric of Temporality," *Blindness and Insight*, p. 192.

16. De Man, "The Rhetoric of Temporality," *Blindness and Insight*, p. 207.

17. See de Man, "The Rhetoric of Blindness," in *Blindness and Insight*, pp. 102–41.

18. Jacques Derrida, *Mémoires: For Paul de Man* (New York: Columbia University Press, 1986), p. 130.

19. De Man, "Heidegger's Exegeses of Hölderlin," in *Blindness and Insight*, pp. 246–66. Hereafter cited in the text as *BI*.

20. For his readings of Hölderlin, see Martin Heidegger, *Poetry, Language, Thought*, trans. Albert Hofstadter (New York: Harper & Row, 1971).

21. On this distinction between "error" and "mistake," see Stanley Corngold, "Error in Paul de Man," *Critical Inquiry*, Vol. 8 (1982): 489–507; and in response to Corngold, "A Letter from Paul de Man," pp. 509–13 in the same issue.

22. Derrida's *Mémoires* has some pertinent remarks about the history and mixed fortunes of the term "deconstruction," especially as it figures in de Man's later work.

23. Beda Alleman, *Hölderlin und Heidegger* (Zürich: Atlantis Verlag, 1954).

24. See my book *The Contest of Faculties*, especially pp. 40–46 and 185–88.

25. This is a central theme of the essays collected in de Man's *The Resistance to Theory*.

26. Antonio Gramsci, *Selections from the "Prison Notebooks,"* trans. Quintin Hoare and Geoffrey Nowell-Smith (London: Lawrence & Wishart, 1971). The principal references to Hendrik de Man may be found on pp. 160, 197, 287, 376, 387, 418–19 and 430.

27. Peter Dodge, *Hendrik de Man, Socialist Critic of Marxism* (New Jersey: Princeton University Press, 1979). Hereafter cited in the text as Dodge. This book takes the form of a series of excerpts from de Man's work at crucial points in his career, with a commentary relating that work to political events in Belgium and elsewhere. See also

Dodge, *Beyond Marxism: The Faith and Works of Hendrik de Man* (The Hague: Martinus Nijhoff, 1966); and A.M. van Peski, *Hendrik de Man* (Bruges-Utrecht: Desclée de Brouwer, 1969).

28. For an account of this period and the consequent upheaval in his thinking, see Hendrik de Man, *The Remaking of a Mind: A Soldier's Thoughts on War and Reconstruction* (London: Allen & Unwin, 1919).

29. Hendrik de Man, *The Psychology of Socialism*, trans. Eden and Cedar Paul (London: Allen & Unwin, 1928).

30. T.S. Eliot, "Tradition and the Individual Talent," in *Selected Essays* (London: Faber & Faber, 1964), p. 11.

31. See also de Man's chapter "Promises (*Social Contract*)," in *Allegories of Reading: Figural Language in Rousseau, Nietzsche, Rilke, and Proust* (New Haven: Yale University Press, 1979), pp. 246–77.

32. A full translation of the *Plan du travail* is given in Dodge, *Hendrik de Man*, pp. 290–99.

33. Eagleton, *The Function of Criticism*, p. 101.

34. Juliet Flower MacCannell, "Portrait: de Man," in Robert Con Davis and Ronald Schleifer, eds., *Rhetoric and Form: Deconstruction at Yale* (Norman: University of Oklahoma Press, 1985), pp. 51–74; p. 74.

35. MacCannell, "Portrait: de Man," p. 73.

36. Eagleton, *The Function of Criticism*, p. 101.

2 De Man and the Critique of Romantic Ideology

1. Paul de Man, "Sign and Symbol in Hegel's *Aesthetics*," *Critical Inquiry* Vol. 8, no. 4 (1982): 761–75. Hereafter cited in the text as SS. De Man takes up some connected lines of argument in his essay "Hegel on the Sublime," in Mark Krupnick, ed. *Displacement: Derrida and After* (Bloomington: Indiana University Press, 1983), pp. 139–53.

2. Paul de Man, "Phenomenality and Materiality in Kant," in Gary Shapiro and Alan Sica, eds., *Hermeneutics: Questions and Prospects* (Amherst: University of Massachusetts Press, 1984), pp. 121–44. Hereafter cited in the text as PMK. For a discussion of related topics in Kant, see de Man, "The Epistemology of Metaphor," *Critical Inquiry*, Vol. 5, no. 1 (1978): 13–30.

3. See G.W.F. Hegel, *Aesthetics*, trans. T.M. Knox (Oxford: Clarendon Press, 1975).

4. S.T. Coleridge, *The Statesman's Manual* (New York: Harper & Bros., 1875), p. 438. Cited by de Man, *Blindness and Insight: Essays in the Rhetoric of Contemporary Criticism*, 2nd ed. (London: Methuen, 1983), p. 192. Hereafter cited in the text as *BI*.

5. See Jacques Lacan, *Ecrits: A Selection*, trans. A. Sheridan (London: Tavistock, 1977).

6. M.H. Abrams, "Structure and Style in the Greater Romantic Lyric," in F.W. Hillis and H. Bloom, eds., *From Sensibility to Romanticism* (New York: Oxford University Press, 1965), pp. 530–59.

7. Abrams, "Structure and Style," p. 551.

8. Earl Wasserman, "The English Romantics: The Grounds of Knowledge," *Essays in Romanticism*, Vol. 4 (1964). Cited in *BI*, p. 198.

9. Abrams, "Structure and Style," p. 536.

10. See W.K. Wimsatt, "The Structure of Romantic Nature Imagery," in *The Verbal Icon: Studies in the Meaning of Poetry* (Lexington: University of Kentucky Press, 1954).

11. Wimsatt, *The Verbal Icon*, p. 110.

12. W.K. Wimsatt, "Battering the Object: the Ontological Approach," in M. Bradbury and D. Palmer, eds., *Contemporary Criticism* (London: Edward Arnold, 1970).

13. See Wimsatt, *The Verbal Icon*.

14. T.S. Eliot, "The Metaphysical Poets," in *Selected Essays* (London: Faber & Faber, 1964), pp. 241–50.

15. Hans-Georg Gadamer, *Truth and Method*, trans. G. Barden and J. Cumming (New York: Seabury Press, 1975).

16. See especially Hans-Robert Jauss, *Toward an Aesthetics of Reception*, trans. Timothy Bahti (Minneapolis: University of Minnesota Press, 1982). De Man's essay on Jauss first appeared as the Introduction to this volume, pp. vii–xxv. It was reprinted in *The Resistance to Theory* (Minneapolis: University of Minnesota Press, 1986), pp. 54–72. Hereafter cited in the text as *RT*.

17. For a compact and informative survey of the field, see Robert C. Holub, *Reception Theory* (London: Methuen, 1984).

18. F.R. Leavis, "Literary Criticism and Philosophy," (reply to René Wellek), *Scrutiny*, Vol. 6 (1937): 59–70.

19. Paul de Man, "The Return to Philology," in *RT*, pp. 21–26; p. 23.

20. See for instance de Man, "Hypogram and Inscription," (on Riffaterre's poetics), in *RT*, pp. 27–53.

21. At this point de Man refers principally to the following texts of Nietzsche: *On the Genealogy of Morals*, trans. Walter Kaufmann (New York: Random House, 1967); *The Will to Power*, trans. Kaufmann and R.J. Hollingdale (New York: Random House, 1967); also his early lectures on rhetoric, translated by Philippe Lacoue-Labarthe and Jean-Luc Nancy in *Poétique*, Vol. 5 (1971). See *Allegories of Reading: Figural Language in Rousseau, Nietzsche, Rilke, and Proust* (New Haven: Yale University Press, 1979). Hereafter cited in the text as *AR*.

22. The distinction has its origin in J.L. Austin, *How to Do Things with Words* (London: Oxford University Press, 1963). Its implications for philosophy and literary theory have been debated by (among others) de Man, Jacques Derrida, John Searle, Jonathan Culler, and Stanley Fish. For two sharply divergent views of the topic, see Mary Louise Pratt, *Toward a Speech-Act Theory of Literary Discourse* (Bloomington: Indiana University Press, 1977); and Shoshana Felman, *The Literary Speech-Act: Don Juan with Austin, or Seduction in Two Languages*, trans. Catherine Porter (Ithaca: Cornell University Press, 1983).

23. Immanuel Kant, *Selections*, ed. Theodore M. Greene (New York: Scribners, 1957). Hereafter cited in the text as *KS*. This edition is good as a readily available source for comparative reading of the three *Critiques*. See also principally the *Critique of Judgment*, trans. J.H. Bernard (New York: Hafner, 1951).

24. On the role of metaphor, fictions, and analogies in Kant, see also J. Hillis Miller, *The Ethics of Reading* (New York: Columbia University Press, 1987).

25. Marcel Proust, *Du Côté de chez Swann* (Paris: Pléiade, 1954). De Man gives his own translation of the passages from pp. 82–88.

26. John Sallis, *Spacings — Of Reason and Imagination in Texts of Kant, Fichte, Hegel* (Chicago: University of Chicago Press, 1987), p. 12.

27. Peter Szondi, *Poetik und Geschichtsphilosophie I* (Frankfurt am Main: Suhrkamp, 1974), p. 396. Passage cited by de Man in SS, p. 765.

28. See especially T.W. Adorno, *Negative Dialectics*, trans. E.B. Ashton (London: Routledge & Kegan Paul, 1973); and the essays collected in *Prisms*, trans. Samuel and Shierry Weber (London: Neville Spearman, 1967).

29. Paul de Man, "Aesthetic Formalization in Kleist," in *The Rhetoric of Romanticism* (New York: Columbia University Press, 1984), pp. 263–90. Hereafter cited in the text as *RR*. De Man provides his own translation of passages from Kleist's "Essay on the Puppet Theatre." There is a version by Eugene Jolas in *Partisan Review*, Vol. 14 (1947): 57–62.

30. Friedrich Schiller, *On the Aesthetic Education of Man, in a Series of Letters*, trans. E.M. Wilkinson and L.A. Willoughby (Oxford: Clarendon Press, 1967), p. 300. Cited by de Man, *RR*, p. 263.

3   Deconstruction and Philosophy

1. Paul de Man, *The Resistance to Theory* (Minneapolis: University of Minnesota Press, 1986). Hereafter cited in the text as *RT*.

2. John Locke, *An Essay Concerning Human Understanding*, ed. John W. Yolton (London and New York: Oxford University Press, 1961), Vol. 2, Book II, p. 87. Cited by de Man in "The Epistemology of Metaphor," *Critical Inquiry*, Vol. 5, no. 1 (1978): 13–30; p. 15.

3. Samuel Johnson, "*Preface* to the Plays of William Shakespeare," in W.K. Wimsatt, ed., *Johnson on Shakespeare* (Harmondsworth: Penguin, 1969), pp. 57–98; p. 68.

4. De Man gives his own translation of this passage in *Allegories of Reading: Figural Language in Rousseau, Nietzsche, Rilke, and Proust* (New Haven: Yale University Press, 1979), pp. 110–11. Hereafter cited in the text as *AR*. There is a sizable excerpt from Nietzsche's essay "Of Truth and Lie in an Extra-Moral Sense" in Walter Kaufmann, ed. *The Portable Nietzsche* (Viking: New York, 1954), pp. 42–47.

5. For an influential statement of this thoroughgoing neo-pragmatist position, see Richard Rorty, *Philosophy and the Mirror of Nature* (Princeton: Princeton University Press, 1980); and *Consequences of Pragmatism* (Minneapolis: University of Minnesota Press, 1982).

6. Robert Moynihan, "Interview with Paul de Man," *The Yale Review*, Vol. 73, no. 4 (1984): 576–602; p. 598.

7. See Paul de Man, "Sign and Symbol in Hegel's *Aesthetics*," *Critical Inquiry*, Vol. 8, no. 4 (1982): 7611–75; Raymond Geuss, "A Response to Paul de Man," *Critical Inquiry*, Vol. 10, no. 2 (1983): 375–82; de Man, "Reply to Raymond Geuss," *Critical Inquiry*, Vol. 10, no. 2 (1983): 383–90.

8. De Man, "Reply to Raymond Geuss," p. 384.

9. Geuss, "A Response to Paul de Man," p. 381.

10. De Man, "Reply to Raymond Geuss," p. 384.

11. De Man, "A Modern Master" (review of Jorge Luis Borge's *Labyrinths* and *Dreamtigers*), *The New York Review Of Books*, Vol. 8, no. 7 (19 November 1964); 8–10.

12. Stefano Rosso, "An Interview with Paul de Man," reprinted in de Man, *The Resistance to Theory*, pp. 115–21; p. 120.

13. See for instance Geoffrey Hartman, "Crossing Over: Literary Commentary as Literature," *Comparative Literature*, Vol. 28 (1976): 257–76; also Hartman's books *The Fate of Reading and Other Essays* (Chicago: University of Chicago Press, 1975); and *Criticism in the Wilderness* (New Haven: Yale University Press, 1980).

14. For a useful extended bibliography, see Linda Hutcheon, "Beginning to Theorize the Postmodern," *Textual Practice*, Vol. 1, no. 1 (1987): 10–31. Of particular interest in this connection are the books and articles by Terry Eagleton, Hal Foster, Harry R. Garvin, Ihab Hassan, Fredric Jameson, David Lodge (*The Modes of Modern Writing*, cited below), Hayden White, and Alan Wilde.

15. Roland Barthes, *S/Z*, trans. Richard Miller (London: Jonathan Cape, 1975). For representative statements of this poststructuralist position, see Catherine Belsey, *Critical Practice* (London: Methuen, 1980); Rosalind Coward and John Ellis, *Language and Materialism: Developments in Semiology and the Theory of the Subject* (London: Routledge & Kegan Paul, 1977); and Colin MacCabe, *James Joyce and the "Revolution of the Word"* (London: Macmillan, 1978).

16. See Jean-François Lyotard, *The Post-Modern Condition: A Report on Knowledge*, trans. Geoff Bennington and Brian Massumi (Minneapolis: University of Minnesota Press, 1983).

17. See Gérard Genette, *Figures of Literary Discourse*, trans. A. Sheridan (Oxford: Basil Blackwell, 1982).

18. For Roman Jakobson's best-known discussion of this topic, see his paper "Linguistics and Poetics," in Thomas A. Sebeok, ed., *Style in Language* (Cambridge: M.I.T. Press, 1960), pp. 350–77.

19. David Lodge very usefully extends and clarifies Jakobson's argument in his book *The Modes of Modern Writing: Metaphor, Metonymy and the Typology of Modern Literature* (London: Edward Arnold, 1977).

20. De Man's late essays on this topic will appear in *Aesthetic Ideology*, Andrzej Warminski, ed., (Minneapolis: University of Minnesota Press, forthcoming).

21. See for instance Richard Ellmann, *Yeats: The Man and the Masks* (New York: Macmillan, 1948); T.R. Henn, *The Lonely Tower* (London: Macmillan, 1950); Frank Kermode, *Romantic Image* (London: Routledge & Kegan Paul, 1957). De Man's doctoral dissertation at Harvard was devoted largely to a critique of the assumptions underlying this organicist-developmental reading of Yeats's poetry. An excerpt appears under the title "Image and Emblem in Yeats" in de Man, *The Rhetoric of Romanticism* (New York: Columbia University Press, 1984), pp. 145–238.

22. John Sallis has some pertinent remarks on this topic in his book *Spacings — of Reason and Imagination in Texts of Kant, Fichte, Hegel* (Chicago: University of Chicago Press, 1987).

23. Paul de Man, "Phenomenality and Materiality in Kant," in Gary Shapiro and Alan Sica, eds., *Hermeneutics: Questions and Prospects* (Amherst: University of Massachusetts Press, 1984), pp. 121–44; p. 128. Hereafter cited in the text as PMK.

24. See for instance Mary Louise Pratt, *Toward a Speech-Act Theory of Literary Discourse* (Bloomington: Indiana University Press, 1977). Similar ideas have been developed and discussed by (among others) Jonathan Culler, Stanley Fish, Richard Ohmann, and John R. Searle.

25. See Michel Foucault's notably un-Kantian essay on Kant, "What Is Enlightenment?," in Paul Rabinow, ed., *The Foucault Reader* (New York: Pantheon, 1985), pp. 32–50.

26. Michel Foucault, *The Archaeology of Knowledge*, trans. A. Sheridan (New York: Harper & Row, 1972), pp. 202–3.

27. See especially the essays and interviews collected in Foucault, *Language/Counter-Memory/Practice*, trans. Donald F. Bouchard and Sherry Simon (Ithaca: Cornell University Press, 1977).

28. Michel Foucault, *The Order of Things: an Archaeology of the Human Sciences*, trans. A. Sheridan (New York: Random House, 1973), p. 318. Hereafter cited in the text as *OT*.

29. Paul de Man, "Pascal's Allegory of Persuasion," in Stephen J. Greenblatt, ed., *Allegory and Representation* (Baltimore: Johns Hopkins University Press, 1981), pp. 1–25; p. 13. Hereafter cited in the text as PAP.

30. This text appears under the title "The Mind of the Geometrician" in *Great Shorter Works Of Pascal*, trans. Emilie Caillet (Philadelphia: Westminster Press, 1948), pp. 189–211.

31. See Frank Lentricchia's chapter on de Man in *After the New Criticism* (Chicago: University of Chicago Press, 1980).

32. Paul de Man, *Blindness and Insight: Essays in the Rhetoric of Contemporary Criticism*, 2nd ed. (London: Methuen, 1983).

33. Kurt Gödel, *On Formally Undecidable Propositions of Principia Mathematica and Related Systems*, trans. B. Meltzer (New York: Basic Books, 1962).

4 Aesthetic Ideology and the Ethics of Reading

1. J. Hillis Miller, *The Ethics of Reading: Kant, de Man, Eliot, Trollope, James, and Benjamin* (New York: Columbia University Press, 1987), pp. viii and 138. Hereafter cited in the text as *ER*.

2. See for instance René Wellek, "Destroying Literary Studies," *The New Criterion* (December, 1983): 1–8.

3. Immanuel Kant, *Foundations of the Metaphysics of Morals*, trans. Lewis White Beck (Indianapolis: Bobbs-Merrill, 1978), p. 19.

4. On Kafka's parable and its Kantian connections, see also Jacques Derrida, "Devant la loi," in A. Phillips Griffiths, ed., *Philosophy and Literature* (Cambridge: Cambridge University Press, 1984).

5. On this topic see Stanley Corngold, "Error in Paul de Man," *Critical Inquiry*, Vol. 8 (1983): 489–507; and in response "A Letter from Paul de Man," pp. 509–13 in the same issue.

5. George Eliot, *Adam Bede* (Harmondsworth: Penguin, 1980), pp. 221–30.

7. Eliot, *Adam Bede*, p. 223. The Penguin editor, Stephen Gill, makes some similar points in his Introduction about the far from straightforward or perspicuous character of Eliot's mimetic doctrine. But he then turns around and rejects such talk of "aesthetic distancing" since it tends to imply that "reading *Adam Bede* is like reading *The Golden Bowl* or *The Good Soldier*." On the contrary, Gill argues: "only through George Eliot's eyes do we observe the world which she presents as simultaneously a real world, historically

placed, specifically realized, accurate in verifiable detail, and a fictional world, artistically ordered by a *knowable* author, George Eliot" (p. 23). The assumption here — that these two kinds of truth-claim go unproblematically together — underpins all versions of expressive realism, and of course differs markedly from Miller's account.

8. Anthony Trollope, *The Warden* (London: Oxford University Press, 1980), p. 189.

9. Henry James. *The Art of the Novel: Critical Prefaces* (Boston: Northeastern University Press, 1984), p. 5.

10. James, *The Art of the Novel*, pp. 347–48.

11. Paul de Man, Preface to Carol Jacobs, *The Dissimulating Harmony* (Baltimore and London: Johns Hopkins University Press, 1978), p. xi.

12. Paul de Man, *The Resistance to Theory* (Minneapolis: University of Minnesota Press, 1986). Hereafter cited in the text as *RT*.

13. See de Man, "Form and Intent in the American New Criticism," in *Blindness and Insight: Essays in the Rhetoric of Contemporary Criticism*, 2nd ed. (London: Methuen, 1983), pp. 20–35. His interview with Robert Moynihan (*The Yale Review*, Vol. 76 [1984]: 576–602) has some interesting retrospective comments on de Man's debt to New Critical close-reading practice.

14. J. Hillis Miller, *The Disappearance of God: Five Nineteenth-Century Writers* (Cambridge: Harvard University Press, 1963); and *Poets of Reality: Six Twentieth-Century Writers* (Cambridge: Harvard University Press, 1965).

15. W.K. Wimsatt, "Battering the Object: The Ontological Approach," in M. Bradbury and D. Palmer, eds., *Contemporary Criticism* (London: Edward Arnold, 1970).

16. See J. Hillis Miller, "The Geneva School," *Critical Quarterly*, Vol. 8 (1966): 305–21.

17. J. Hillis Miller, "Ariadne's Thread: Repetition and the Narrative Line," *Critical Inquiry*, Vol. 3 (1976): 57–77. The implications of this essay are worked out at greater length in Miller's *Fiction and Repetition: Seven English Novels* (Oxford: Basil Blackwell, 1982).

18. See especially M.H. Abrams, *Natural Supernaturalism: Tradition and Revolution in Romantic Literature* (New York: Norton, 1971). For his response to Miller's critique, see Abrams, "The Limits of Pluralism II: The Deconstructive Angel," *Critical Inquiry*, Vol. 3 (1977): 425–28.

19. For a broadly representative collection of essays, see Harold Bloom, Geoffrey Hartman, J. Hillis Miller, *et al*, *Deconstruction and Criticism* (London: Routledge & Kegan Paul, 1979).

20. Paul de Man, "Phenomenality and Materiality in Kant," in Gary Shapiro and Alan Sica, eds., *Hermeneutics: Questions and Prospects* (Amherst: University of Massachusetts Press, 1984), pp. 121–44. The topic is explored further in de Man, "Sign and Symbol in Hegel's *Aesthetics*," *Critical Inquiry*, Vol. 8, no. 4 (1982); and "Hegel on the Sublime," in Mark Krupnick, ed., *Displacement: Derrida and After* (Bloomington: Indiana University Press, 1983), pp. 139–53.

21. James, *The Art of the Novel*, pp. 336–37.

22. For these comments on Schiller, see de Man, "Aesthetic Formalization: Kleist's *Uber das Marionettentheater*," first published in his posthumous volume of essays *The Rhetoric of Romanticism* (New York: Columbia University Press, 1984), pp. 263–90. A forthcoming collection, *Aesthetic Ideology*, edited by Andrzej Warminski (Minneapolis:

University of Minnesota Press) will contain the text of a lecture on Kant and Schiller, along with essays on Hegel, Pascal and others.

23. See de Man, "The Dead-End of Formalist Criticism," in *Blindness and Insight*, pp. 229–45.

24. De Man, "Aesthetic Formalization," p. 265. Hereafter cited in the text as AF.

25. See T.S. Eliot, "Tradition and the Individual Talent" and "The Metaphysical Poets," in *Selected Essays* (London: Faber & Faber, 1964), pp. 3–11 and 241–50.

26. Miller has more to say on this topic in his essay "The Search for Grounds in Literary Studies," in Robert Con Davis and Ronald Schleifer, eds., *Rhetoric and Form: Deconstruction at Yale* (Norman: University of Oklahoma Press, 1985), pp. 19–36.

27. Terry Eagleton, *Criticism and Ideology* (London: New Left Books, 1976).

28. See especially the closing chapter of Eagleton's *Literary Theory: An Introduction* (Oxford: Basil Blackwell, 1984). For his hostile commentaries on de Man, see *The Function of Criticism* (London: New Left Books, 1984), pp. 100–6; and, most recently, *Against the Grain: Selected Essays* (London: New Left Books, 1986), pp. 53–56, 136–38, 156–62.

29. Frank Lentricchia, *Criticism and Social Change* (Chicago: University of Chicago Press, 1983).

30. In this connection, see the chapter on de Man in Lentricchia, *After the New Criticism* (Chicago: University of Chicago Press, 1980).

31. See particularly Hans-Robert Jauss, *Toward an Aesthetics of Reception*, trans. Timothy Bahti (Minneapolis: University of Minnesota Press, 1982). De Man's essay on Jauss — reprinted in *RT* — first appeared as an Introduction to this volume.

32. De Man, *The Rhetoric of Romanticism*, p. viii.

5   Against a New Pragmatism

1. See Stanley Fish, *Is there a Text in this Class? The Authority of Interpretive Communities* (Cambridge: Harvard University Press, 1980).

2. Steven Knapp and Walter Benn Michaels, "Against Theory," in W.J.T. Mitchell, ed., *Against Theory: Literary Theory and the New Pragmatism* (Chicago: University of Chicago Press, 1985), pp. 11–30.

3. Fish, *Is There a Text in this Class?*, pp. 361–62. (Cited by Knapp and Michaels, "Against Theory," p. 27.)

4. Fish, *Is There a Text in this Class?*, pp. 367–68.

5. Knapp and Michaels, "Against Theory," p. 27.

6. Stanley Fish, "Consequences," in *Against Theory*, pp. 106–31; p. 126.

7. Fish, "Consequences," p. 127.

8. On this topic see Michel Foucault, "What Is Enlightenment," in Paul Rabinow, ed., *The Foucault Reader* (New York: Pantheon, 1985), pp. 32–50.

9. E.D. Hirsch, Jr., *Validity in Interpretation* (New Haven: Yale University Press, 1967), p. 216. (Cited by Knapp and Michaels, "Against Theory," p. 13.)

10. Knapp and Michaels, "Against Theory," p. 13.

11. See Jacques Derrida, "Signature Event Context," *Glyph*, Vol. 1 (1977): 172–97;

John R. Searle, "Reiterating the Differences," *Glyph*, Vol. 1 (1977): 198–208; and Derrida's response to Searle, "Limited Inc abc," *Glyph*, Vol. 2 (1978): 162–254.

12. See Paul de Man, *Allegories of Reading: Figural Language in Rousseau, Nietzsche, Rilke, and Proust* (New Haven: Yale University Press, 1979), p. 294.

13. Knapp and Michaels, "Against Theory," p. 24.

14. Fish, "Consequences," p. 126.

15. See for instance Clare Dalton, "An Essay on the Deconstruction of Contract Doctrines," *Yale Law Journal*, Vol. 94 (1985): 997–1114; Ronald Dworkin, "Law as Interpretation," *Critical Inquiry*, Vol. 9 (1982–83): 179–200; Stanley Fish, "Working on the Chain Gang: Interpretation in the Law and in Literary Theory," *Critical Inquiry*, Vol. 9 (1982–83): 201–16; Peter Goodrich, *Legal Discourse: Studies in Linguistics, Rhetoric and Legal Analysis* (London: Macmillan, 1987); Allan C. Hutchinson, "From Cultural Construction to Historical Deconstruction," *Yale Law Journal*, Vol. 94 (1984): 209–37; Bernard Jackson, *Semiotics and Legal Theory* (London: Routledge & Kegan Paul, 1985); Christopher Norris, "Suspended Sentences: Textual Theory and the Law," in *The Contest of Faculties* (London: Methuen, 1985); R.M. Unger, "The Critical Legal Studies Movement," *Harvard Law Review*, Vol. 96 (1983); James Boyd White, *When Words Lose their Meaning: Constitutions and Reconstitutions of Language, Character and Community* (Chicago: University of Chicago Press, 1984). See also the following journal numbers devoted specifically to issues in the province of law, rhetoric, and literary theory: *Texas Law Review*, Vol. 60 (1982); *Stanford Law Review*, Vol. 36 (1984); *Southern California Law Review*, Vol. 58 (1985).

16. For a representative collection of essays, see David Kairys, ed., *The Politics of Law: A Progressive Critique* (New York: Pantheon Books, 1982). Also — of more specific interest in this context — Mark Tushnet, "Critical Legal Studies and Constitutional Law: An Essay in Deconstruction," *Stanford Law Review*, Vol. 36 (1984): 623–64.

17. See Stanley Fish, "Working on the Chain Gang."

18. Joseph William Singer, "The Player and the Cards: Nihilism and Legal Theory," *Yale Law Journal*, Vol. 94 (1984): 1–70; p. 61.

19. Stephen L. Carter, "Constitutional Adjudication and the Indeterminate Text: A Preliminary Defense of an Imperfect Muddle," *Yale Law Journal*, Vol. 94 (1984): 821–72; p. 855.

20. See H.L.A. Hart, *Essays in Jurisprudence and Philosophy* (Oxford: Clarendon Press, 1983).

21. Paul de Man, "Promises (*Social Contract*)," in *Allegories of Reading*, pp. 246–77.

22. De Man, "Promises (*Social Contract*)," p. 271.

23. Carter, "Constitutional Adjudication," p. 830.

24. Singer, "The Player and the Cards," p. 26.

25. Singer, "The Player and the Cards," p. 58.

26. See Hans-Georg Gadamer, *Truth and Method*, trans. Garrett Barden and John Cumming (London: Sheed & Ward, 1975).

27. See for instance Jürgen Habermas, *Communication and the Evolution of Society*, trans. Thomas McCarthy (London: Heinemann, 1979).

28. The most influential statement of this view may be found in Peter Winch, *The Idea of a Social Science and its Relation to Philosophy* (London: Routledge & Kegan Paul, 1958).

29. Jacques Derrida, "Of an Apocalyptic Tone recently adopted in Philosophy," *Oxford Literary Review*, Vol. 6, no. 2 (1984): 3–37; p. 33.

30. Jacques Derrida, "The Principle of Reason: The University in the Eyes of its Pupils," *Diacritics*, Vol. 19 (1983): 3–20; p. 9.

31. See Immanuel Kant, *The Conflict of the Faculties*, trans. and ed. Mary J. Gregor (New York: Abaris Books, 1979). Hereafter cited in the text as *CF*.

32. For the use of these speech-act distinctions in a Kantian context of argument, see Derrida, "Of an Apocalyptic Tone."

33. See Paul de Man, "Phenomenality and Materiality in Kant," in Gary Shapiro and Alan Sica, eds., *Hermeneutics: Questions and Prospects* (Amherst: University of Massachusetts Press, 1984), pp. 121–44.

34. See Jacques Derrida, "The Parergon," *October*, No. 9 (1979): 3–40.

35. Pierre Bourdieu, *Distinction: A Social Critique of the Judgment of Taste*, trans. Richard Nice (Cambridge: Harvard University Press, 1984), pp. 493–94.

36. Derrida, "The Principle of Reason," p. 13.

37. T.W. Adorno, *Negative Dialectics*, trans. E.B. Ashton (London: Routledge & Kegan Paul, 1973), pp. 85 and 158. These passages are cited in Rainer Nägele's illuminating essay "The Scene of the Other: Theodor Adorno's Negative Dialectic in the Context of Poststructuralism," in Jonathan Arac, ed., *Postmodernism and Politics* (Minneapolis: University of Minnesota Press, 1986), pp. 91–111.

38. See Jürgen Habermas, "Right and Violence: A German Trauma," *Cultural Critique*, No. 1 (Fall, 1985): 36–57.

39. Sotirios A. Barber, *On What the Constitution Means* (Baltimore and London: Johns Hopkins University Press, 1984), p. 37. Hereafter cited in the text as *WCM*.

6 "The Temptation of Permanence"

1. T.W. Adorno, "The Sociology of Knowledge and its Consciousness," in *Prisms: Cultural Criticism and Society*, trans. Samuel and Shierry Weber (London: Spearman, 1967), p. 32.

2. T.W. Adorno, "Subject-Object," in Andrew Arato and Eike Gebhardt, eds., *The Essential Frankfurt School Reader* (Oxford: Basil Blackwell, 1978), p. 499.

3. T.W. Adorno, *Minima Moralia: Reflections from a Damaged Life*, trans. E.F.N. Jephcott (London: New Left Books, 1974), p. 81.

4. Adorno, *Minima Moralia*, p. 16.

5. T.W. Adorno, *Philosophy of Modern Music*, trans. Anne G. Mitchell and Wesley V. Blomster (London: Sheed & Ward, 1973), p. 69.

6. Adorno, *Minima Moralia*, p. 18.

7. Adorno, *Minima Moralia*, p. 81.

8. Jacques Derrida, *Mémoires: For Paul de Man* (New York: Columbia University Press, 1986).

9. Derrida, *Mémoires*, p. 142.

10. Derrida, *Mémoires*, p. 142.

11. Jacques Derrida, *Of Grammatology*, trans. Gayatri Chakravorty Spivak (Baltimore: Johns Hopkins University Press, 1976).

12. Derrida, *Of Grammatology*, p. 138.

13. Derrida, *Mémoires*, p. 143. For de Man's reading of Derrida's reading of Rousseau, see *Blindness and Insight: Essays in the Rhetoric of Contemporary Criticism*, 2nd ed. (London: Methuen, 1983). Hereafter cited in the text as *BI*.

14. Cited by Derrida, *Mémoires*, p. 130.

15. See Frank Lentricchia, *Criticism and Social Change* (Chicago: University of Chicago Press, 1983).

16. For a brief account of this debate, see George Steiner, *Heidegger* (London: Fontana, 1978).

17. See for instance David Halliburton, *Poetic Thinking: An Approach to Heidegger* (Chicago: University of Chicago Press, 1981).

18. I am much indebted to Ortwin de Graef for his help in providing copies of this material.

19. Cited by de Graef in his Introduction to these early essays and reviews (typescript copy).

20. Paul de Man, *The Rhetoric of Romanticism* (New York: Columbia University Press, 1984), p. viii.

21. Paul de Man, *Allegories of Reading: Figural Language in Rousseau, Nietzsche, Rilke, and Proust* (New Haven: Yale University Press, 1979), p. ix. Hereafter cited in the text as *AR*.

22. See F.W. Nietzsche, *The Birth of Tragedy* and *The Case of Wagner*, trans. Walter Kaufmann (New York: Vintage Books, 1967).

23. Paul de Man, "The Temptation of Permanence," trans. Dan Latimer, *Southern Humanities Review*, Vol. 17 (1983): 209–21. Hereafter cited in the text as TP.

24. See the essays collected in Martin Heidegger, *Poetry, Language, Thought*, trans. Albert Hofstadter (New York: Harper & Row, 1971).

25. See T.W. Adorno, *The Jargon of Authenticity*, trans. Knut Tarnowski and Frederic Will (London: Routledge & Kegan Paul, 1973).

26. André Malraux, *The Walnut Trees of Altenburg*, trans. A.W. Fielding (London, 1952).

27. André Malraux, *The Voices of Silence*, trans. Stuart Gilbert (New York, 1953).

28. See Edmund Husserl, *The Crisis of the European Sciences and Transcendental Phenomenology*, trans. D. Carr (Evanston: Northwestern University Press, 1970).

29. Paul de Man. "The Return to Philology," in *The Resistance to Theory* (Minneapolis: University of Minnesota Press, 1986), pp. 21–26; p. 24. Hereafter cited in the text as RP.

30. Rainer Maria Rilke, *Briefe* (Wiesbaden, 1950), pp. 898–99. (Passage translated by Dan Latimer.)

31. Paul de Man, Preface to Carol Jacobs, *The Dissimulating Harmony* (Baltimore and London: Johns Hopkins University Press, 1978), p. xi.

32. Walter Benn Michaels, "Saving the Text," *Modern Language Notes*, Vol. 93 (1978): 780.

33. De Man refers briefly to this late work-in-progress in his interview with Stefano Rosso, *The Resistance to Theory*, pp. 115–21; p. 121.

7   Postscript

1. Peter Dodge, *Hendrik de Man, Socialist Critic of Marxism* (New Jersey: Princeton University Press, 1979).

2. Lentricchia's comments are cited by Jon Wiener, "Deconstructing de Man," *The Nation*, January 9, 1988, pp. 22–24.

3. For de Man's treatment of this passage from Nietzsche, see *Blindness and Insight: Essays in the Rhetoric of Contemporary Criticism*, 2nd ed. (London: Methuen, 1983), pp. 149–50.

4. Wiener, "Deconstructing de Man."

5. Raul Hilberg, one of the specialist historians quoted here, has more recently disputed the accuracy of Wiener's evidence. In a letter to *The Nation* (April 9, 1988), Hilberg asserts that Wiener attributes to him the words of a correspondent from the *New York Times*. These are not matters that can or should be discussed in a mere footnote, especially where the media have already been responsible for so much misinformation and casual second-hand reporting. As this book went to press I received a copy of Jacques Derrida's fine and compassionate essay "Like the Sound of the Sea Deep within a Shell: Paul de Man's War" (*Critical Inquiry*, Vol. XIV [1988], pp. 590–652). I would strongly recommend this article to anyone who seeks a better understanding of de Man's involvement with *Le Soir* and the issues raised by his wartime writings.

6. Julia Kristeva, *Powers of Horror: Essays on Abjection* (New York: Columbia University Press, 1982).

7. On the right-wing Flemish separatist movement and its wider European context, see for instance I.L. Carsten, *The Rise of Fascism* (Berkeley and Los Angeles, 1967), pp. 204–18; Jean-Michel Etienne, *Le Mouvement rexiste jusqu'en 1940* (Paris, 1968); Michel Géoris-Reitshof, *Extrême droite et néofascisme en Belgique* (Brussels, 1962); David Littlejohn, *The Patriotic Traitors* (London, 1962); Jean Stengers, "Belgium," in H. Rogger and E. Webber, eds., *The European Right* (Berkeley and Los Angeles, 1965).

8. Geoffrey Hartman, "Blindness and Insight," *The New Republic*, March 7, 1988, pp. 26–31; p. 31.

9. Michael Dummett, *Frege: Philosophy of Language* (London: Duckworth, 1981).

10. De Man, "Walter Benjamin's 'The Task of the Translator'," in *The Resistance to Theory* (Minneapolis: University of Minnesota Press, 1986), pp. 73–93 p.87.

11. Michael Sprinker, *Imaginary Relations: Aesthetics and Ideology in the Theory of Historical Materialism* (London: Verso, 1987), p.248.

12. Minae Mizumura, "Renunciation," in "The Lesson of Paul de Man," *Yale French Studies*, No. 69 (New Haven: Yale University Press, 1985), pp.81–97; pp. 96–97.

13. See especially Victor Farias, *Heidegger et le Nazisme* (Paris: Verbier, 1987).

14. Jacques Derrida, *De l'esprit: Heidegger et la question* (Paris: Galilée, 1987). Hereafter cited in the text by page number.

15. See de Man, *Allegories of Reading*, p. 227.

16. Jacques Derrida, *Mémoires: For Paul de Man* (New York: Columbia University Press, 1986), p.100. Hereafter cited in the text by page number.

Index of Names

Abrams, M.H., 10, 31–3, 113, 116, 201–2, 206
Adorno, T.W., v, 61, 72, 145, 149–52, 167, 176, 209, 210
Alleman, Beda, 14, 200
Althusser, Louis, 120, 176, 192
Arac, Jonathan, 209
Aristotle, xxii, 1, 78, 81, 107
Arnold, Matthew, 39
Artaud, Antonin, 181
Auden, W.H., 110
Austin, J.L., 43–4, 136, 202

Balzac, Honoré de, 76
Barber, S., 147–8, 209
Barthes, Roland, 76, 204
Beckett, Samuel, xxi
Beethoven, Ludwig van, 151
Belsey, Catherine, 204
Benjamin, Walter, xxi, 119, 122, 191, 211
Bernstein, Eduard, 19, 20
Bismarck, 183
Blanchot, Maurice, 40, 75
Bloom, Harold, 206
Bonnefoy, Yves, xxv
Borges, Jorge Luis, 74–7, 203
Bourdieu, Pierre, 144, 209
Bowles, William Lisle, 33
Brooks, Peter, 199
Brower, Reuben, 175–6
Burke, Kenneth, 1–2, 120
Burt, E.S., xiii

Calvino, Italo, 75–7
Carter, Stephen L., 135–7, 208
Céline, L.-F., 181–2
Cioran, E.M., xxi

Coleridge, Samuel Taylor, xv–xvi, 10, 30, 31, 33, 35, 200–1
Corngold, Stanley, 200, 205
Culler, Jonathan, xix, xxiii–iv, 202, 204

Dalton, Clare, 208
de Graef, Ortwin, 158–9, 210
de Man, Hendrik, 17–21, 24–6, 152, 156, 159, 178, 200–1
de Man, Marc, 189
Derrida, Jacques, xxiii, xxv, 11, 22, 131–2, 136, 139–40, 143–5, 149, 153–6, 173, 175, 178, 193–8, 208–11
Descartes, René, 65, 90, 97, 170
Dodge, Peter, 17–21, 24–5, 178, 200–1
Donne, John, 36, 117
Dummett, Michael, 190–1, 193, 211
Dworkin, Ronald, 208

Eagleton, Terry, 1–4, 16, 17, 25, 26, 85, 120, 199, 200, 201, 204, 208
Eliot, George, 106–8, 205–6
Eliot, T.S., xxiv, 22, 29, 34–6, 113, 117, 178, 191–2, 207
Eluard, Paul, 189
Empson, William, 115, 199
Engels, F., 20
Euclid, 99

Felman, Shoshana, 199, 202
Fish, Stanley, 126–30, 133–4, 137, 139, 175, 202, 204, 207, 208
Foucault, Michel, 77, 89–95, 205, 207
France, Anatole, 133–4
Frege, Gottlob, 190–1, 193, 211
Freud, Sigmund, 30
Frey, Hans-Jost, xix

Index of Topics

(I have not provided entries for certain topics [like 'deconstruction'] which occur too often for any detailed accounting.)

Critical Legal Studies, 133–48
'criticism of consciousness', 34, 112, 206

'defamiliarization' (formalist poetics and reception-theory), 37, 67, 85–6, 122
'deviation' (poetic language: Jakobson on), 80–2
dialectic (Hegel), 30–2, 150–51
differance (Derrida), 154
Dionysian principle (Nietzsche), 162–3
discourse (Foucault on), 89–94, 101
disinterest (aesthetic: Kant on), 57, 59, 143–5; (rhetoric of in Husserl), 171
'dissociation of sensibility' (T.S. Eliot on), 36, 117
doxa (Plato), 65
Dreyfus Affair, 188
dwelling (Heidegger), 165–9

'edifying' philosophy (Rorty on), 138
eidetic inspection (Husserl), 171
Enlightenment tradition (Kant to Husserl), 130, 139–48, 170–74
errors (in reading), xix, 13, 87, 105, 149, 172, 193–4, 205
ethics, 38, 48, 50–54, 57, 63, 96, 100, 154, 193, 205
'ethics of reading' (Derrida on Heidegger and de Man), 193–7; (Hillis Miller on), 102–24
Erinnerung (Hegel), 32
existentialism, xx, 6, 49, 53–4, 96

faculties, Kantian doctrine of, 45–9, 53–9, 64–5, 140–45
figural language, xv, xviii, xxii, 49–51, 66, 69–70, 79–85, 89, 105, 119–20, 123, 160–63
Flemish separatist movement, 185–6, 211
foregrounding (formalist and phenomenological aesthetics), 81, 86, 122
forgetting (Nietzsche on), 4–5, 179–80
formalism, 29, 64, 67, 80–3, 121, 132
'forms of life' (Wittgenstein), 139
foundations (philosophical), 65–6, 78–9, 86–101, 170–74
framing (aesthetic: Kant on), 143–4

Frankfurt School, 72, 145–6
'free play' (in Kantian aesthetics), 55–6, 86, 123; (mistaken understanding of), 105, 115, 136

genealogy (Nietzsche), 69, 160–64; (Foucault), 90
generic distinctions, 51–3, 68–71
genetic readings, 160–64
genius, ideology of, 28–30, 44–6, 56, 59–64, 107, 187
geometry, 45, 79, 90–1, 95–9
grammar (in relation to logic and rhetoric), 54, 65, 78–85, 88–9, 132, 136; (Foucault on), 93
'heresies' (New Critical), xv
hermeneutic circle, 34, 148, 160, 175
hermeneutics 11–14, 34, 36, 39, 42, 61, 63–4, 111, 131–3, 138–9, 141–2, 148, 156–8, 160, 165, 175
history, 16–17, 21, 23, 52, 63, 77, 117, 119–20, 152–76, 178–80, 183–6, 192–8; (and modernity: Nietzsche on), 4–9, 156, 179–80, 200
horizon of meaning (aethetics and reception-theory), 37–8
hypotyposis, 104

'ideal speech-situation' (Habermas), 138–9, 145–6
ideology, v, 1, 16, 51, 54, 58, 63, 87, 91, 107, 120–21, 141, 152–76 *passim*, 190, 191–2
illocutionary force (speech-act theory), 82
imagery (Romantic nature-poetry), 33, 202
immanent critique (Adorno), viii, 149–52
indeterminacy (in law), 135, 137, 147
intentionality, xxi, 34, 131–2
interiorization, xxiv, 7, 21, 31–3, 35
'interpretive communities' (Fish), 134
irony, xiv, xv, 26, 28, 39, 67, 112, 157, 173

'jargon of authenticity' (Heidegger), 167, 210
judicial review, 129

'language-games' (Wittgenstein), 139